D1108008

The Modern Theater
Architecture, Stage Design, Lighting

The Modern Theater
Architecture, Stage Design, Lighting

by Hannelore Schubert

Translated by J. C. Palmes

Praeger Publishers
New York · Washington · London

Design of jacket: Hanns Lohrer, Stuttgart

Praeger Publishers, Inc.
111 Fourth Avenue, New York, N.Y. 10003, U.S.A.
5 Cromwell Place, London S.W. 7., England

Published in the United States of America in 1971
Originally published as 'Moderner Theaterbau'
© 1971 by Karl Krämer Verlag, Stuttgart
Translation © 1971 by Karl Krämer Verlag, Stuttgart, Germany

Library of Congress Catalog Card Number: 74–111072
All rights reserved

Printed in Germany

Foreword

This book is about the position of theatre building after World War II. On the one hand, it offers a documentary survey, which brings together for convenience and comparison what has hitherto been widely dispersed; and, on the other, it traces the various lines of development and divergence. The documentary section is confined to the German-speaking world. This has no significance other than the superabundance of material available, which made selection a necessity. For the same reason pure reconstructions, whether in the form of extensions or variations, were completely excluded, so that the wealth of selected subject-matter could be clearly presented.

This restriction to one cultural region was not inspired by local patriotism. But it cannot be overlooked that the theatres built since the war in Germany, Austria and Switzerland represent a self-contained chapter of postwar architecture. Despite the constant stimulus which came from abroad and was widely reflected, these theatres form a homogeneous group. While in Switzerland a few competitions—notably the one for the Schauspielhaus in Zürich—became international occasions, the Germans looked only to themselves. No foreign architect has built a theatre in Germany since the war.

The author is very conscious that here the word 'Germany' stands for West Germany only. It had been her intention to include East German material in this volume, but all efforts to make contact with the theatres of the German Democratic Republic proved fruitless. So there was no other course but frankly to accept the deficiency. There has been no question, however, of establishing a criterion on the basis of the standards achieved in the Federal Republic of Germany and German-speaking countries. The documentary section is admittedly confined to this region, but what has been planned and realized here will be related to the international situation. In this respect the narrow limits have been broken, so that one can be judged by the other.

The main emphasis throughout the present volume has been laid on theatres which have been built. But all seemingly important schemes of recent years have been assigned a special section. A separate chapter is devoted to projects and utopias of the past century, for the theatre is not only reality; it is the unrealized dream, whose existence is apparent in many subsequent creations. Mannheim is unthinkable without Mies van der Rohe's bold conception, and Scharoun's plans for Kassel are still discussed today.

Historical factors are deliberately excluded. The evolution of the theatre since ancient times has been dealt with in countless handbooks and other works, and could only be lightly touched upon here. History is only meaningful when its role is clearly apparent in planning innovations and impinges upon the buildings and theories of modern theatre architecture. The fact that the present situation can only be explained as a development of bygone times is naturally not forgotten.

This is a book therefore which is intentionally limited to the immediate 'here and now' in the hope that, from the systematically precise documentation of the present, a contribution may result which points beyond this limitation.

Work on the volume has extended over several years, and entailed great difficulties in obtaining material. To all those who have helped and encouraged her, the author extends her sincerest thanks: to the architects and the technical directors of the theatres, and especially to Fräulein Traute Ziegler and Fräulein Nora von Mühlendahl of the publishers' staff, upon whom so many tedious details have inevitably devolved in guiding the book to its completion.

Hannelore Schubert

Contents

Introduction

Hardly a single German theatre survived the war undamaged. All who experienced the aftermath remember how plays were produced in all kinds of rooms: foyers, municipal and school halls, and similar makeshift theatres—a theatrical adventure still regarded with a certain nostalgia. It is not the task of this book, however, to evaluate the effect of this enthusiasm. Certainly, in the lively committed atmosphere of a theatre without mechanical aids and only the most rudimentary resources, the impossible proved feasible, and in many cases the very limitations became a positive asset. It generated a style which can only be associated with the simple stages of the postwar era. The 'Darmstädter Stil', essentially the creation of G. R. Sellner, is a case in point. After the currency reforms which brought stability to the value of money, the reconstruction of existing theatres and the building of new ones was promptly set in motion. Everywhere the interest was so great that the justification for the expenditure (which was often considerable) was hardly ever questioned. People wanted art to have a fitting home again, and to enjoy a theatre in which they could mirror themselves as individuals and as a society, and—incidentally—perhaps also, to present a world on the stage which was not, or not yet, attainable in everyday life.

Thus, as early as 1950, the first reconstructed theatres opened their doors, among the most important and also most interesting solutions being the Laves-Theater in Hanover, shown here as a representative example of all the reconstructed buildings (see page 93 et seq.). The first of the new schemes were also initiated.

On architectural grounds it may be regrettable that the damage to the larger, principal houses was nowhere so extensive as to justify an international competition: the Staatsoper in Berlin was rebuilt to old plans, the Schauspielhaus in the Gendarmenmarkt has so far not been reconstructed, while the Städtische Oper in West Berlin, so far as the stage area was concerned, was restored piece by piece and the whole thing finally assembled somehow with the auditorium tacked on in front. The new building of the Staatsoper in Hamburg was restricted to the auditorium, which was placed in front of the old picture-frame stage. In Munich the National Theatre was rebuilt, and the State Opera in Vienna was resurrected according to the old plans. The undamaged Schauspielhaus of Zürich has retained its original, and now inadequate, accommodation. A competition, one of the few of international status, was not held until 1964 (see page 200 et seq.), but the resultant new design is still unrealized. Frankfurt built its opera inside the half-destroyed Schauspielhaus. At Stuttgart the opera-house survived, and after a wearisome, dilatory competition, only a new building for a playhouse was planned and built.

Thus, from the outset, the organization of big international competitions for the design of important houses was non-existent. The sole completely new major scheme is the 'double-house' of Cologne.

So the story of German postwar theatre architecture—whether of reconstructions or of new buildings—has been an episode in the evolution of the German municipal theatres, a provincial affair. This fact should not be forgotten, particularly when international comparisons are drawn. What occurs in Sydney and New York should be compared with Berlin, Munich and Vienna, but not with Gelsenkirchen, Ingolstadt and St. Gallen. The theatres, which were planned and erected in the crucial period between 1950 and 1960, are predominantly medium-sized and small houses of 'mixed activity', where all types of theatre, opera, plays, operettas and ballet are presented. They seldom seat more than a thousand people; the separation into two complementary and completely equipped houses only begins in towns of the size of Cologne, and even then the furnishing of the second theatre, the playhouse, is more modest.

The few buildings designed as single-purpose houses are for plays. The first of this type was opened in Stuttgart in 1962, and was followed in 1963 by the Freie Volksbühne in Berlin, the Schauspielhaus in Frankfurt and, in 1969, by the Schauspielhaus in Düsseldorf. In smaller places, everything is performed in one theatre, and this always means that one or other art form has to accept a compromise. If there is a so-called 'second house', it is almost invariably some kind of makeshift. At Mannheim there is no gridiron or understage machinery, and at Gelsenkirchen the second house is a studio, not a 'small house'.

This special situation explains why postwar theatre building in Germany has remained a strictly internal matter. On the unique occasion of the competition for the Schauspielhaus at Düsseldorf, an attempt was made to attract international talent, but circumstances did not allow it to develop. For Mannheim there was Mies van der Rohe's magnificent design—but Mies planned an exemplary theatre, which might have stood some chance of realization in Berlin before the war, in a city where it would merely have been one theatre among many and where such perfection can be absorbed. Mannheim, however, did not want a show piece, but a serviceable town theatre, and so the grand design was condemned to failure from the beginning.

The development of the German town theatre is entirely a reflection of German small state particularism. It has no parallel elsewhere. It explains why the building of these theatres has become the concern of a 'closed society', why so few international suggestions have been adopted and why, too, these buildings—however much they may be admired individually—play a minor part in the international scene. But the weak turn to the strong for good solutions, and from the character of the job and the factors involved, theatres have resulted which offer characteristic solutions for this particular building type.

In the German-speaking world, that is Germany, Austria and Switzerland, the theatre implies repertory, in which a season of works (in the larger

Introduction

houses, several seasons) is regularly performed. In ideal conditions this gives an opportunity for presenting both the modern and the old. The tragedies of antiquity, classical drama, baroque opera and musical plays are all undertaken, and also modern pieces, written for the conventional stage as well as for the experimental theatre.

This is where the problem of theatre building starts: a theatre should emerge in which all forms of theatrical art and all periods may find appropriate representation. It was simpler in the nineteenth century. The merits of the proscenium (picture-frame) stage, which fulfilled all artistic and period needs, were not contested. Semper's (see page 11) or Fellner and Helmer's splendid, closely integrated, architectural achievements for the theatre were not due to this uncontroversial nature of the formal programme.

For us in the twentieth century the task is more difficult. The makeshift solutions of the postwar era have shown up the defects of the picture-frame stage. Modern methods of presentation require different types of stage for the production of particular plays.

It is, in this connection, a striking fact that the significant ideas in the development of theatre forms have come almost exclusively from architects, who seem to have devoted more thought than directors and producers to the suitability of the contemporary type of theatre. Nearly all public discussions on this question have been instigated by architects rather than directors. This may be partly explained by the infrequent inclusion of directors of makeshift theatres in preparatory planning for the new building, and hence their slight interest in it. There is often a change in directors during the construction phase and each director has a different conception of acting.

Finally, the fact remains that the director must observe a neutral attitude to a competition. He cannot work with the architect in evolving new forms (as Gropius and Piscator once did), but is able at most to modify the prize-winning design, in collaboration with the architect, before it is built.

In very recent times, the artists have joined in demands for new forms of theatre. Thus the composer and conductor Pierre Boulez, in a lively interview, appealed for the destruction of all old opera-houses, because they obstructed the possibility of new forms of opera. L. Nono, K. H. Stockhausen and B. A. Zimmermann are seeking new horizons in opera, and the youngest generation of producers are turning away from the established theatre and exploring fresh opportunities in stagecraft. Indeed there are many increasingly insistent voices which consider the present type of repertory theatre and policy of artistic variety outmoded, and aim at a concentration of the theatre. This would be achieved by confining the town theatre to one type of performance at a time and, if need be, presenting the individual works in 'runs', so as to make more efficient use of resources. (At the Freie Volksbühne in Berlin and—somewhat differently—at the Schauspielhaus in Düsseldorf this is already done.)

Of late the idea of the 'street-theatre' has been constantly raised in discussions. The endeavour to free the theatre from its splendid isolation has led to proposals for a modern version of the medieval travelling players' wagon. In the designs of the Berlin students' competition echoes of this theme often recur (see page 19 et seq.), but the question remains whether such conceptions are practicable and, in particular, whether the open-air theatre can be organized as a permanent institution in Northern countries. If so, the charm of these solutions would lie in the immediacy and spontaneity of the situation. Oskar Fritz Schuh made a first attempt at the 1970 Salzburg Festival to relax the formality of an established institution by improvizations of similar intention, and one awaits with interest the outcome of his venture.

Projects of the Past Hundred Years

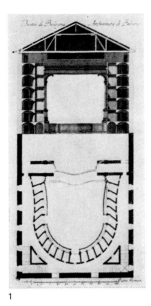

To make clear in which direction the opposition to traditional forms is moving and what attracts the utopians, a general view of plans introduced in the last hundred years must be provided. The initial form was the picture-frame stage, with the auditorium arranged as a balcony- and-box theatre, a concept of the early eighteenth century. This type of theatre, a reflection of court society of the period, with its strict separation of actors and audience, who faced each other across the apron of the stage, and its hierarchically divided public, survived throughout the nineteenth century. The 'royal' box was reserved for monarchs or heads of state, and the stalls now had seats, but the privileged were accommodated henceforth in the balconies and boxes. The often inadequate view from seats at the sides and the opposition to a class-segregated audience, with certain rows enjoying particular advantages, led in the end to a new form of auditorium.

There was more concern about the rigid separation of stage and public than with the subdivisions of the auditorium. Here efforts were especially directed towards the reduction of the distance between them, bringing the players to the public, and introducing the public to the theatrical 'happening' and involving them in it. These endeavours were particularly concentrated upon plays. Opera has remained to this day conservative in its structure. Because of the essential visual requirements, the orchestra has always been placed in the orchestra pit, with the conductor on the boundary between public and stage. This signified that all houses of 'mixed activity' were unable to abandon this arrangement, and consequently the form of most postwar new theatre buildings was predetermined.

The latest developments in television drama, however, have released the orchestra from its fixed position. In the production of the 'Soldaten' by Bernd Alois Zimmermann in Munich, a second orchestra was not located in the orchestra pit, but in another room, where it was 'co-ordinated' by electro-acous-

1–3
Antonio Galli Bibiena (1700-1774): Teatro Comunale, Bologna

4
Gottfried Semper: Hoftheater Dresden, 1837–1841

1

2

3

4

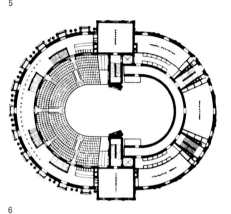

5

Projects of the Past Hundred Years

tical methods. The possibility certainly exists—in television it is already a fact—of ultimately separating stage and orchestra, so that opera too would be freed from the traditional picture-frame stage.

Despite previously immutable attitudes, important innovations stemmed from the operatic theatre. Richard Wagner built his Festspielhaus in Bayreuth as an arena. He wanted a popular theatre, and so the traditional divisions were deliberately abolished. Even today the theory of a people's theatre is bound up with the form of the arena. This new development in the organization of the auditorium substantially improved the range of vision but the

jekt 4000', while Hans Poelzig followed similar ideas in his theatres for Max Reinhardt—the Grosses Schauspielhaus in Berlin, and the design for the Salzburger Festspielhaus. The association of Reinhardt and Poelzig is not accidental. The great rooms were a complement to a theatrical event, which aimed at grandiose effects and impressive mass scenes.

While the actors were moved out from the 'frame' to the forestage, there was also a desire to rid them of scenery and rely more on the effect of the spoken word. Scenery was thought disturbing; uncluttered imagination should be given free rein. Today, seventy-

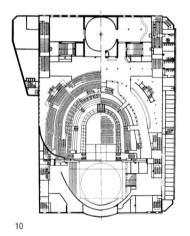

6

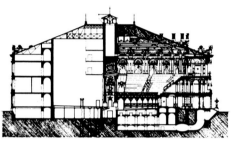

7

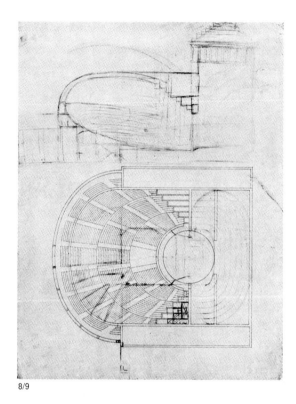

8/9

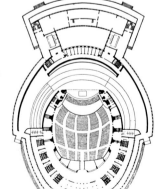

12

10

11

abolition of the circles (balconies) in the larger houses thrust the public further away from the stage. This could be more readily tolerable in opera than in a play, when significant details may be lost to the more distant part of the auditorium.

The revulsion against the framed stage led in other ways to new forms of auditorium. The first result was the incorporation of the proscenium area into the stage zone, the logical consequence of this being the deep extension of the stage-apron into the auditorium. The circular arrangement of seats in arena-shaped houses invited an almost similarly shaped stage. We find a plan of this type by Andreas Streit in his 'Reform-Theater' of 1887. Adolf Loos translated it into gigantic terms in his 'Theaterpro-

5
Friedrich Kranich the Younger: Festival Theatre Bayreuth, 1872–1876

6–7
Andreas Streit: Reform-Theater Vienna, 1887

8–9
Adolf Loos: Theatre project for an audience of 4000, 1898

10–11
Hans Poelzig: Grosses Schauspielhaus, Berlin, 1919

12
Hans Poelzig: Design for Salzburg Festival Theatre, 1920–1921

Projects of the Past Hundred Years

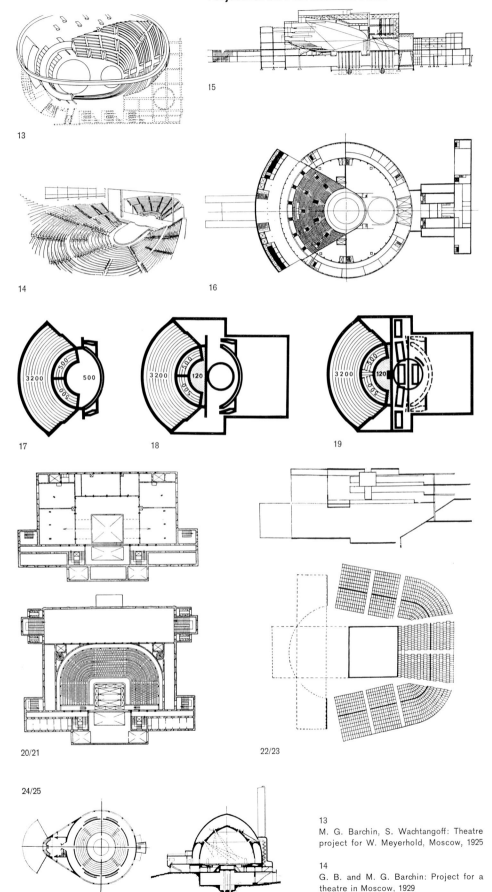

13
M. G. Barchin, S. Wachtangoff: Theatre project for W. Meyerhold, Moscow, 1925

14
G. B. and M. G. Barchin: Project for a theatre in Moscow, 1929

five years later, now that the old make-believe stage-sets have vanished, we find the bareness of a scene, in which the actor performs in an empty space, a positive disadvantage. After the war the policy was still to incorporate the proscenium, but so to arrange it that it could be provided with scenery. This was done by placing the safety-curtain in front of the proscenium area with a flying system in close proximity, and by ingenious use of lighting in the auditorium. Nowadays, in contrast to the past, the actor is no longer required to perform in isolation on the stage-apron, as if in a 'vacuum'.

The arena-form of stage, projected deep into the auditorium, particularly interested architects and theatre people of the twenties. In Russia there were a number of such projects; for example, the theatre developed in 1925 in Moscow for Meyerhold by Barchin and Wachtangoff. Another, by G. B. and M. G. Barchin of 1929, brought the arena-shaped galleries right on to the stage, so that the ring round the stage lying in the middle of the oval is complete. All the designs for the State Theatre at Kharkov (1931) provided for arena-shaped solutions. The proscenium area was in many instances planned to be varied and extended by novel means far into the auditorium. It is also possible that an arena-type layout was a condition of the competition, but the programme of this important and, in its day, much discussed event is no longer available.

Two schemes for a U-shaped theatre were submitted in the 1920s by Kreislinger and Rosenbaum, and by Farkas Molnar, in which the theory of the arena-theatre was further developed. Molnar worked at the Bauhaus where he met Gropius, whose Total-theater represented a logical synthesis of many forms of theatre debated at the time. The 'Intimate Theater', evolved by Norman Bel Geddes, belongs to the same category. The 'Théâtre en rond', established in Paris in the thirties, put these theories into practice with very modest resources, while many ideas of this time live on in the American college theatres (see page 57), and even the recently constructed Kellertheater at the Bonn Center reflects Molnar's views.

15–16
Zdenko von Strizic, Karl Ebbecke: Competition design for the Kharkov State Theatre, 1931

17–19
Alfred Karsten, Erich Hengerer, Carl Meyer: Competition design for the Kharkov State Theatre, 1931—three variations of the stage

20–21
Wilhelm Kreislinger, Fritz Rosenbaum: Design for an arena-stage 1925

22–23
Farkas Molnar: Design for a U-theatre, 1924

24–25
Norman Bel Geddes: 'Intimate Theatre', 1924

Projects of the Past Hundred Years

The concept of drawing the players away from a fixed stage area was more and more radically applied, with the audience and actors confronting each other with an increasingly immediate directness. This led to solutions like the 'Kugeltheater' of Andreas Weininger, in which the plane of the stage was split up into a central system of spiral stairs and platforms, surrounded on all sides by the audience.

In the German-speaking world the arena-stage was slow to gain acceptance. Several big competitions for playhouses were held at Essen, Düsseldorf, and Zürich. Only in Essen was the idea adopted of an arena-like stage projected into the auditorium (in this instance put forward by more than one entrant). Eckhard Schulze-Fielitz made proposals to this end, Fritz Bornemann evolved an interesting design for a round theatre; Bruno Lambart and Eisele, and P. Lanz and L. Schlör similarly took up the idea. In all other competitions however, at the very most only a meagre forestage area could be used as stage.

In the Ford Foundation competition of 1962, which was to clarify fundamental questions of the modern theatre, the arena-stage was once again brought into prominence by E. Durell Stone. Otherwise it has lost its actuality.

A variant of these layouts is offered by houses in which the acting area is designed to be flexible. A part of the stalls can be adapted as a stage, and a section of the audience can be shifted round on seating wagons into the stage-area proper. Barchin's project provided for this, and the Totaltheater of Gropius could be similarly manipulated (see page 17). In recently built houses this form of adaptable arena-stage is often found.

In the Mannheimer Schauspielhaus seat wagons have been installed, so that the audience can be placed on the stage, and a central stage results (see page 116 et seq.). In the 'Small House' at Gelsenkirchen there is also a central arena stage (see page 122 et seq.), and in the Berliner Akademie a

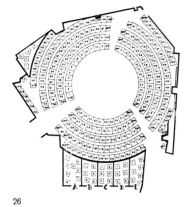

26

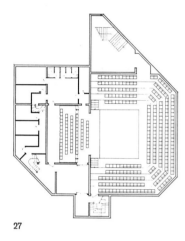

27

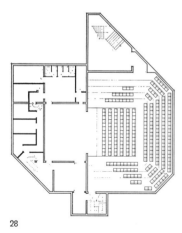

28

29

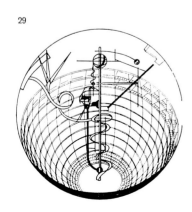

30/31

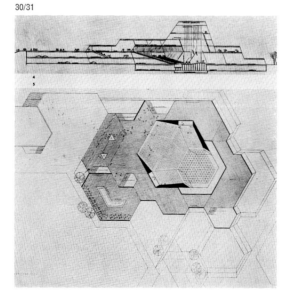

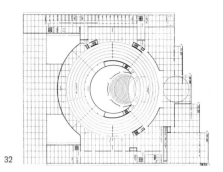

32

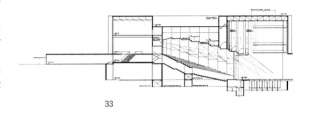

33

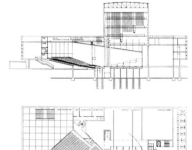

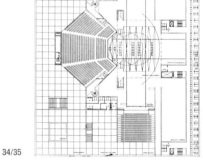

34/35

26
'Théâtre en rond', Paris

27—28
Theatre in the Bonn Center, 1969–1970

29
Andreas Weininger: Project for a spherical theatre, 1924

30—31
Eckhard Schulze-Fielitz: Competition design for Essen Opera House, 1959

32—33
Fritz Bornemann: Competition design for Essen Opera House, 1959

34—35
P. Lanz, L. Schlör: Competition design for Essen Opera House, 1959

Projects of the Past Hundred Years

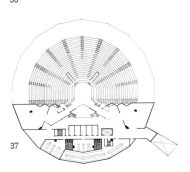

36

37

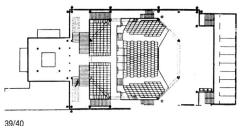

39/40

43

44

bridge-stage for use on two sides (see page 180 et seq.). However, one thing is common to all these stages; almost without exception, they are used in the traditional manner. In the Düsseldorf 'Small House' (see page 169 et seq.), in the 'Cellar Theatre' at Bonn (see page 14) and the Studio at Ulm (see page 175 et seq.), the same kind of flexible staging is provided, and it remains to be seen whether the producers will accept it.

Another tendency is reflected in an increase in the width of stage space and the provision of several adjacent playing areas. Henry van de Velde gave the first impetus to this development in his Werkbundtheater at Cologne in 1914, in which two significant ideas were exploited for the first time: the portal is no longer treated as an ornate stage frame, but as a simple post-and-beam construction, making the separation of auditorium and stage as imperceptible as possible; two columns divide the stage

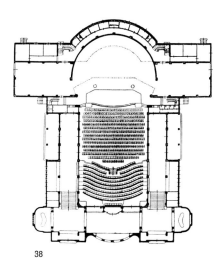

38

into three sections, a larger 'main stage' in the middle, and two, slightly angled, smaller 'secondary stages'. Thus the play can be performed without interruption on several stages consecutively or simultaneously. It was certainly not by chance that the 'Faust' which derives from the cycle of medieval mystery plays was first performed here. For these, too, demanded several sets or platforms erected next to one another, with the public gathered in front.

Auguste Perret created a similar form of theatre for the Paris Decorative Arts Exhibition of 1925. But the most logical plan stems from the Austrian Oskar Strnad, who in 1918 designed a scheme for a playhouse in which the audience sat on an arena-shaped, steeply raked bank of seats, around which the stage, divided into a number of separate segments, formed a ring. The central part carrying the audience could be turned so that the play proceeded without intervals from scene to scene. An open-air stage of this kind has been built at Tampere in Finland where it is used every summer. Gropius also took up the idea of the revolving theatre, with the special object of achieving, with the help of the rotatable section, the greatest possible number of variations in the shape of the stage. The 'Théâtre mobile' of Jacques Polieri brought this concept up to date: rotatable audience-core and ring-form stage. The concept was very recently put into practice by André Wogenscky in the Maison de la Culture at Grenoble (see page 28). Here the audience-core, as it had been with Strnad, is rotatable, while the circular stage can also be revolved. This theatre is intended as a 'Small House' and serves as a playhouse. The opera has preserved the traditional 'peep-show' stage.

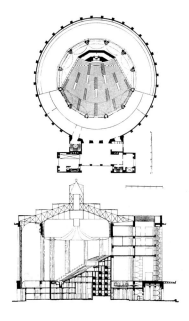

41/42

36—37
Edward Durell Stone: Design commissioned by the Ford Foundation on the theme of 'The Ideal Theatre', 1962

38
Henry van de Velde: Theatre for the Werkbund Exhibition, Cologne, 1914

39—40
Auguste Perret: Théâtre pour l'Exposition des Arts Décoratifs, Paris, 1925

41—42
Oskar Strnad: Design for a playhouse, 1918

43
Open-air theatre, Tampere, 1959

44
Jacques Polieri: 'Théâtre mobile', 1960

Projects of the Past Hundred Years

The exceptionally wide 'Cinerama'-screen of Hans Scharoun may be regarded as the ultimate consequence of the van de Velde stage. There is no division into separate sections, but the flat broad expanse of stage inevitably implies an increased width of scene, and suggests a subdivision into a number of settings. For Kassel (see page 212) a stage of this type was proposed, and at Mannheim Scharoun planned something similar. In the building for Wolfsburg, now in process of realization, Scharoun has abandoned his staging ideas on technical grounds (see page 214 et seq.).

The notion of offering producers the widest possible choice of theatrical expression with the minimum operating costs has constantly exercised architects' minds since the twenties. Thus, from the collabora-

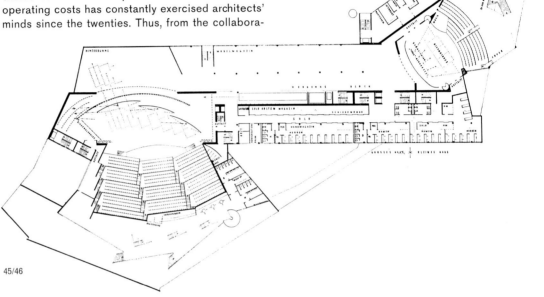

45/46

45—46
Hans Scharoun: Competition design for the National Theatre, Mannheim, 1953

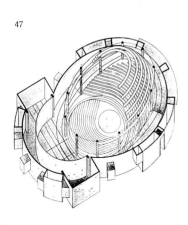

47

tion of Gropius and Piscator, grew the conception of the Totaltheater. The partnership between these two sympathetically matched artists led to the first, and until now most consistently planned, application of this theory. The project epitomizes all the multifarious endeavours to discover a new theatre seen in the first half of the present century.

Flexibility for the auditorium, as for the stage, is similarly the aim of the much discussed design by A. P. von Laban and E. Stoecklin for Krefeld of 1951, although other influences are apparent here. In 1944 a new theatre came into being in Malmö, by Erik Lallerstedt and Sigurd Lewerentz, of which the auditorium can be reduced by movable partitions from eleven hundred to six hundred or four hundred seats. In this way the theatre—it has a conventional stage—can be altered from a large house to one of an intimate type. Laban and Stoecklin adopted this idea, suspending segmental divisions in the curved auditorium, so that this could be varied. In addition, as with the arena-stages mentioned above, the stalls can be incorporated in the stage. The idea

of auditorium-flexibility has been taken up comparatively seldom. Knud Munk returned to it in his first-prize award-winning design for an opera house in Göteborg in 1969 (see page 48), and in America there are several theatres in which this principle has been applied (see page 57 et seq.).

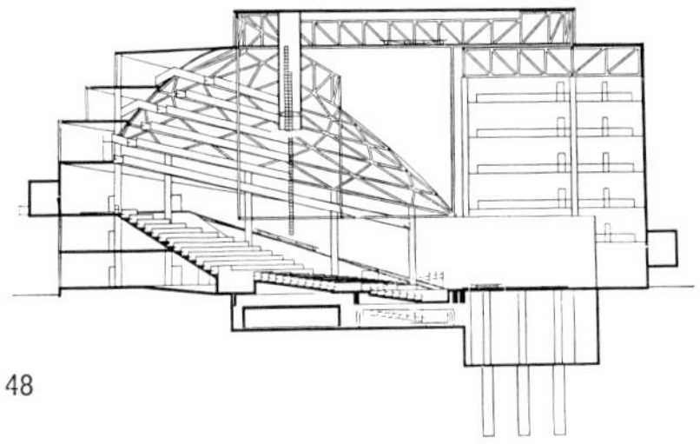

48

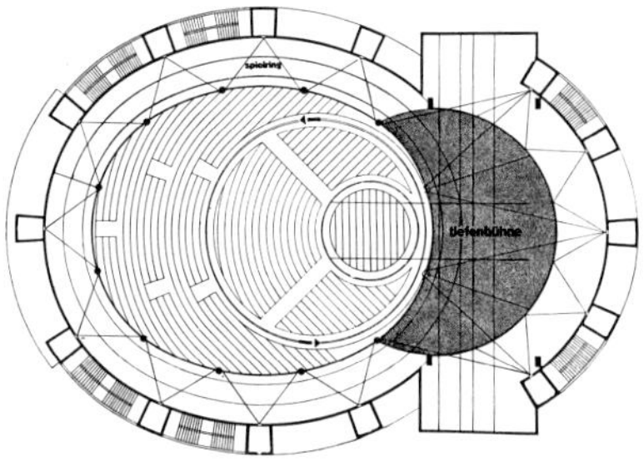

49

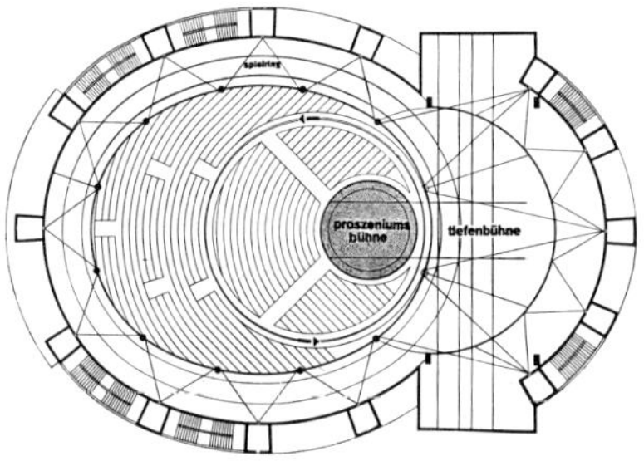

50

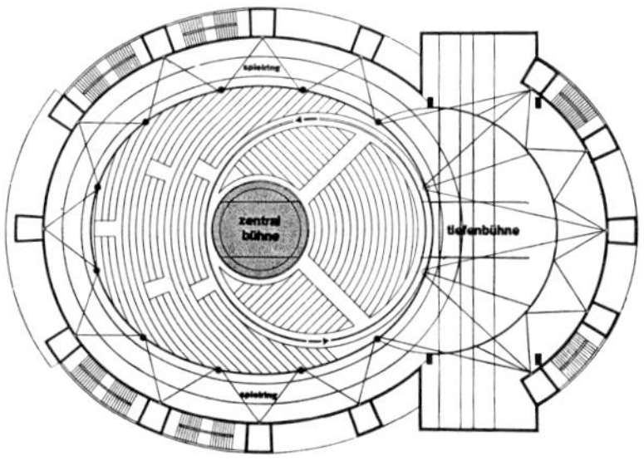

51

52

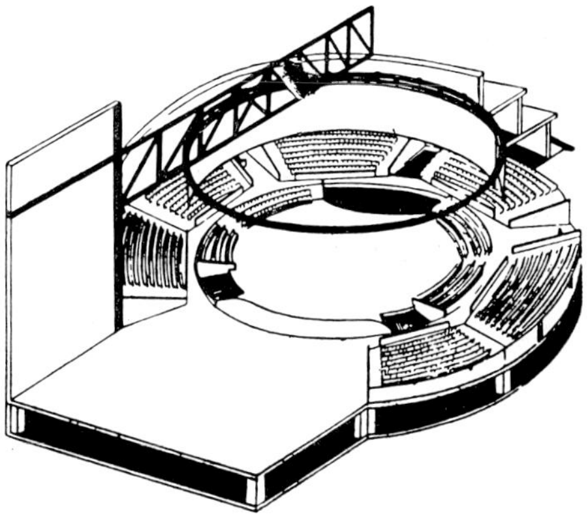

53

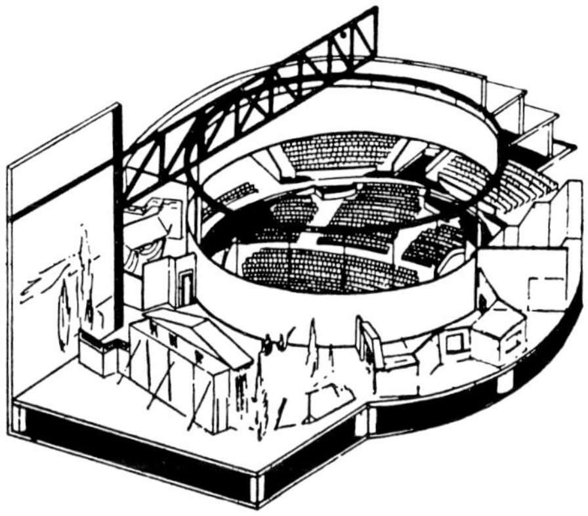

54

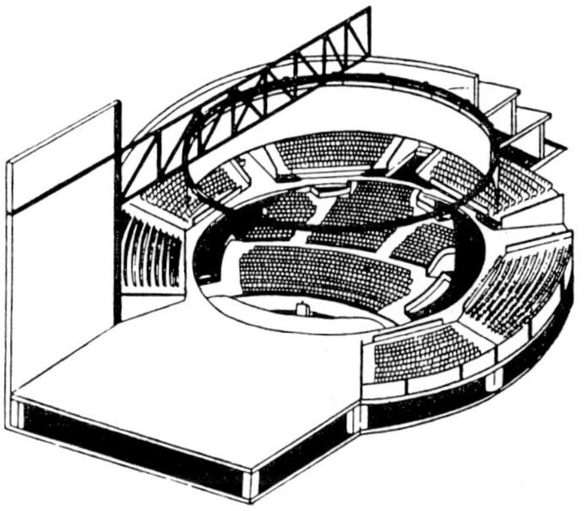

55

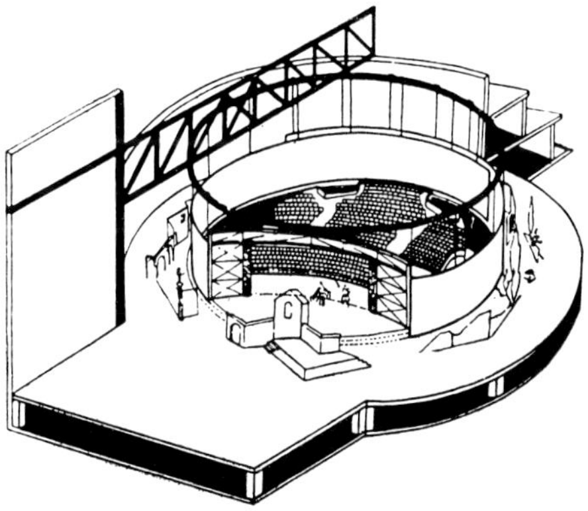

56

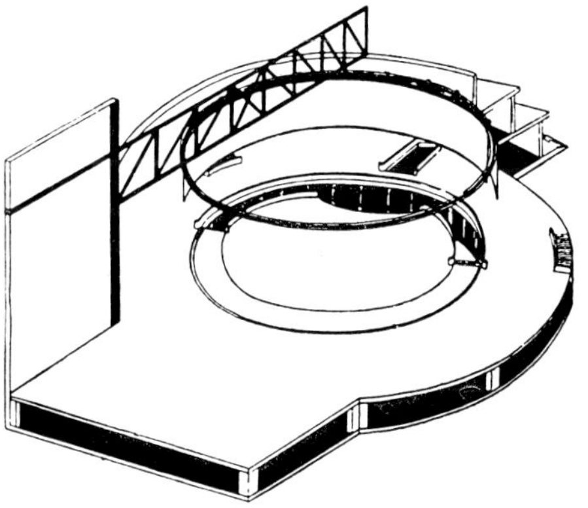

57

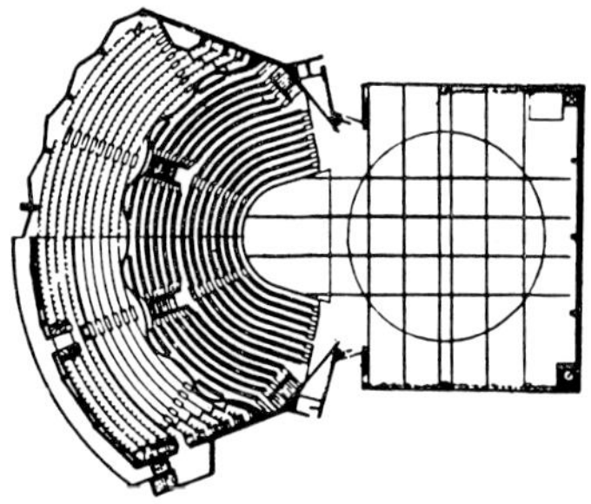

58

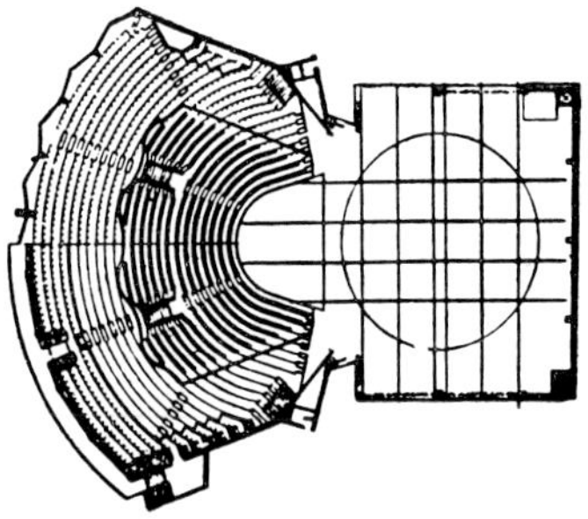

59

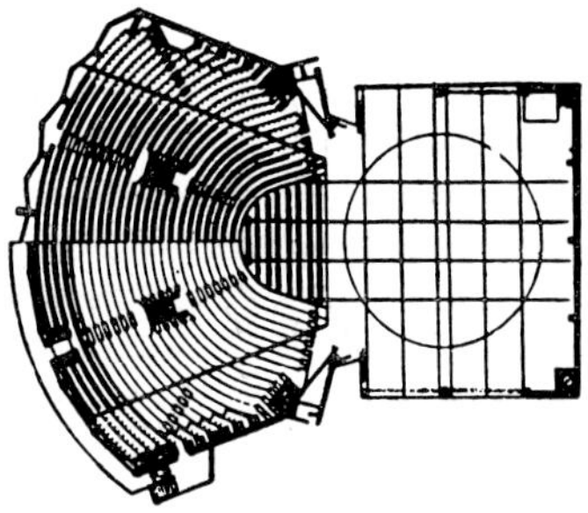

60

47–51
Walter Gropius: Design for the 'Total-theater', 1927

52–57
André Perottet von Laban, Erwin Stoecklin: Design for a municipal theatre at Krefeld, 1951
Festival theatre
Arena theatre
Congress/concert hall
Grand spectacular
Intimate theatre
Exhibition

58–60
Erik Lallerstedt, Sigurd Lewerentz: City Theatre, Malmö, 1944

17

Projects of the Past Hundred Years

The first Basle competition of 1953 revealed proposals aimed at making the stage area as flexible as possible and capable of alteration from the picture-frame to the open stage; for example, the Vischer, Weber, Bignens scheme. A little later, in 1955, Roman Clemens, who was the architect for the exhibition of the Darmstadt Theatre Symposium, elaborated the 'Theaterprojekt B', in which he set out a solution for the stage 'frame'. This was the point of departure for subsequent practical developments. The technical advance in the evolution of the stage opening has been an important contribution of German postwar theatre architecture.

The idea of making the stage flexible enough to be used both as picture-frame and as open and arena

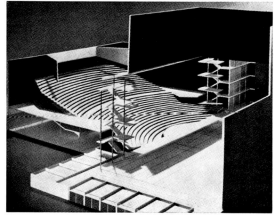

62

61

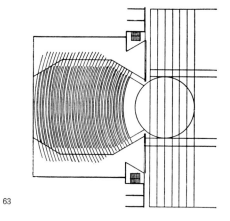

63

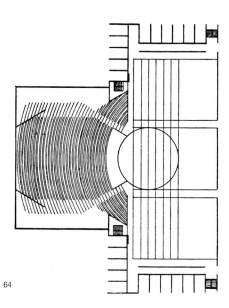

64

65/66

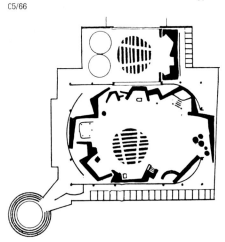

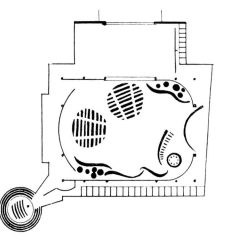

Projects of the Past Hundred Years

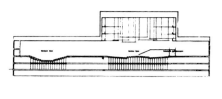

theatre originates from a stylistic interpretation of stagecraft, which places practical propriety first. The intention is to present each individual play on the form of stage appropriate to it: classical drama in an arena, nineteenth-century naturalistic in a picture-frame. At the same time there is a desire to master new forms of stagecraft and to create the instruments proper to them.

Today there is a tendency towards another conception of stagecraft. Assuming that a complete reconstruction is not feasible, the chosen play is allotted to a traditional stage and the setting and style of performance are adjusted to the play. Alternatively, the stage is systematically constructed for the experiment. When this is not possible, one moves into a simple room, which does not render the producer unnecessary by a superfluity of built-in technical aids, but provides a very high degree of dramatic freedom by the addition of mobile equipment.

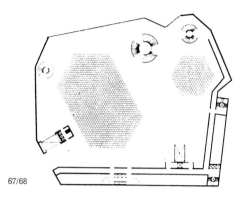

67/68

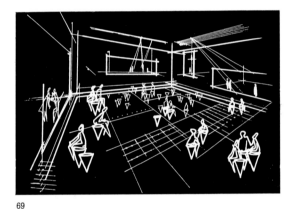

69

67–68
Werner Ruhnau: 'Mobiles Theater', competition design for Düsseldorf playhouse, 1959–1960

69
Jaacov Agam: Design for a theatre with several stages in counterpoint, 1963

70–71
Georg Renken: Competition design for a 'Theatre of Tomorrow', 1964–1965

70/71

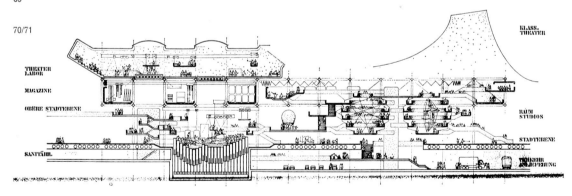

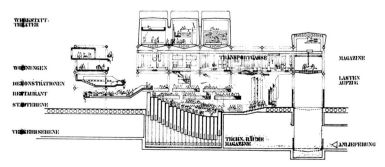

72–73
Norbert Wörner: Competition design for
a 'Theatre of Tomorrow', 1964–1965

74–75
Peter Blake: Competition design for 'The
Ideal Theatre', sponsored by the Ford
Foundation, 1962

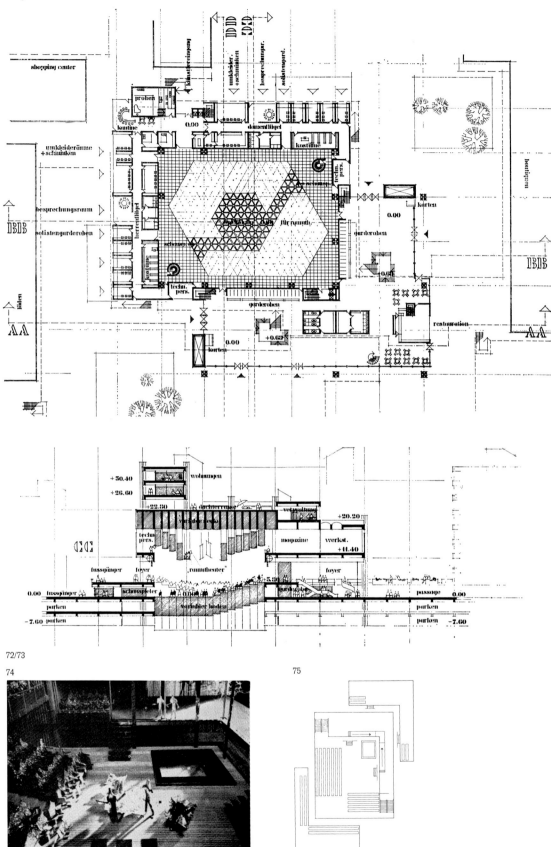

72/73

74

75

Projects of the Past Hundred Years

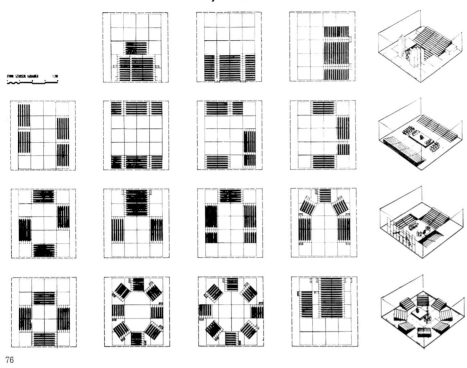

76

77–80

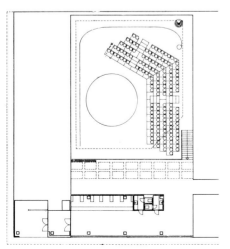

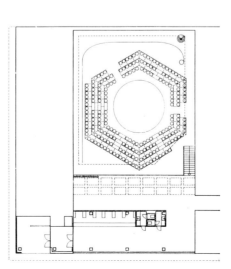

81

76
Weber, Rubinov: Competition design for the studio of the National Theatre, Budapest, 1965

77–81
Toivo Korhonen: Theatre laboratory, Tampere University, 1967

Recent theorists tend therefore to regard the entire theatre as a single unit, uniting public and stage in a large hall in order to create in it the necessary situations for the plays to be presented. In 1958 R. von Dobloff developed a 'Free Theatre' of this sort, and Werner Ruhnau a similar scheme with greater technical resources (Düsseldorf competition 1960). Jaacov Agam, in his design of 1963, once again reduced the technical apparatus. The entries for the Berlin students competition disclosed analogous proposals, e.g. those of Georg Renken and Norbert Wörner. All these projects stem from the plan of the television studio: a large hall is so arranged that all the mechanical equipment is located in the ceiling, leaving the floor area freely adaptable.

In his Düsseldorf plans Ruhnau went a step further by rendering the whole floor flexible by means of hydraulic platforms. This theatre caters for every conceivable situation for audience or stage, but the cost of the basic equipment is exceptionally high, and its operation would probably be very complicated in a repertory theatre. The projects of Peter Blake for the Ford Foundation competition and of the East German architects, Weber and Rubinov, for the Studio of the National Theatre in Budapest (1965 competition) are much more realistic. Here, too, the plain hall is the starting point, the various positional changes for the audience being brought about by wagons. A workshop-theatre of this kind has also been built. Toivo Korhonen built it at the University of Tampere—a space with many technical installations, which can be masked by a round curtain, while the mechanized ceiling remains exposed.

Projects of the Past Hundred Years

82—85
Ludwig Mies van der Rohe: Competition
design for the National Theatre,
Mannheim, 1953

It is clear that such schemes should not merely be regarded as theatrical utopias, for practical experience shows the increasing dissatisfaction of the younger generation with the status quo. They appear indeed to be an accurate reflection of their ideas, and it may be that there is a chance here to marry and realize the aims of producers and architects outside the established, institutionalized, theatre.

Mies van der Rohe's design for Mannheim illustrates an exception to this attitude. His concern is less with the revolution in the physical form of stages—in this case, both are basically conventional—than with communication with town and public. The theatre is open to the town and seeks to establish close links with the public 'outside', the richness of materials and architectural form reinforcing the contrast with workaday existence.

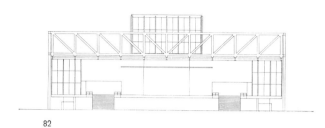

82

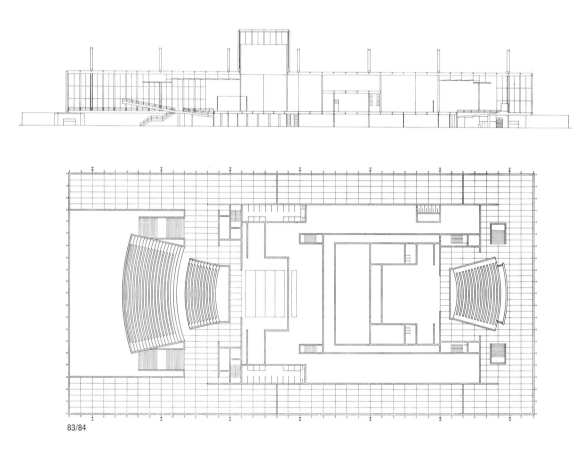

83/84

85

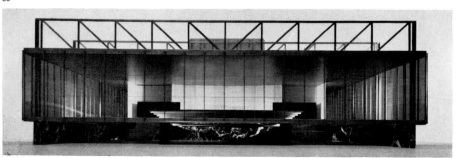

22

The International Scene

The International Scene

Within the context of this book it is impossible to give a description of the international position of theatre-building in the sense of a comprehensive survey. What follows is no more than a sketch, showing the most significant tendencies in various countries, but with no intention of providing an exhaustive picture. The aim is to offer opportunities for comparison, and to pinpoint resemblances and differences.

It has already been pointed out (see page 8) that theatre-building in the German-speaking world differs fundamentally from that of other lands. Nowhere else is the 'theatrescape' so extensive, with so many theatres in such close proximity as in the great commercial centres. For example, within a radius of one hundred kilometres of Frankfurt are five theatres: Wiesbaden, Darmstadt, Mannheim, Mainz and Koblenz. In the Ruhr, where the individual towns have grown into a single economic unit, it is the same: Cologne, Düsseldorf, Duisburg, Essen, Bochum, Oberhausen, Wuppertal and Dortmund are not more that two hours' car drive apart. It should further be stressed that most German theatres are not metropolitan theatres, but average-town houses for 'mixed activities'. This geographical and artistic situation may well be unique.

The position of Italy is historically not unlike that of Germany. The ambitions of the independent city-states and principalities lay in encouraging the arts, and in many towns very large theatres were the result. In Italy, however, comparatively few were destroyed in the war, so there was no need to build new ones. In Milan, Venice, Florence, Bologna, Genoa, Rome and Naples, the problem has largely been the preservation of the existing theatres.

Thus only two smaller theatres in Milan have become noteworthy among new buildings, both for the striking originality of their floor-plans (one must disregard the 'Piccolo Teatro', for its conventional character contrasts strangely with the remarkable performances given there by Giorgio Strehler).

The 'Teatro Sant'Erasmo' in Milan, built by Antonio Carminati and Carlo de Carli, is the first Italian theatre with a central stage, an 'intimate' theatre for straight plays. The 250 seats are stepped upward on two sides, as in a lecture-hall, with a few on the other two sides at stage-level spread round the octagonal stage. The technical equipment of the latter is very modest.

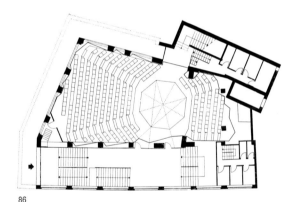

86

87

86–87
Antonio Carminati, Carlo de Carli: Teatro Sant'Erasmo, Milan, 1952–1953
Ground-floor plan, view from the stage into the hall

88–90
Vittorio Caneva, Gianni Grilletto, Vittorio Lattuada: Teatro alle Maschere, Milan, 1955
Ground-floor plan, stalls, view into the hall

91
B. and M. Boguslawski, B. Gniewiewski, M. Leszczynska: Competition design for Madrid Opera House, 1961

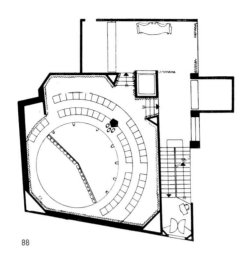

88

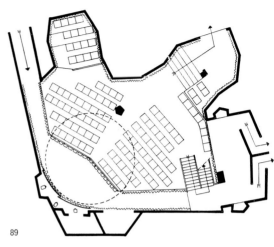

89

90

91

A second theatre of progressive design to appear in Milan is the 'Teatro alle Maschere', by Vittorio Caneva, Gianni Grilletto and Vittorio Lattuada, with an auditorium of only eighty-nine seats. Because of the confined space the stage was placed in a corner, with shallow-raked stalls on two sides. An original feature is the circular balcony, its opening embracing the entire stage. These two Italian theatres, however, are not in any true sense typical and representative solutions. They are interesting isolated cases, which owe their existence to the initiative of particular theatrical companies and managements, rather than to a widespread influential movement.

In Spain no new theatre building has attracted notice since the war, although a considerable stir was created by the international competition for an opera house in Madrid, which was held in 1961 (but unhappily without leading to a new building). The first prize went to a Polish group of architects: Boguslawski, Gniewiewski and Associates, the team which won first prize in Budapest in 1965. While the top award was conferred upon a strictly cubic solution with a spacious rectangular plan, on the basis of a completely systematic wagon-stage, the artistic importance of this competition lay more in the attempt to express the theme of a theatre architectonically than in the academic elaboration of the designs. Thus the third prize was gained by a Spanish team, led by J. L. Aranguren, for an entry in which the various rooms form a composition of cube-like steps; and the first honourable mention by the Swiss architect Justus Dahinden, in whose project a flat raft-like structure is combined with a truncated shell, under which the rooms of the stage area are grouped. Many of the entries submitted treated the problem simply as an exercise in architectural form, and made clear also that such monumental conceptions must remain visions, unless they conform to the practical requirements of theatre building.

92

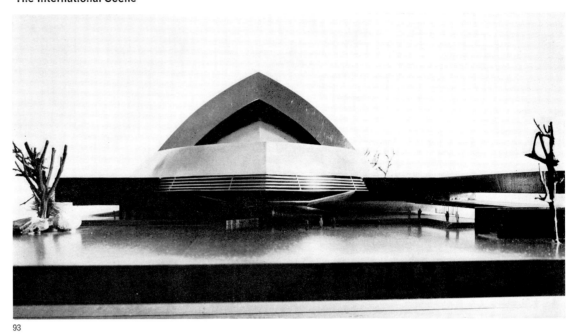

93

92
J. L. Aranguren, J. A. Corrales, J. M. Garcia de Paredes, A. de la Sote, R. Vazquez Molezun: Competition design for Madrid Opera House, 1961

93
Justus Dahinden: Competition design for Madrid Opera House, 1961

94
Claude Paillard (Atelier CJP), Hansjörg Gügler: Municipal theatre St. Gallen, 1964–1968

94

As a German-speaking country, Switzerland is included in the documentary section (see pages 107, 165). While in Germany the most active period of building new theatres was in the fifties and early sixties, in Switzerland it has only just begun. First to be opened was the Stadttheater at St. Gallen in 1968, which occasioned far more than local interest. The Stadttheater (municipal theatre) of Basle is under construction, and the new theatre for Winterthur is in the final planning stage (both are documented in the chapter on projects to be built, see page 208 et seq.). The two new buildings for Zürich have not yet been started. As long ago as 1961 a competition was held for the Opera House, and one followed in 1964 for the Schauspielhaus (playhouse, see page 198 et seq.). Although the competition designs have been further developed, their realization has been postponed for the present, because both sites are affected by a new traffic scheme, which has not yet been finally decided. While in Germany, therefore, only the late-comers, the theatres affected by the theatrical and economic crisis, are still at an early stage, in Switzerland the building of two important new theatres is yet to start.

France is organized very differently. Paris is the undisputed hub of the country, and sets the pattern for the theatrical world. In the provinces only a few of the larger towns have their own permanent companies. All the others have limited seasons or touring companies. This corresponds to the German 'Tourneetheater', which gives guest-performances and makes short 'stands' in the municipal theatres. As in many towns there are no theatres, and to counteract the increasing cultural monopoly of Paris, an interesting series of theatres have been built within the framework of the 'Maisons de la Culture'. Occasionally these are multi-purpose halls, but often they are genuine theatres built as part of a comprehensive community centre.

95

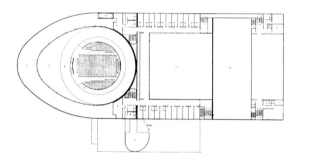

96

97

98

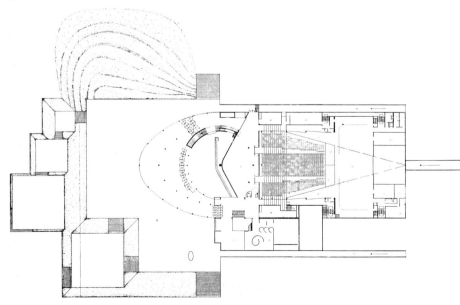

At Grenoble, André Wogenscky, for many years associated with Le Corbusier, built a magnificent Maison de la Culture with two theatres (Grenoble has its own company). While the larger house, for opera, with steeply sloping stalls, adheres to the principle of the traditional 'peep-show' stage, the smaller theatre, with a seating capacity of six hundred, embodies an interesting experiment, which puts into practice the ideas of Oscar Strnad and Jacques Polieri. It has a round, slanting, audience 'turntable', surrounded by a ring-stage, also rotatable, which widens elliptically on one side into the main stage. A second elliptical ring embraces the latter and serves as a store-room for scenery and properties, and as backstage. In Grenoble a principle often demanded for the German stage has been followed. The large house has been traditionally designed but a studio has not been considered adequate for the smaller and a full-sized theatre of six hundred seats has been built. Completed in 1968, it is undoubtedly one of the most significant of postwar theatres.

There are other interesting examples among the Maisons de la Culture. Pierre Sonrel erected the first of these buildings at Amiens, all of which were sponsored by André Malraux. Its main features are two theatres, the larger having an extremely unusual form of auditorium. In the front part, which includes the first rows of stalls, the orchestra pit and proscenium, two revolves have been installed. Thus the house can be used conventionally as a picture-frame theatre or, for plays, seats can be placed on these circle-segments, while enabling a large bridge-like stage to project into the auditorium. The use of this forward stage is made possible by direct lighting above the stalls. On the other hand the 'small house' is arranged in the traditional manner like a lecture-theatre.

At Rennes, where Jacques Carlu and Michel Joly were the architects responsible, a Maison de la Culture was opened in December 1968, which reveals a number of special features. Here, too, the large house has been planned conventionally for a picture-frame stage, but the traditional flies have been replaced with batteries of spot-lights. The smaller house, with about six hundred seats, is an oval-form arena theatre, which can serve both as an enclosed amphitheatre with central stage, and as a traditional theatre, whose forestage can be extended as required into the auditorium. Adequate lighting for every variety of scene is ensured by open flies.

95–99
André Wogenscky: Maison de la Culture, Grenoble, 1968
View from south-west, section, fourth floor, upper ground-floor, audience turn-table

100–103
Pierre Sonrel: Maison de la Culture, Amiens, 1966
Ground-plans, 6.65 and 3.50 m level; large and small halls

99

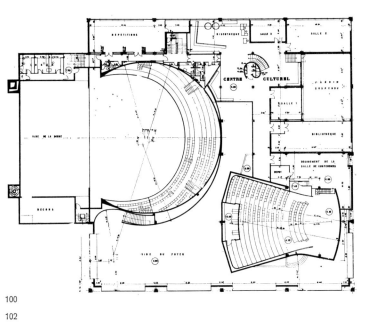

100

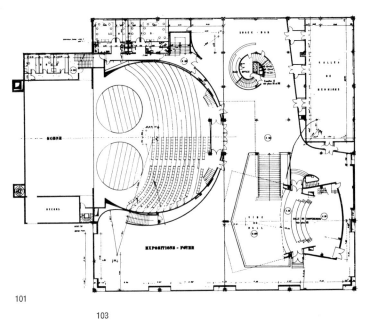

101

102

103

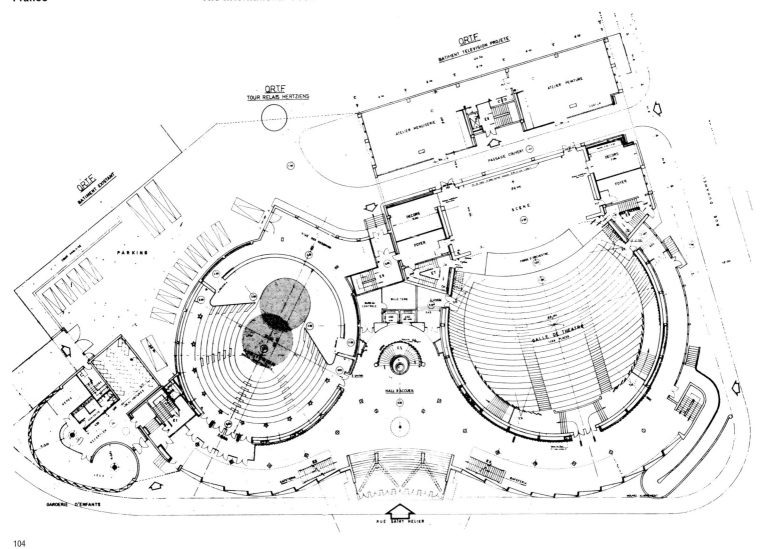

104

104—106
Jacques Carlu, Michel Joly: Maison de la Culture, Rennes, 1968
Main floor, large and small halls

105

These three French provincial examples illustrate the possibilities offered in a smaller scheme, when the programme is approached with a really unprejudiced and open mind. These Maison de la Culture, which may be compared with the German situation rather than the American college theatre, reflect more of the ideas of modern stagecraft than all the postwar new buildings in Germany.

In Belgium there have been few new theatres since the war. The Théâtre National in Brussels by Jacques Cuisinier has become well known, a theatre which in its organization closely follows the lines of the German Volksbühnen. It was fitted into space allocated for it in the Centre Rogier, a large commercial and office complex, in 1961. The various premises of the theatre are distributed through ten storeys of a wedge-shaped structure. It comprises a larger, conventional house with picture-frame stage, and a smaller theatre, its stage thrust deep into the auditorium and thus adaptable to open-stage use. This may imply laborious reorganization, but as all plays run for six to eight weeks, no great complications ensue.

106

107
Jacques Cuisinier: National Theatre, Brussels, 1961
Third floor

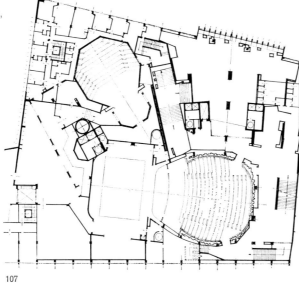

107

108

In England—as in France—the artistic centre is the capital, London. Plans for the National Theatre, actively pursued since 1951, are now slowly taking shape. A design by Denys Lasdun and Partners is in course of execution. The comprehensive Thames-side scheme incorporates three houses: a traditional theatre with picture frame stage for an audience of about nine hundred, a large house with 1165 seats, and a studio. In the biggest theatre, in which classical drama, Shakespeare and modern theatre will be played, the stage is placed above a corner in an angle, the revolving section being thrust forward into the auditorium, so that the rows of seats embrace the stage in an approximate semicircle. To a large extent the concept of Wright's theatre in Dallas (see page 62) has been adopted, but the 'theater in the quarter-round' of Norman Bel Geddes may also have been a model. The studio is a workshop of the type coveted by modern producers (two hundred seats): a rectangular hall, with a technical room on the narrow side, but otherwise completely flexible and adaptable to the widest variety of theatrical purposes. Thus the London National Theatre forms an entity of three completely distinct stages, on which every conceivable form of theatre can be presented.

England, however, can no longer rely on the magnetic power of the metropolis. Indeed precisely the opposite is apparent in the tendency to make the provinces culturally attractive to enlightened members of the technological and business communities who cannot live in London. Unlike France, whose Maisons de la Culture are the result of state initiative, England depends upon private support for her theatre, or at least to a considerable extent on private sources.

A good example of such patronage is the Octagon Theatre at Bolton (in the industrial region of Liverpool) by Geoffrey H. Brooks. It was planned for completion early in the 1970s as part of a community centre, but was opened in 1967 thanks to the enthusiastic endeavours of the impatient townspeople. It comprises 335 to 425 seats and can be exploited in various ways: as a central arena-stage (when it forms an elongated octagon) or as a traditional proscenium stage set in one angle of the octagonal figure. The economical, objective, functional appointments (and the low building costs) of the house show what abundant theatrical possibilities can be provided with modest means.

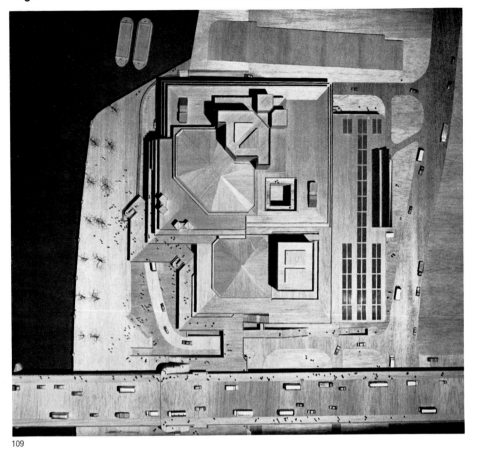

109

108–111
Denys Lasdun and Partners: National Theatre, London (under construction)
Model from north (p. 31), site plan model, floor-plans of lower theatre (street level) and upper theatre

110

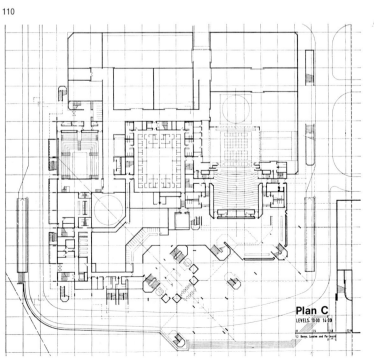

Plan C
LEVELS 10·00 14·00

111

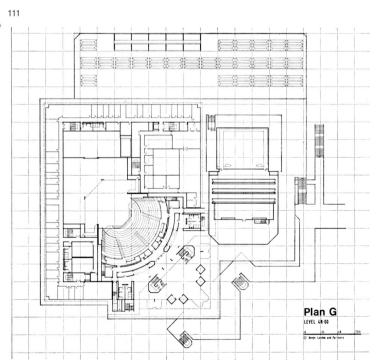

Plan G
LEVEL 48·00

112

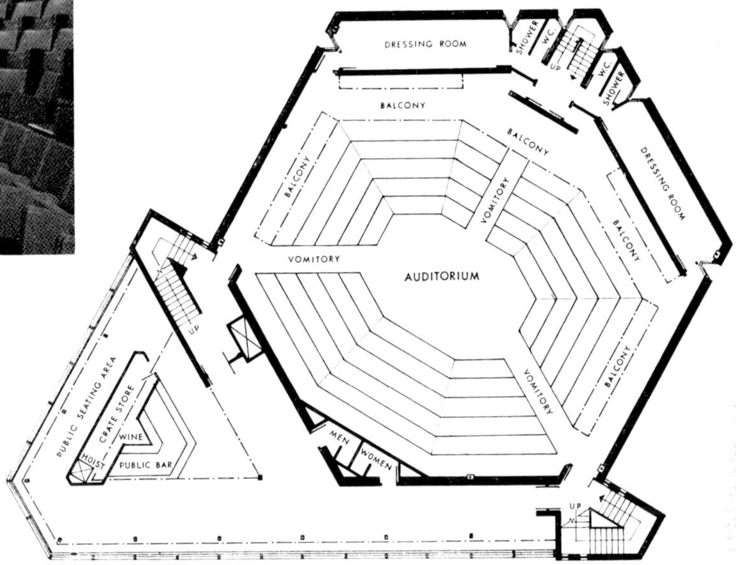

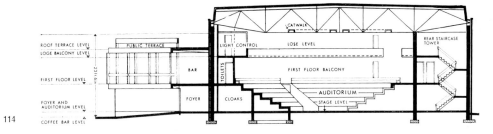

113

112–115
Geoffrey H. Brooks: Octagon Theatre,
Bolton, 1967
View of stage and auditorium, principal
floor plan, section, main entrance

114

115

The International Scene

A better known example of a parallel kind is the Chichester Festival Theatre by Powell and Moya built in 1962. For about £ 130,000 a completely functional theatre was erected with 1365 seats, none of which is more than sixty feet from the stage. The building is basically a hexagon, with the stage inserted into one of the points. The construction is startingly exposed, no part of the technical

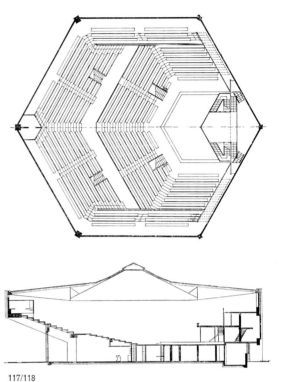

116

117/118

119

116–119
Philip Powell, Hidalgo Moya: Festival Theatre, Chichester, 1962
View from north-west, upper storey, section, view of stage and auditorium from side rows

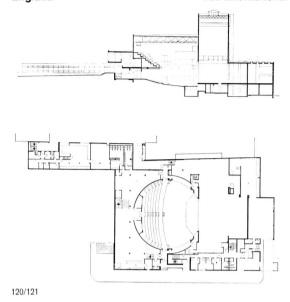

120/121   122

120–123
Peter Moro and Partners: Nottingham Playhouse, 1964
Section, lower floor, view from west, auditorium

123

equipment being hidden—the sort of theatre that one would go far and wide to find in the German provinces.

Another theatre of high architectural quality must be mentioned here, the Nottingham Playhouse, built in 1964 by Peter Moro and Partners. There are few theatres which are so clearly expressed stylistically, with such finely balanced proportions and which, in particular, have been planned with such technical precision. The transition from the circle of the auditorium (723–756 seats) to the rectangle of the stage is extremely well solved by the suspended lighting drum, which strikingly repeats the theme of the circular house. As at Gelsenkirchen internal walls are faced with a black slatted wood grille, but with a surer sense of form, enhanced by translucent strips of light. In contrast to the simple wall cladding, the balcony parapets and the box curtains are gold, while the seating is brilliant blue. Both produce a festive atmosphere in the house, although this was not deliberate. The cheerful effect is in no way impaired by the many spotlights mounted along the face of the balcony parapet. Practical needs and convenience have not been sacrificed to aesthetics.

35

124

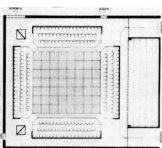

125

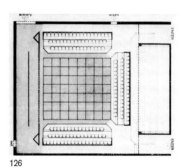

126

127

124–130
Peter Moro and Partners: Gulbenkian Centre, University of Hull, 1969
Perspective section, possible stage variations, general view, auditorium and stage

128

129

130

A students' theatre, extraordinarily well thought out and thoroughly detailed, was built in 1969 by Peter Moro and Partners for the University of Hull. The problem lay in combining in a single building a picture-frame stage and an arena-stage of the utmost flexibility. Moro solved it by placing a free circulation space round a squared central platform of almost chess-board character, any section of which can be lowered when not required, and erecting a fly-tower above it. This free zone is adaptable to every purpose; e.g. as stage or standing space for seat-wagons (indeed part of it can be used for the audience). The room can be opened on one side to expose a gallery of five rows of additional seats. With the aid of a few 'telari', a cyclorama, and a rigid-framed curtain, many different types of stage can be arranged—an ingenious combination of heterogeneous forms of theatre, which have also been well planned architecturally.

The theatre of the University of Southampton, built in 1964/65 to the designs of Sir Basil Spence, deserves to be mentioned more for the exceptionally logical assimilation of the bulky fly-tower into the scheme as a whole, than for the unusual form of stage. The outer walls, running counter to one another, interlock to enclose, on the one hand, the auditorium and, on the other side, the stage-tower, linking these two spatial elements smoothly together. Also noteworthy is the novel handling of the auditorium, in which the stalls progress without interruption into the balcony, but are embraced by the side arms of the latter.

The new Abbey Theatre in Dublin by Michael Scott and Partners must not be forgotten—an Irish reaffirmation, in its disciplined austerity, of the qualities of English theatrical architecture.

131–134
Sir Basil Spence: Nuffield Theatre, University of Southampton, 1964–1965
View from south-east, ground floor, section, view of auditorium from stage

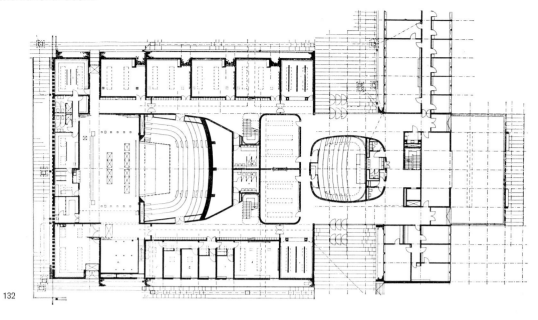

132

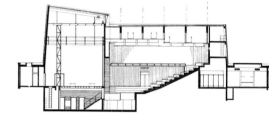

133

131

134

135

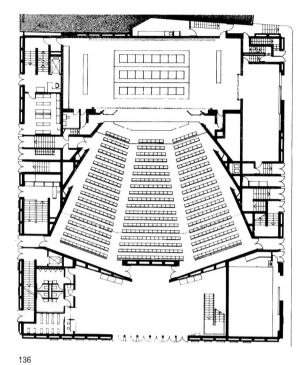

136

135–136
Michael Scott and Partners: The new
Abbey Theatre, Dublin

137

138

137–140
F. P. J. Peutz: Heerlen Theatre, 1961
View of auditorium from balcony, entrance front, principal floor, section

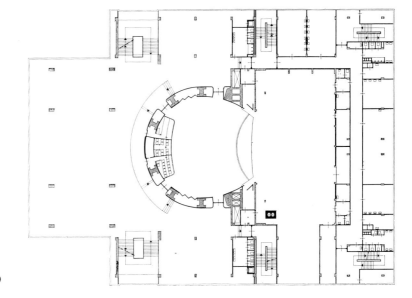

139

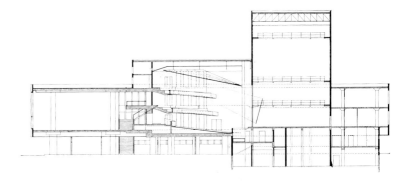

140

In contrast to her neighbour Belgium, Holland has built quite a number of new theatres since the war. Admittedly Amsterdam's opera still has no appropriate home, but in provincial towns several new theatres appeared at the beginning of the sixties. In 1961 F. P. J. Peutz built a theatre in Heerlen, which compels attention by its clarity and precision of line. In general, the new Dutch theatres are less remarkable for experiments in staging and architectural imagination than for functional objectivity and solidity of execution. In character Heerlen is related to the Mannheim theatre, with its strict rectangular forms, the huge glazed surfaces of the façades, and an almost parsimonious sobriety. At about the same time a new theatre was built at Nijmegen (architects, B. Bijvoet and G. H. M. Holt). This is spaciously sited, with a foyer wing (which can be used separately from the theatre) extending across the open public square. The same architects were responsible for the theatre at Tilburg, completed in the early 1960s. Here, too, the foyer extension forms an annex which can be isolated from the theatre and provides a certain architectural individuality. In the stage-and-auditorium block the motif of gently curving movement has been adopted from Münster for the fly-tower, the pronounced curvature of the auditorium contrasting with the shallow curve of the taller feature. The most recently finished (1963) of this group of new buildings is the Municipal Theatre of Eindhoven, by G. G. Geenen and L. R. T. Oskam. It is the most ambitious in conception, with two houses, the larger being particularly elaborate in its technical and subsidiary appointments. The smaller is interesting, because the little stage is provided with a generous forestage area, which can be transformed into a genuine arena-stage by removing some of the seating.

141

141—143
B. Bijvoet, G. H. M. Holt: Nijmegen Theatre, 1962
View from east, section, ground-floor

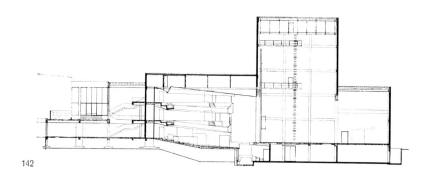

142

143

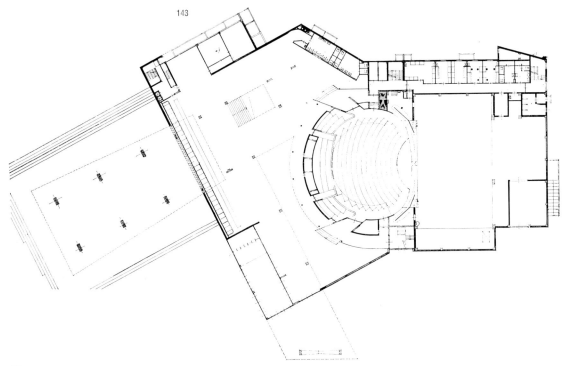

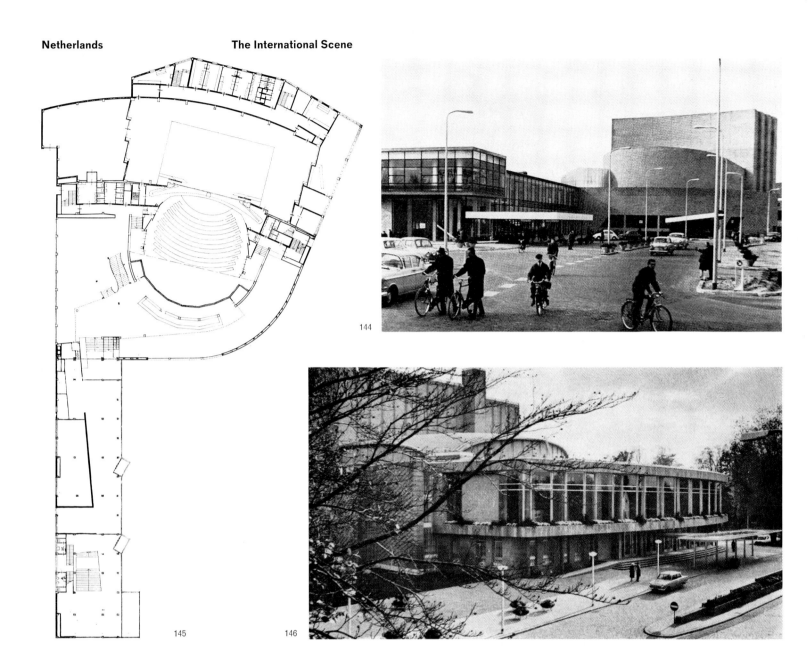

145

146

144

147

144—145
B. Bijvoet, G. H. M. Holt: Tilburg
Theatre, 1962
Ground-floor, view from north-east

146—150
C. G. Geenen, L. R. T. Oskam: Eindhoven
Theatre, 1963
Entrance front, large hall. P. 42: ground-
floor, section, basement (small hall)

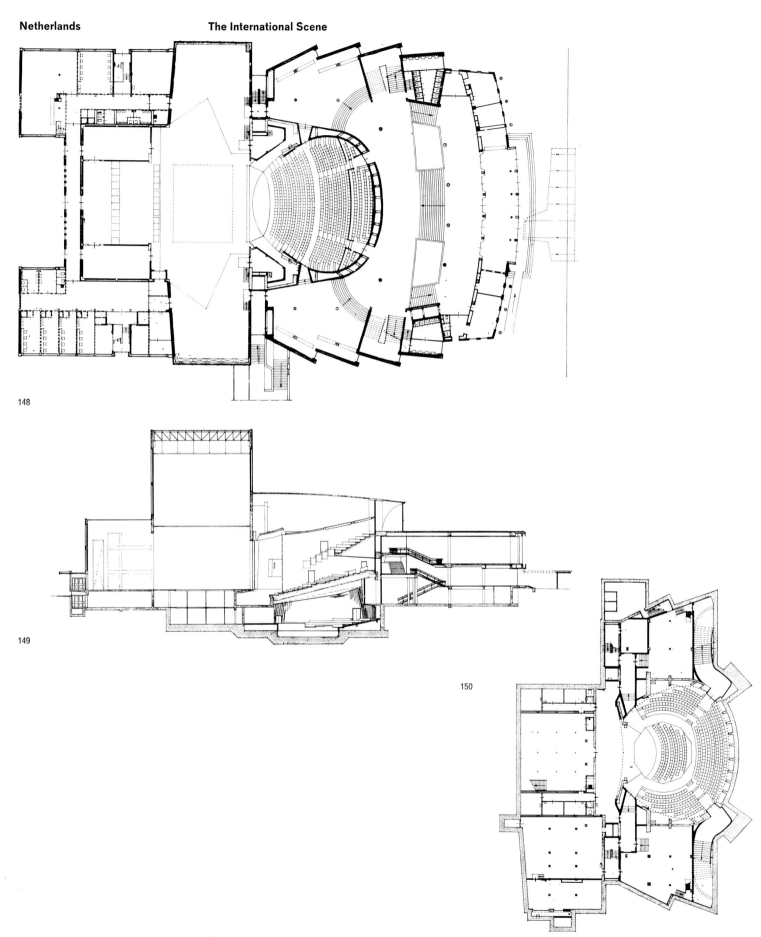

148

149

150

151

152

153

154

151–158
Timo Penttilä: National Theatre, Helsinki, 1967
Entrance front, large house, studio, ground-floor. P. 44: large house (section), possible variations of studio stage

In Scandinavia only a few new theatres have emerged since the war, no doubt because this period did not represent a cultural hiatus for these countries. The most important realization has been in Finland, where a new National Theatre was built in 1967 at Helsinki. On a splendid open parkland site, the architect Timo Penttilä was able to develop a comprehensive plan, in which most of the spatial elements are deployed at ground level. The large house is designed for a traditional picture-frame stage with an exceedingly wide proscenium opening of more than sixty feet, recalling Scharoun's big-stage schemes. The sight-lines, moreover, remain good with the width narrowed to forty feet, although the auditorium, only fifteen rows deep, has an extremely shallow rake. The layout of the studio is most interesting. The seating is arranged in an arena-like half-circle, which can easily be extended to a three-quarter round. Only light sliding partitions are used

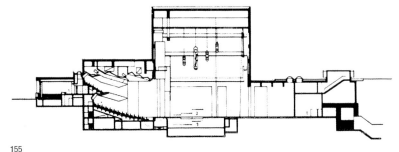

155

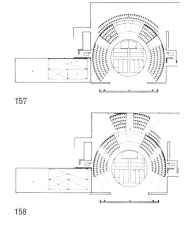

156

157

158

At Turku there is an enchanting smaller theatre, which was built in 1962 for 6,800,000 Finnish marks to the designs of architects R. V. Luukkonen and Helmer Stenros. It is completely equipped with workshops and scene-stores, and wholly constructed of Finland's superb and characteristic materials, wood and copper. It is also no hotchpotch of modernistic clichés, but a clear-cut conception of an architectural standard which can by no means be taken for granted in the theatre domain in Germany.

Toivo Korhonen, whose university buildings at Tampere drew admiring attention, included a 'theatre-laboratory' in the scheme. It is equipped like a television studio, a rectangular room full of unconcealed technology, an acting-machine adaptable to practically any purpose. A large cyclorama, which can be moved along a circular track in the ceiling, makes it possible to mask much of the mechanized wall surface, as required (see page 21).

to screen the stage, since the safety-curtain could be dispensed with. The seat-rows are arranged on five wagons, so that the room can be quickly and frequently varied. The ceiling, in the manner of television studios, is equipped in its entirety for technical purposes. The foyer and grand staircase are especially attractive, while the wide-opening glass walls offer an unobstructed view of the beautiful park.

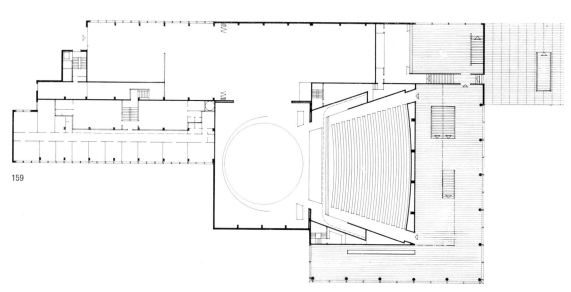

159

160

159–160
R. V. Luukkonen, Helmer Stenros: Turku Theatre, 1962
Upper floor, view of auditorium

161

162

163

161–163
Erik Lallerstedt, Sigurd Lewerentz: City Theatre, Malmö, 1944
Entrance front, views of auditorium

Sweden completed her most important theatre of recent times in 1944: the theatre at Malmö, designed by E. Lallerstedt and Sigurd Lewerentz—a building which has been constantly referred to, but nowhere really imitated. It is remarkable for the spatial adaptability of the auditorium, the capacity of which can be reduced from eleven hundred to six hundred or four hundred seats. This is very simply achieved by pull-out folding partitions, which can be easily operated manually by one man (see page 17). The scheme also includes an 'Intimate Theatre' with 204 seats, so all kinds of performances can be presented from the studio play to grand opera. The straightforward architectural treatment has successfully resisted criticism for twenty-five years. The spacious foyer faces the city through wide, clearly articulated glazed walls. The auditorium, handled with disciplined simplicity, is lined with light-coloured, delicately grained, wood.

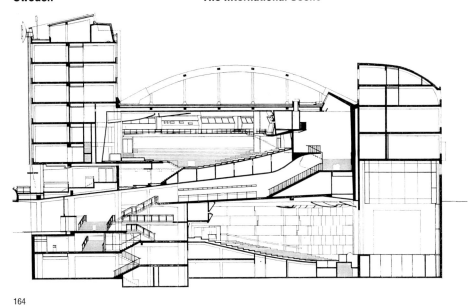

164

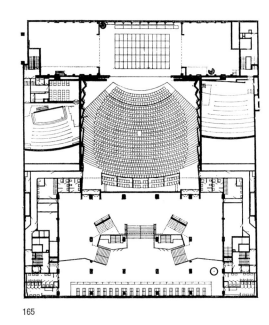

165

166

The Folketshus in Stockholm by Sven Markelius was finished in the early sixties. This large structure, comprising congress hall, assembly rooms and restaurants, also houses the City Theatre with all the ancillary stage offices. Sited in a busy street, the theatre fits inconspicuously into the townscape shallow, picture-frame stage. The equipment is con- steeply in wide rows before a broad, but rather behind an office-frontage. The auditorium rises ventional.

Two competitions have attracted notice in Sweden in recent years. One of these, held in 1965, for a theatre at the university town of Umea, produced many interesting ideas. In particular, the project of the Swedish architect I. Häussler, for whom the well-known Stockholm producer Per Edström acted as consultant, is still much discussed. The inter- esting feature of this scheme is that it combines three theatres, which can be arranged and 'played' completely differently by moving the seat-wagons

167–172
Immanuel Häussler: Competition design
for theatre at Umea, 1965
Possible stage variations; floor plans,
17.05 and 12.25 m level; section

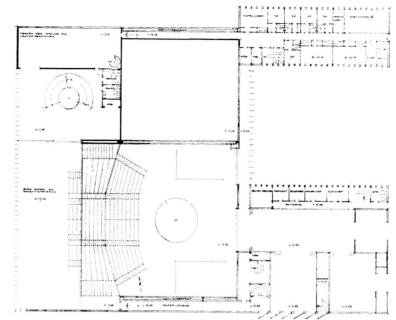

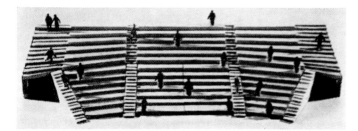

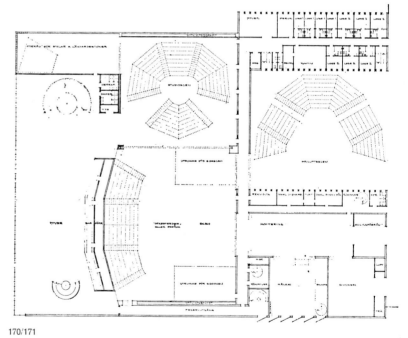

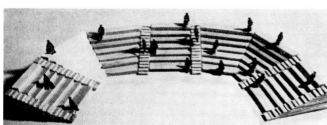

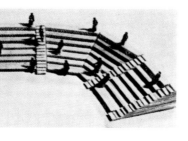

167–169

170/171

172

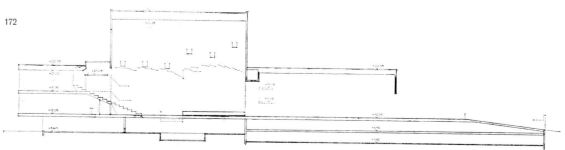

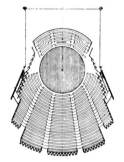

173

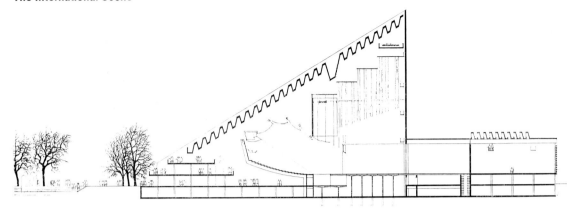

176

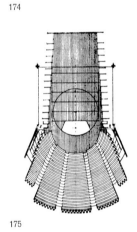

174

175

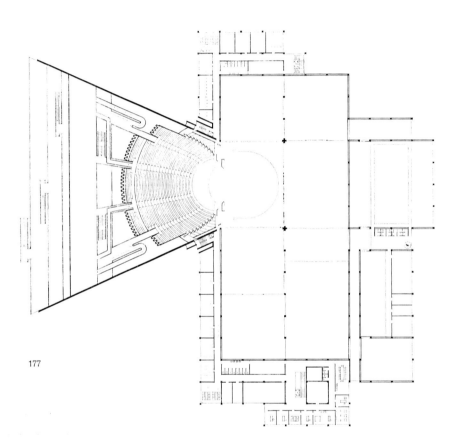

177

173–177
Knud Munk: Competition design for theatre at Göteborg, 1969
Possible stage variations; section; floor plan, 21.90 m level

from one to the other. Only for the largest house is a more or less fixed layout prescribed, although it too may be varied at the boundary between audience and stage.

The competition for a new theatre in Göteborg, decided in 1969, has also been a source of eager debate. Knud Munk won the first prize with a visually impressive design. While all workshops and ancillary stage areas are concentrated in a flat low building, a great sloping roof rises from above the entrance hall to the top of the fly-tower, tapering towards the apex in the manner of a single-sided pyramid. Inside is suspended an amphitheatrical auditorium, disposed as at Malmö (but less ame-

nable to variation), and a stage which borrows many ideas from the Kharkov competition (see page 13).

In Norway a competition took place in 1967 for a cultural centre at Skien, the Ibsenhuset. Here a small playhouse was incorporated in a group of lecture and exhibition rooms. The design by Asmund Skard and Ole Stoveland, awarded the first prize, is adroitly adjusted to the steeply falling site, so that from the entrance-front the centre appears to be a largely low and flat building. On the valley side, however, it 'digs into' the ground, absorbing the whole of the stage complex. In the final version the continuous flat roof has been abandoned to house a grid above the stage.

178

179

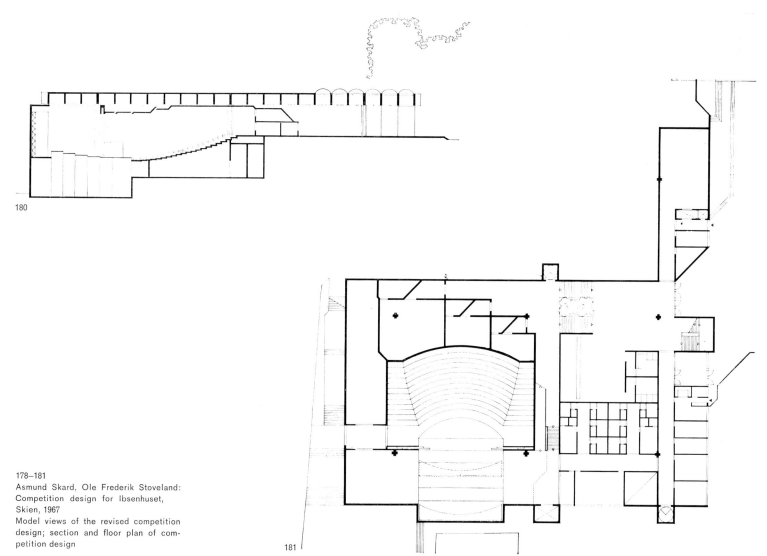

180

178—181
Asmund Skard, Ole Frederik Stoveland:
Competition design for Ibsenhuset,
Skien, 1967
Model views of the revised competition
design; section and floor plan of com-
petition design

181

182

183

182–184
Bohdan Pniewski: National Theatre, Warsaw, 1954–1965
Main entrance front, auditorium view, floor plan at stage level

184

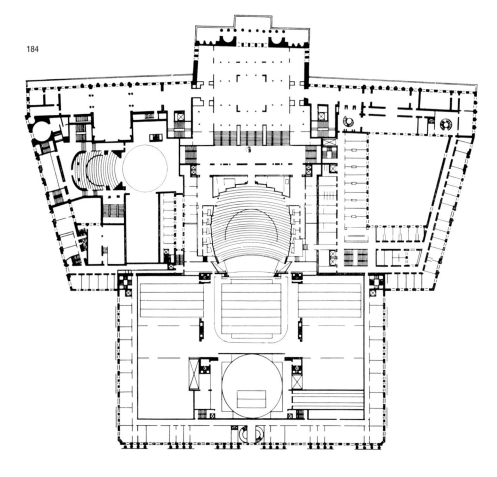

In Poland, following the destruction of the last war, a considerable number of theatres have been rebuilt. The best-known is the Warsaw National Theatre (architect Bohdan Pniewski), which was reopened in 1965 on the occasion of its bicentenary. It comprises a large house for opera and ballet, and a smaller playhouse. Only Antonio Corrazzi's façade survives from the old building. This is a new creation therefore, but one which incorporates what remains from the past and adapts itself to the circumstances.

The large theatre is designed with raised and steeply raked stalls, two spacious balconies and nearly 1900 seats. In layout it conforms to the strict form of picture-frame stage, inherited from the nineteenth century. The dimensions, however, are vastly increased. The principal stage is some 90 x 120 feet, and can be extended to a depth of 170 feet. Appropriate technical appointments of the highest standard are provided. The little house is located in a wing and also has the traditional type of 'peepshow' stage, but of substantially more human scale.

Another large new theatre was built after the war at Lodz (architects W. Korski, J. Korski and R. Symborski) — a building with an impressive colonnaded façade, but inside far more restrained than this monumental introduction might suggest. The extensive area of the stalls is subdivided by numerous gangways and covered by a deeply projecting balcony. Acoustic elements, handled in a robustly ornamental fashion, adorn the ceiling. The spacious stage, surmounted by a high grid, opens into an extensive backstage.

185

186

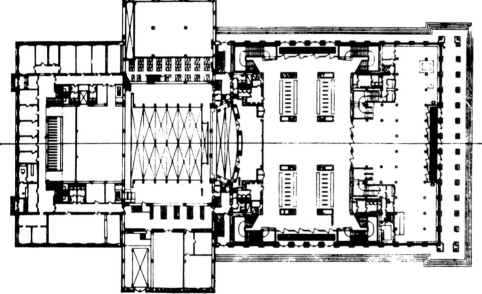

187

185–188
W. Korski, J. Korski, R. Symborski: Theatre at Lodz, 1958–1962
View of auditorium from stage, main entrance front, entrance
floor, section

188

Poland

189–192
Lech Kadlubowski, Daniel Oledzki: Theatre at Danzig, 1966
View of auditorium, main entrance front, ground-floor, section

190

191/192

189

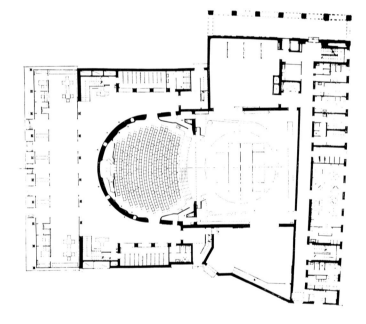

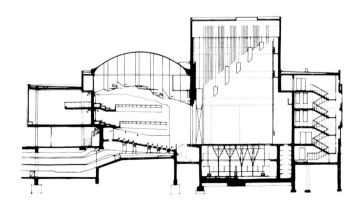

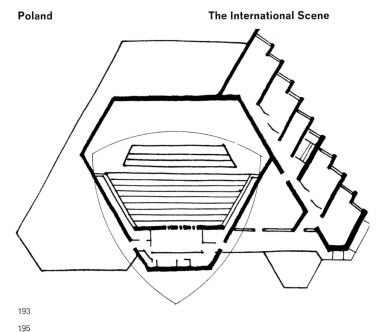

193

195

194

193—195
Wiktor Jackiewicz: Theatre at Lasku, 1968
Floor plan at stage level, auditorium, main entrance front

The new theatre at Danzig, by Lech Kadlubowski and Daniel Oledzki, stands in deliberate contrast to the rehabilitated and reconstructed buildings of the old city, presenting a completely glazed front to the old square. The broad cube of the foyer is stepped up and beyond the auditorium dome to a high fly-tower. The almost circular auditorium is placed inside the large rectangular foyer, the stalls being partially ringed by two deep-projecting balconies. The stage proper is spaciously planned, but has no backstage and has only narrow access-ways to the wing-spaces. The plan of the old house determined in many respects the organization of the new.

A small playhouse was built in 1968 at Lasku (architect Wiktor Jackiewicz) to an asymmetrical plan, with the stage brought right into the auditorium. The theatre achieves its effect from the contrast of plain brick and exposed concrete frame. The roof framework, too, is exposed, as is the technical equipment built into it.

196

In Czechoslovakia, the theatres of the capital, Prague, were not destroyed, but in the provinces there have been many new buildings and reconstructions. Of these, the most significant is the new theatre at Brno, which was completed in 1965 after twenty years of planning and building, and is today recognized as one of the most important modern examples in the country (architects Otakar Oplatek, Vilém Zavrel). Rich materials characterize this lavish creation. The auditorium has 1383 seats. The sharply ascending rows of stalls merge at the sides into prominent boxes and are partly oversailed by a balcony. The generously proportioned stage, which is mainly used for opera and ballet, is of the picture-frame type, with a number of wing-spaces and a revolve. The lighting installation reflects the high standard of Czech lighting technique. (This has been a field of constant experiment in Czechoslovakia.)

The new theatre at Gottwaldow by M. Repa and F. Rozhon dates from 1967. Gottwaldow is a new

196–199
Otakar Oplatek, Vilém Zavrel: Theatre at Brno, 1945–1965
Main entrance front, ground-floor and first floor plans, view of auditorium

197/198

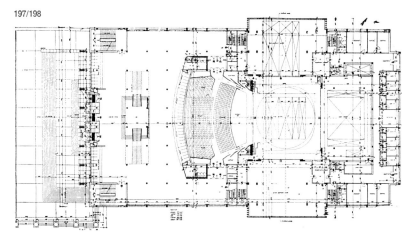

199

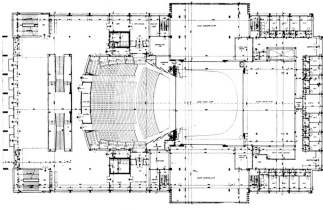

industrial centre and, as in the West, efforts are inevitably directed towards making such places attractive by an active cultural programme. The auditorium is developed as a steeply ascending succession of stalls, the back row merging directly into the balcony, which has a middle section resembling boxes—a solution which looks like a modern variant of the Prinzregententheater in Munich. The dark wood panelling, contrasting with the light balcony parapet, makes a pleasant impression. The layout of the stage is certainly unusually conventional for 1965. The forestage area extends exceptionally far beyond the orchestra pit, however, and the safety curtain is set well behind the prominent position of the proscenium opening.

200–202
Miroslaw Repa, Frantisek Rozhon:
Theatre at Gottwaldow, 1965–1967
Auditorium, ground-floor plan

200

201

202

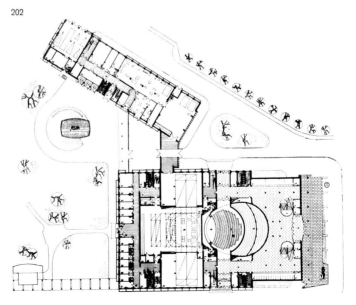

203
Zbigniew Bac, Wiktor Jackiewicz, Elz-
bieta Krol, Krystyna Plawska-Jackiewicz:
Competition design for theatre at Novy
Sad, 1961

204—205
Miklos Hofer, Ferenc Vajda: Budapest
National Theatre, competition 1965, de-
sign to be built
Floor plan + 4.40 and 0.00 m, section

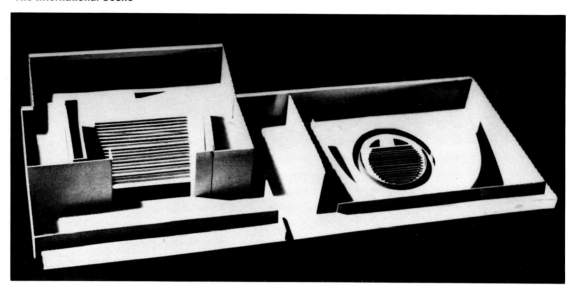

203

204/205

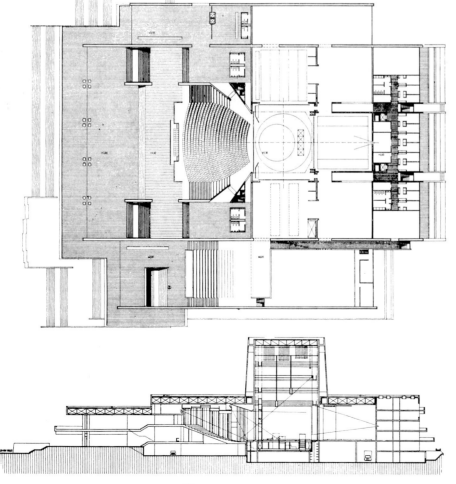

Jugoslavia was able to rely on the continuing life of
her old theatres after the war. In 1969 the renovated
opera house at Zagreb was open again. It was designed, like the theatres of Graz and Budapest, by
Fellner and Helmer and erected about the turn of
the century. Only at Novy Sad has a competition
been held during the postwar period; this was won
by the Polish team of Bac, Jackiewicz, Krol and
Plawska. The smaller house is of interest, because
it proposes a variant of the 'Théâtre Mobile' of
Polieri, but the design is not so logically worked
out as at Grenoble.

In 1965 Hungary announced a large and important
competition for the new National Theatre in Budapest—a playhouse to seat twelve hundred people,
and a studio. It was open to all architects from
European socialist countries and gives a useful
conspectus of architectural tendencies and possibilities in the Eastern block of states. It led to no
definite result, however, no first prize being awarded. The second prize was shared and went to the
Polish team of Boguslawski/Gniewiewski, whose
scheme presented a strictly correct, almost pedan-
tic solution, and to the Hungarian Miklos Hofer, who
was commissioned to develop his proposals further.
The design by Hofer and Ferenc Vajda—we show
here the final revised version—also offers a strictly
rectangular layout, with a completely equipped, generously planned wagon-stage, and is distinguished
by its spaciousness. In the projects section
(see page 21) we illustrate the studio project by
Weber and Rubinov, two East German architects,
whose entry was among the premiated designs.

206
Max Abramovitz, Wallace K. Harrison, Philip Johnson, Eero Saarinen: Lincoln Center for the Performing Arts, New York, 1957–1966
Air view, with New York State Theatre (top left), Metropolitan Opera (top right), Philharmonic Hall (bottom left), Vivian Beaumont Theatre (bottom right)

207–210
Wallace K. Harrison: Metropolitan Opera, New York, 1966
Main entrance front facing Lincoln Plaza. P. 58: section, upper floor, view of auditorium

206

207

If one wants to report upon theatre-building in the United States, it is essential to distinguish official architecture from that of college and private theatres. Only from the tension between these two poles—and the intrusive presence of Broadway commercialism—can theatre architecture in America be understood.

Thus the Lincoln Center in New York is indeed, to all outward appearances, the most important theatrical centre, but it should not be taken as representative of the whole continent. On the contrary, it would be totally unjust to represent the stylistic tastelessness and antiquated architectural posturing of the Lincoln Center as typical of the whole country.

The Lincoln Center, an amalgam of cultural institutions, accommodates three large theatres: the Metropolitan Opera, the Vivian Beaumont theatre and the New York State theatre. The 'Met' is characterized

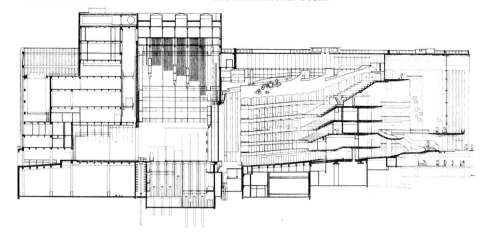

210

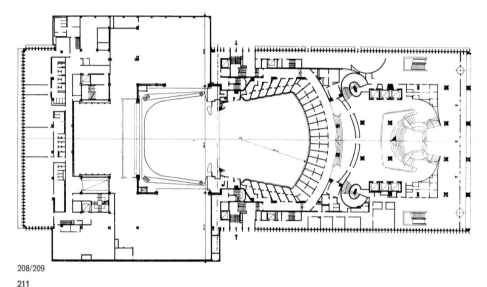

208/209

211

by extravagant splendour and an agglomeration of stylistic anachronisms, recalling many buildings beyond the iron curtain (like the Moscow underground railway stations), although these are outshone by the costliness of the materials. In fact the two countries have one thing in common: the desire to find a substitute for a non-existent tradition. America has no theatrical tradition and, in order to create one, harks back to a historical precedent which implies tradition in Europe: namely the temple of the Muses, as we have known it from the distant past. And everything, but everything, has to be magnified in the hypertrophic fever of the twentieth century. The equipment is sumptuous to be barely conceivable, the capacity of the building gigantic—3788 seats in the opera, plus standing-room for 175, i.e. an audience of almost 4000—and the stage and technical installations are provided with every imaginable refinement (architect Wallace K. Harrison).

The Vivian Beaumont theatre is much more interesting, designed by Eero Saarinen in collaboration with Joe Mielziner. This theatre, which is combined with a library and museum to form a composite block, is a novelty for New York. It is the first independent, non-commercial theatre in the city.

With its big stage, and three ancillary stages, the house seems at first sight to exemplify the picture-frame convention and wagon principle. But the fore-stage can be so completely transformed by means of 'disappearing' seat-wagons that the picture-frame stage can be changed into an arena-stage projecting deep into the hall. The division between stage and auditorium—which incidentally is more discreetly appointed than at the 'Met'—is contrived by a safety-curtain separated into sections, which can be omitted individually to allow a proscenium opening of any width. It is also possible, by completely closing the curtain, to perform on the forestage only. In any case American fire regulations are less exacting than in Europe. The studio theatre, which is sited underneath the main auditorium, also has an arena-stage thrust out into the audience area.

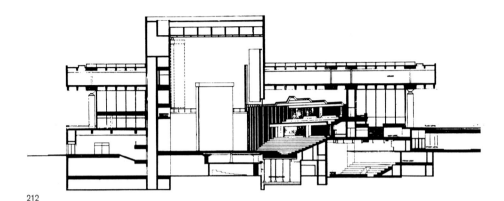

212

211—214
Eero Saarinen, Joe Mielziner: Vivian Beaumont Theatre, New York, 1965
Auditorium (p. 58), section; floor plans, understage (studio-theatre right) and stage level

213/214

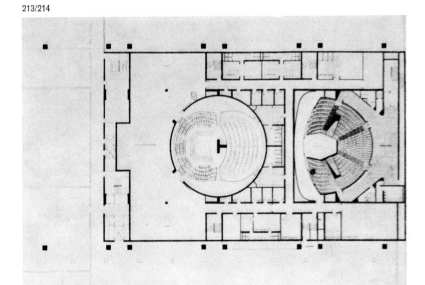

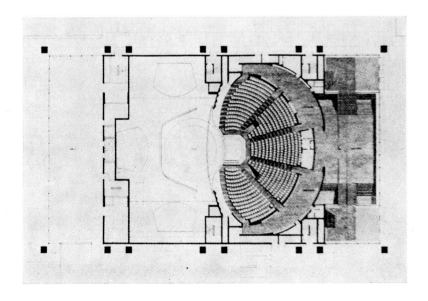

213/214

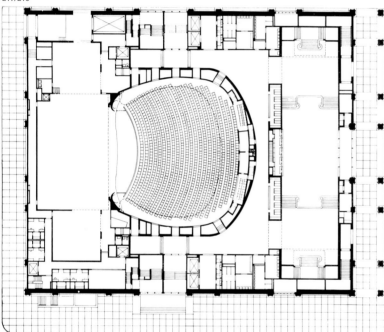

215

216

217/218

The third theatre of the Lincoln Center is the New York State by Philip Johnson, which is not far behind the Metropolitan in dubious eclecticism, for there is no lack of pomp and splendour. This is at once obvious in the reinforced concrete columns of the entrance front, clad in Roman travertine, and later in the goldleaf facings of the balcony parapets. The house is principally intended for operetta and ballet. The stage is conventionally equipped as a picture-frame, with two wing-spaces and no backstage; the auditorium has five horseshoe-shape balconies; a great globe of light, in place of the earlier chandelier, hangs from the ceiling. In the foyer, too, everything is extravagant and expensive. The filigree of the gallery supports in front of the brillant windows and walls, recalls the Crystal Palace of Joseph Paxton.

In the same class—and a whole series of buildings could be mentioned here—is the Music Center in

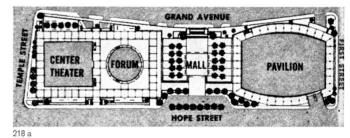

218 a

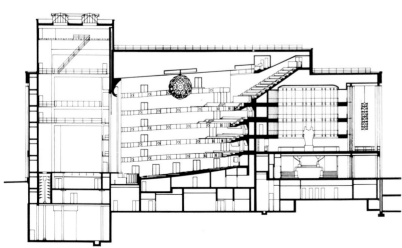

215–218
Philip Johnson: New York State Theatre, 1964
Glimpse into foyer, main entrance front facing Lincoln Plaza, ground-floor, section

218 a
Welton Becket & Ass.: Music Center, Los Angeles, California, 1964–1966

219

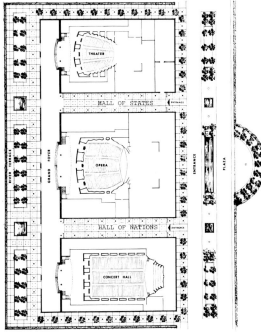

222

220

221

Los Angeles, in design equally 'square' and un-imaginative. The John F. Kennedy Center for the Performing Arts in Washington DC by Edward D. Stone is similarly staid and uninspired in plan. The stages reflect the usual picture-frame arrangement, and the auditoria are organized as balcony theatres. The appointments, however, promise to be rather more restrained and simpler than those of the Lincoln Center.

219—222
Edward Durell Stone: John F. Kennedy Center for the Performing Arts, Washington DC, under construction since 1966
Photos of models: main entrance front, auditorium views (opera house and playhouse), principal floor plan

223

224

The other element in American theatre architecture is utterly unconventional and full of ideas. This is the private and college theatres, which are built all over the country (and almost everywhere) by private initiative.

One such is the Kalita Humphreys theatre in Dallas, Texas, opened in 1960, designed by Frank Lloyd Wright and differing widely from the conventional conception. The building is erected on a truncated rhombus, with the circular fly-tower standing in the shallow angle of one side. It extends right into the auditorium, so that the stage apron is surrounded on three sides by the public. As the revolve reaches to the very front of the stage, happenings on stage can be brought directly to the audience. The auditorium of this theatre holding barely three hundred people has an unusually intimate character.

A 'theatre-fortress', with marked sculptural qualities, has appeared in Houston, Texas (architect Ulrich Franzen, in collaboration with George C. Izenour, a distinguished American stage-designer). The structure was designed for a private company, closely associated with the city. The large house

225

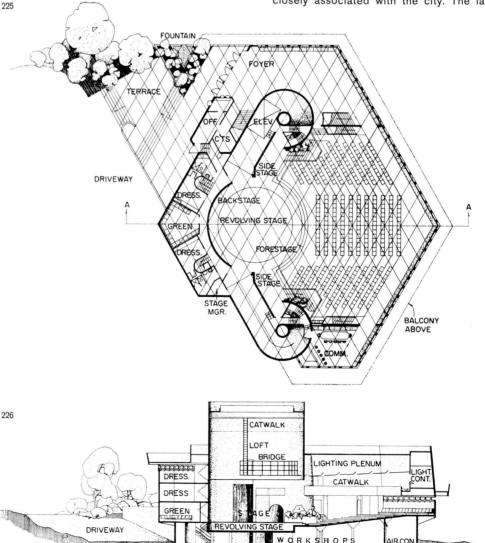

226

223–226
Frank Lloyd Wright: Kalita Humphreys Theatre, Dallas, Texas, 1958–1960
Main entrance front, glimpse of stage and auditorium, ground-floor, section A–A

227–233
Ulrich Franzen: Alley Theatre, Houston,
Texas, 1968–1969
Section, foyer floor, entrance floor
Photos of models: stairs to main foyer,
foyer of small house, view into small
house, principal entrance front

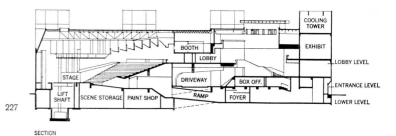

227

SECTION

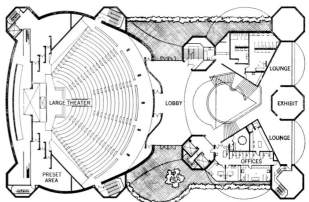

228

LOBBY LEVEL

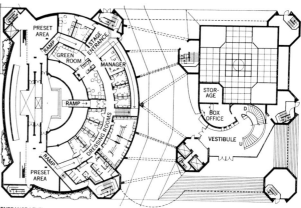

229

ENTRANCE LEVEL

230

233

231

232

234—235
Caudill, Rowlett, Scott: Jesse H. Jones
Hall, Houston, Texas, 1966—1967
Sections, with ceiling raised (concert)
and lowered (theatre)

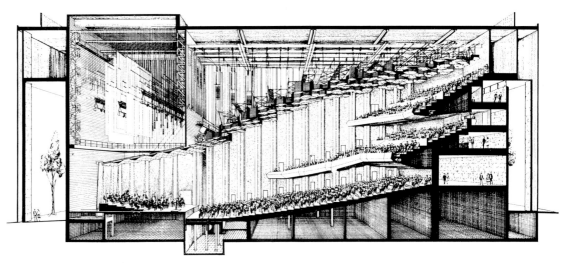

234

235

(eight hundred seats) has an amphitheatrical auditorium confronting a projecting stage, wide but not particularly deep, and flanked only by rather small 'preset areas'. Unusual, but certainly practical, is the placing of the artists' dressing rooms under the slope of the stalls, with direct central access to the stage, in addition to the normal entrance facilities. The small house, a consistently designed arena-theatre of three hundred seats, is concentrated upon a square central acting space. The seats rise steeply on each side in four large blocks. The large foyer with its shallow ramp-like stairs is charming. It can also be used for social gatherings.

Another building in Houston provides an interesting solution of a very different kind: the Jesse H. Jones Hall, built by Caudill, Rowlett and Scott, also in collaboration with George C. Izenour. It is intended for concerts and theatrical performances, and has a variable capacity which is achieved by a descending ceiling and not, as at Malmö, by a system of partitions. In this way one balcony can be 'taken away', so that the number of the audience is reduced from three thousand to eighteen hundred. This type of ceiling also makes it possible to alter the reverberation period according to the requirements of opera, concerts or plays.

Even more adaptable to a multitude of uses is the theatre of the Loretto-Hilton Center at Webster Groves, Missouri, designed by architects Murphy and Mackey with, once again, the collaboration of Izenour. It belongs to a college, and has to serve as assembly hall, lecture-room and for other educational purposes. The auditorium is infinitely variable in size, it being possible to separate the several side spaces, which can be used as classrooms, by fire-proof curtains and a similarly retractable balustrade. The fire-proof curtains are faced with plywood panels to improve the acoustics and, with the

64

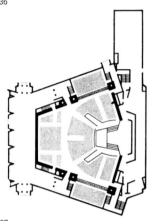

236

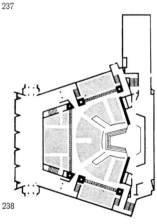

237

238

239

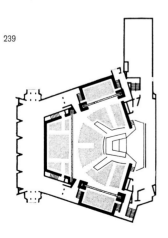

236—240
Murphy and Mackey: Loretto Hilton Center, Webster Groves, Missouri, 1967
Possible stage variations, view of auditorium (as arena-theatre, see bottom floor plan at left)

240

same object, extra curtains can be added for lectures. The number of seats can be raised from five hundred to twelve hundred. Of course these are very expensive devices, but they are worthwhile in this instance, because the theatre can also be used for teaching purposes. The stage is designed as an arena extending deep into the stalls.

The American college theatres are differently organized from German students' theatres. While, in Germany, they are purely amateur affairs, carried on as something additional to study (and often to its detriment), in America they are the first steps towards the professional stage. Dramatic training is a recognized study course, and work on a production is equivalent to a semester. Strictly speaking, only the Folkwang-Schule in Essen and the Reinhardt Seminar in Vienna would be comparable with these American theatres. At the end of the course, the students take their final examinations and, after graduation, either become professional actors or teachers at one of the many colleges. And as all these people are young, and as all the potentialities of a production are discussed stage by stage, these groups are naturally more receptive to experiment than the established town theatre. They are also free from the handicaps of repertory, for when a play is put on after several months of preparation, it is performed continuously for four to eight weeks; then, after a longer interval, the next production appears. Once this is understood, it is no surprise that the most progressive theatre emanates from these American colleges. They are theatre-workshops in the best sense. The best-known, because it was one of the first of this type, is the Experimental Theatre of

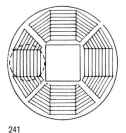

241

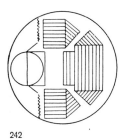

242

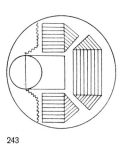

243

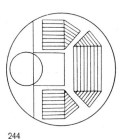

244

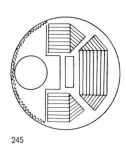

245

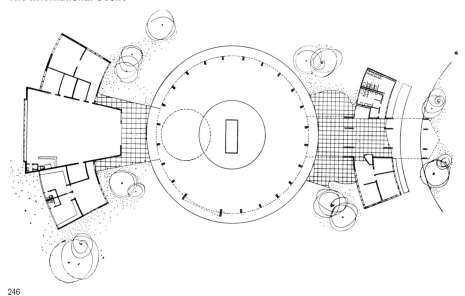

246

247

the University of Miami, Florida, by Robert M. Little and Marion Manley, an arena-theatre with a stage of exceptional flexibility. It can be arranged with a central acting area, drawn to one side as an open stage, or organized as a picture-frame. The hall is circular, and a section of the seating can be shifted around on the wagon principle. In theatre-building discussions in Germany, Miami has constantly been taken as a model, but other achievements of American college theatre have too often been overlooked. They were nevertheless adaptable to German conditions. The Studio at Münster might have become something similar (see page 206), and an analogous idea was first tried out in the Studio at Ulm (see page 175 et seq.). In the small house at Karlsruhe a one-room theatre is proposed, which for the first time will make possible wide variations within the acting space in a theatre of 350 seats (see page 203 et seq.).

241–247
Robert M. Little, Marion I. Manley: Experimental Theatre, University of Miami, Florida, 1950
Possible variations of stage and auditorium, principal floor plan, stage for Elizabethan theatre (Shakespearian stage)

248–251
Harry Weese: Arena Stage Theatre, Washington DC, 1962
General view, with stage-house (left); floor plans at stage level (above, with enlarged stage); view of auditorium and stage

248

251

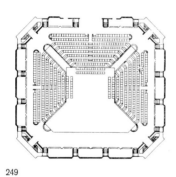

249

250

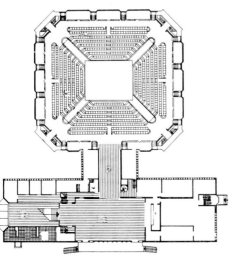

The Arena Stage Theatre in Washington DC by Harry Weese, opened in 1962, is equipped in a similar way to the Experimental Theatre at Miami. Here the arena stage is inserted into a square floor plan (with the corners cut off), and here also it can be drawn back from the middle against a containing wall to form a 'normal' stage.

252

253

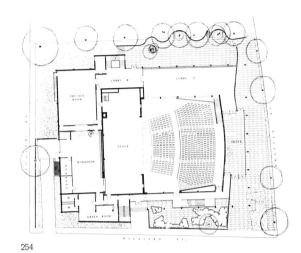

254

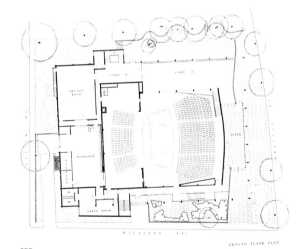

255

256

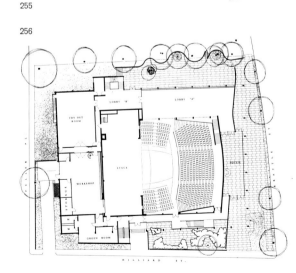

252–256
Hugh Stubbins & Ass.: Loeb Drama Center, Harvard University, Cambridge, Mass., 1960
Entrance side, view of stage and auditorium, plans of principal floor showing possible variations of stage and auditorium

Hugh Stubbins has created a drama centre for Harvard University which is particularly adapted to such mutations. The traditional picture-frame stage can be transformed by means of easily moved seat-wagons into a centrally placed arena. This is a variant which would be most readily translatable to the particular conditions of Germany. In particular, the problem of season-tickets would be solved by the fact that the number of seats remains constant. 'One of the world's most versatile instruments for producing drama of all kinds has recently gone into operation', wrote the Architectural Forum about the new 'Teaching machine' for a theatre at Birmingham, Alabama. This playhouse, which is amphitheatrical in plan, has a revolving-cylinder stage, its middle segment fixed and the two semicircular segments 'lowerable'. A third half-circle lies in the under-stage zone, and can be rotated upward so that three scenes can be presented on the semicircular stages.

257

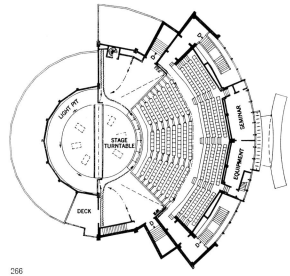

266

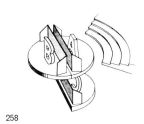

258

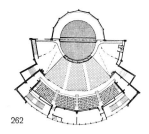

262

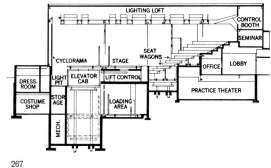

267

259

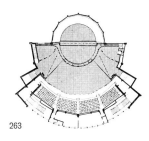

263

260

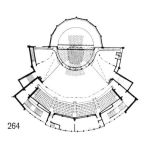

264

It is not quite clear, however, why such complicated machinery had to be built, when a straightforward wagon installation would have sufficed. Here mechanization has become an object in itself (architects: Warren, Knight and Davis; theatrical consultant: Arnold Powell). On the other hand the acting space can be changed and extended into the auditorium by comparatively simple means. The seats are mounted on wagons, which can easily be shifted and rearranged.

261

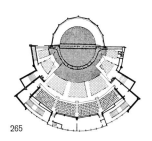

265

257–267
Warren, Knight & Davis: Southern College Theatre, Birmingham, Alabama, 1968
View of auditorium and stage, possible stage variations, stage-floor plan, section

268–271
Jørn Utzon: Sydney Opera House,
planned from 1957, under construction
Section and floor plan (from competition
design), views

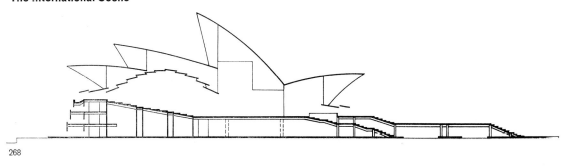

268

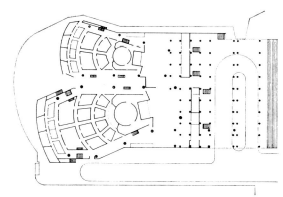

271

269

270

There is no building which has been so much discussed and upon which so little precise documentation is available as the Sydney Opera House, designed by Jørn Utzon and now—after disagreements with Utzon—being built by an Australian team.

The Opera House in Sydney is not theatre architecture in a specific sense, but an architectural monument in Sydney bay, and an impressive structure; but nobody—unless he knew that this shell construction belonged to an opera house—would guess that behind it was a theatre. It might equally well be a memorial hall, a library, a congress hall or a museum.

Under two sequences of shells, which are not strictly parallel, lie a large and a small hall, which also include various subsidiary rooms. The large hall is for opera, symphony concerts, and ballet, and also accommodates restaurants; the small one is for plays, intimate opera, chamber music, concerts and lectures. The twin shell structures therefore shelter in each case a large number of rooms serving a large number of purposes. Unfortunately, the plans of this building which have been published are inadequate to enable a judgement to be made on the various spatial relationships, or an opinion to be expressed on the extent to which the external architecture matches the 'content'.

272

273

272–275
Affleck, Desbarats, Dimakopoulos, Lebensold, Sise: Salle Wilfrid Pelletier, Montreal, 1964
General view (auditorium side), view of auditorium and stage, section, plan of main floor

274

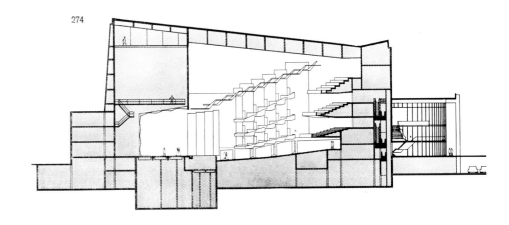

In Canada, one firm of architects has been responsible for three large theatre schemes—a rare event today, unlike the nineteenth century, when Fellner and Helmer did fifty theatres. In the 1960s the partnership of Affleck, Desbarats, Dimakopoulos, Lebensold and Sise designed theatres at Montreal, Charlottetown and Ottawa. In Montreal a three thousand-seat-opera, which is also a concert hall for the Montreal Symphony Orchestra, has been built. The large auditorium, with gently raked stalls and three balconies which slope down at the sides to form a succession of open boxes, faces a comparatively large stage, with only one wing-space and no backstage whatever. The stage-house proper is set rather far back owing to the depth of the orchestra and forestage area. The auditorium roof rises gradually and merges smoothly into the fly-tower. A pierced acoustic ceiling is lowered above the audience to the height of the proscenium opening.

275

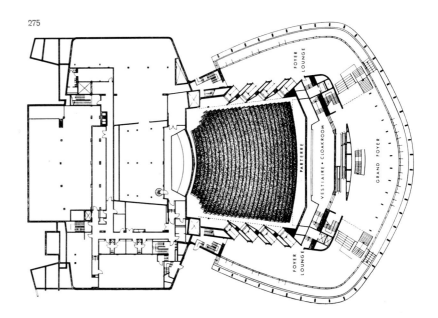

276

The theatre at the Confederation Centre of Charlottetown (for which George C. Izenour was called in as consultant) is essentially more intimate and accommodates no more than one thousand people. The stage lies like a broad band in front of the auditorium, the boundary between the acting area and wing-spaces being adjustable to any requirement. Round a forestage in the form of a circle segment, ringlike extensions can be thrust out, so that the stage can be taken deep into the auditorium. Here, too, the latter is almost the same height as the stage-house, but in this case the roof construction is exposed. Large shells, recalling Calder's mobiles, are suspended in space as sound-reflectors.

276—278
Affleck, Desbarats, Dimakopoulos, Lebensold, Sise: Confederation Centre, Charlottetown, 1964
View of auditorium and stage, section, ground-floor and site plan

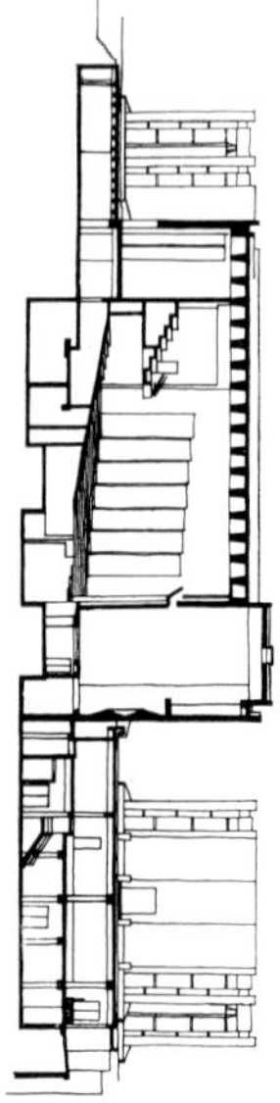

278

277

Grafton Street

Richmond Street

Great
George
Street

CONCOURSE LEVEL

0 10 20 30 40

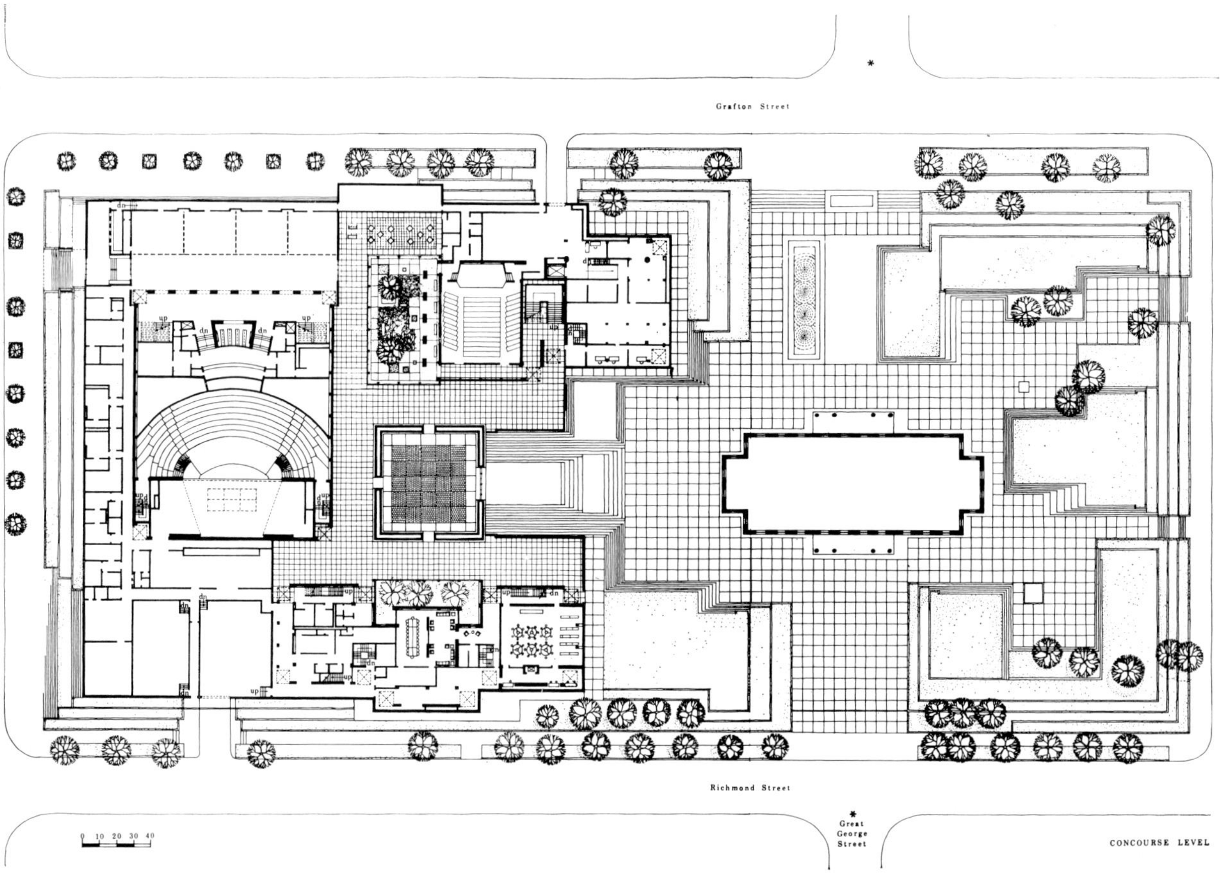

279

280

281

The largest and most impressive of the three works is the National Arts Centre in Ottawa, which includes—in addition to other buildings with a cultural purpose—an opera house (2300 seats), a playhouse (900 seats), and a studio-theatre (300 seats). The auditorium, which is surrounded by three balcony-tiers continuing at the sides as boxes, is separated from the stage by a deep 'pit', behind which is a large stage with three extensive wing-spaces. Once again the fly-tower is only slightly higher than the hall, and an acoustic ceiling, radiating from a central lighting plenum, slopes down towards the proscenium opening.

The playhouse has the amphitheatrical form so characteristic of the American continent and a generously planned stage. The similarly ample forestage area has three separate entrances from the auditorium.

The studio theatre is equally complete in its appointments. The seats are disposed in an irregular hexagon, as in an amphitheatre, around a central stage which can also be backed against one of the main containing walls by exploiting a 'trapped' platform (also hexagonal). Two galleries, extending round the house and accessible by demountable stairs, can be drawn into the performance.

279–283
Affleck, Desbarats, Dimakopoulos, Lebensold, Sise: National Arts Centre, Ottawa, 1969
Opera house auditorium, view of studio theatre, view from north, section through opera house, site and principal floor plan

282

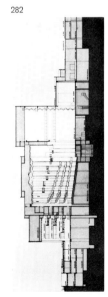

283

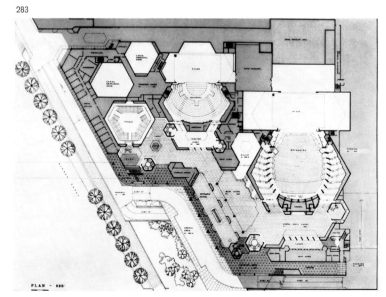

284—288
Oscar Niemeyer: National Theatre,
Brasilia, 1960—1965
Stage of small house, view from south-
west, floor plans (service rooms and
stages), section

284

285

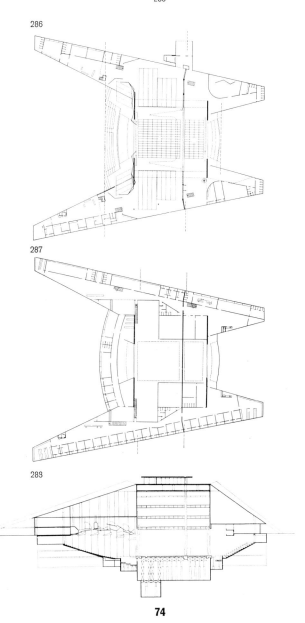

286

287

288

At Brasilia, the new capital of Brazil, the architect
Oscar Niemeyer has carried out a scheme embracing two theatres. Here, as at Sydney, the aim
has been to create an architectural monument, an
attitude inspiring the design of all Brasilia's public
buildings. The combined theatre is a mixture of
Mannheim and Cologne expressed in the handwrit-
ing of Oscar Niemeyer. The layout as a large double-
theatre with stages placed back to back recalls
Mannheim. But whoever is familiar with the experience of Mannheim may question whether the 'sound-
proof wall', which is interrupted by large safety curtains, is in fact sufficient for effective segregation. At
Mannheim, in any case, there is a wide backstage
passage which acts as an insulation layer between
the two houses. At Brasilia also, as at Mannheim,
this plan has the disadvantage for the smaller house
of an inordinate spread of stage. Resembling Cologne is the piling-up of immense building masses
to the culminating point of the fly-tower, which by no
means assumes this form in actuality. In a townscape laid out in broad perspectives and long vistas,
in which something of the pathos of the South also
plays its part, this may be justifiable, however. One
great asset of Mannheim has not been adopted at
Brasilia; the artists' dressing-rooms are at stage
level, but here are located on the floor beneath the
stage and have thus been sacrificed for the benefit
of extravagantly large wing-spaces. In general, one
has the impression of excessive size, and one sus-
pects that this house—like the double-theatre in
Cologne, which is proving so difficult to manage—
will not simplify the producer's task.

Japan / Persia

289–290
Togo Murano: Nissei-Theatre, Tokyo, 1959–1963
View of auditorium, principal floor plan

291–293
Eugene Aftandilian: State Theatre, Teheran, 1967
Section, principal floor plan, auditorium view

The International Scene

As a rule, Japanese theatres cannot be compared with European, because the demands placed upon the stage by the traditional theatre of Japan are quite different from those of the West. The Nissei Theatre in Tokyo, commissioned by an insurance company and built to the designs of Togo Murano in 1959–63, comes nearest—it also includes office accommodation in the same building—to the European conception. The stage is lower and wider than we expect, but technically equipped with many refinements: a wagon-stage, a cylinder-type revolve and a playing surface of variable rake make for multifarious scenic effects. The scene-stores are in cellars, and are reached by lowering the stage, which then acts as a lift. The décor seems fantastic and suggests the forms of Gaudí translated into a modern idiom.

In Persia, the new state theatre of Teheran was inaugurated in 1967, a costly and splendid building, which once again takes up the theme of the old Residenztheater of balcony boxes, state boxes and stalls. The plan (architect Eugene Aftandilian; theatre

289

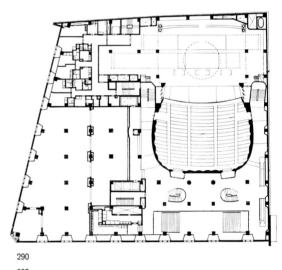

290
293

291

292

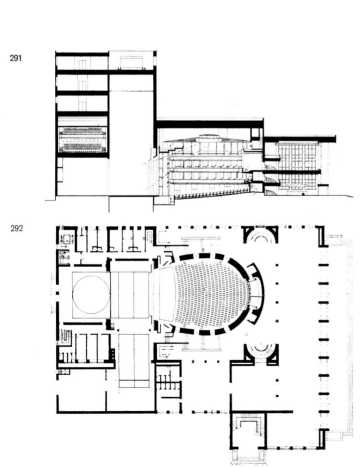

75

294–296
Hayati Tabanlioglu: Istanbul Opera House,
1956–1969
Auditorium view, floor plan (opera),
section

294

technical consultant Manfred Weidner) reflects a conventional opera house, but the theatre has also to answer the varied needs of a multi-purpose hall. As long ago as 1940 Turkey had planned an opera house on the European model for Istanbul. The first scheme, which had already begun to assume physical shape, was so violently criticized, that in 1956 the architect Tabanlioglu, a pupil of Gerhard Graubner, produced a fresh design and was empowered to carry it out. There has thus arisen an extensive complex of buildings, accommodating not only a large house for opera, ballet and plays, but also a concert hall, a studio-theatre and a children's theatre. The layout recalls in many respects the basic plan of Cologne. Above the gently sloping stalls, two tiers of seats merge at the sides into a series of deep balconies thrust out from a comparted wall. The stage is of the wagon type, with a large main stage and generous wing-spaces. The decorative treatment of the rooms is extremely restrained and closely follows European precedents.

295

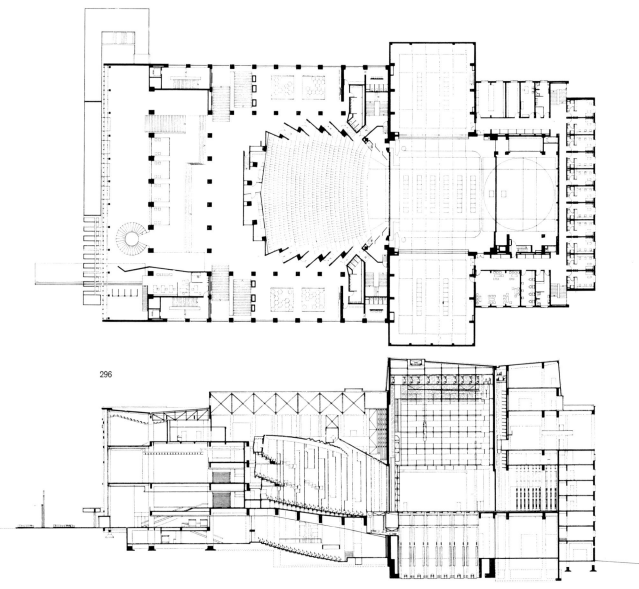

296

Documentation

Theatre Buildings in Germany — Switzerland — Austria

List of Theatres Described

Present Situation

Two factors which have decisively influenced post-war theatre-building in Germany and the German-speaking countries have already been mentioned: the fact that theatre-building is largely a provincial matter and that the organization of the German town theatre has remained one of 'mixed activity' and repertory. The determining principle in the theatre is the relationship of audience and actors, of auditorium and stage. This is a cardinal factor in every project and has already created a straitjacket; for the German municipal theatre, in addition to plays, always presents operetta, and generally opera—or at least it offers stage-space for visiting productions of this sort (e.g. in Ingolstadt, where only a theatrical company is maintained and one 'shops around' for opera in neighbouring towns). The architectural form of the theatre is thus fixed from the start. It remains also, because of the traditional nature of opera, a picture-frame theatre, and the architectural development of the German-speaking theatre since the war can be regarded as simply a question of how can I break away from the picture-frame stage, yet how can I preserve it? Or, in other words: how am I to free acting from the operatic picture-frame, without having to give up opera? All architectural research and experiments have been directed upon the proscenium opening, the boundary which separates actor and audience. A genuine arena-theatre, as is often found in America, has not yet been built in Germany. The fore-stage has been brought into wide use, but the orchestra pit and safety curtain are still proving a double-obstacle. A revision of theatre safety regulations, which should be adjusted to modern standards of technical expertise, is overdue. In America the law is more flexible.

In the meantime other forms of stage are only imaginable in experimental studios. And here lies a further problem. When a second house is built, it is almost without exception a 'small house', in a technical sense economically equipped no doubt (Mannheim, Kassel, Cologne), but capable of becoming eventually a fully fledged second house. The urge to get established is extraordinarily strong, and the studio puts up with any temporary accommodation, in an assembly hall perhaps or a rehearsal room where everything, as far as possible, has to cost nothing.

Gelsenkirchen presents a glaring example of every conceivable misunderstanding. The architects' original design provided for a studio using a rehearsal stage. In the final version, this became a separate studio, which also had to serve for dress rehearsals. This studio became the apple of the architects' eye, and they fitted it out with particular care, with the result that the studio character vanished almost completely in the lavish décor. The first director took a look at the building and concluded, by no means so wrongly, that it was a normal 'small house'. But the technical installations were unsuitable and insufficient, and the number of seats too small for such a purpose. This produced dissatis-faction, and when the amalgamation with Bochum took place, where a studio-theatre had been built, there was talk of alterations costing a million marks to ensure that the two houses would be mutually adaptable and performances could be transferred from one to the other. The idea of a studio for varied experiment disappeared. The architects themselves had finally crushed it by their extravagance (see page 124 et seq.).

One often notices unrealistic behaviour on the part of architects. A good instance of this occurred with the students' competition sponsored by the theatrical journal 'Theater heute', on the initiative of the BDA and the theatre architect Fritz Bornemann (see page 19 et seq.). The competition was intended to solve the problem of designing the 'Theatre of tomorrow', without regard for the existing police regulations. It became clear at the preliminary meeting in Berlin that nobody wanted to listen to the experienced (and not always conservative) stage-people who advised that one should start with the smallest unit, the studio. In the end it was not as a result of the unrealistic programme that the theatre-experts and architects failed to get together. It was merely because nowhere was there revealed any sign of a way out of the present undeniably unhappy condition of contemporary theatre architecture, although many interesting individual solutions were put forward by the students. Had the attempt been made to confine the programme to a strictly limited field for subsequent free and detailed discussion, it would certainly have been productive and enabled the two parties to become more sympathetic partners. The task of making the studio an up-to-date instrument of dramatic art would have been worth considering. How fruitful it can be, if the boundaries are rigidly defined, is shown by the proposed studio at Münster. Unfortunately the scheme has not yet been realized, because there were no funds for this purpose and the stage-offices of the existing theatre had a priority. But there the architects and theatrical profession really had thought constructively about the problem which they had been set, namely how can the studio be combined with the 'institution' of the 'small house'? In addition considerations of rentability and the use of the room as a congress hall had to be taken into account. And this precise brief led to a solution which cannot be ignored in future plans for studio-theatres.

The Münster scheme (see page 206) relies upon a rhombic central platform, trapped in individual sections and equipped with two proscenium wings which are easily moved by hand. Seat-wagons, which can be inserted into 'pockets' under the raked seats, enable multifarious changes to be made to the house. If the wings are pushed forward to about the middle angles of the rhombus, they form the normal picture-frame stage, which can also be partitioned off by a curtain. The house can also be converted with minimal trouble into an arena-theatre with central stage, while the surrounding galleries can be used for lighting or drawn into the performance. Simple to adapt and versatile in its resources, it is regrettable that this proposed theatre will not be built in the foreseeable future and that there is no opportunity to test a system of this kind, for only by experience with such a house can real progress be made.

Architects and theatre-people, however, have seen their chance in Düsseldorf, where the small house has retained a studio character. There had already emerged from the competition designs for the play-house building the much debated project of Werner Ruhnau, who proposed that the whole house should be conceived as one completely flexible unit—a suggestion which has assumed extraordinary importance in later discussions even if current practical considerations and very high building costs stand in the way of realization. The constructed Düsseldorf playhouse (see page 168 et seq.) is different, but interesting none the less: while the large house intimidates the visitor by its gigantic proportions, so that one is reminded of an opera house, the smaller theatre is more human in scale. The latter is a rectangular hall, which narrows a little towards the back. The basic layout corresponds to a picture-frame theatre, and with this arrangement has 244 seats. The proscenium wings, with the curtain, can be rotated through ninety degrees to the wall and, in addition, the two front rows of seats can be removed to form an open stage. A 'bridge' over the auditorium supports the lighting equipment. The room can also be converted into an arena-theatre by sliding the front rows of the stalls away from each other to the sides, leaving free a square, vertically raised, central stage. What is otherwise a picture-frame stage then carries a fourth tier of seats, so that the middle-stage is completely surrounded by the audience, who now have 345 seats at their disposal. The technical appointments are simple and practical. One wonders whether this theatre is proving its worth in practice and, in particular, if its possibilities are being exploited by producers.

Another small house has been built on similar principles: the Cellar Theatre of the 'Bonn Center'. This, too, can be used with a picture-frame stage, and also with open or arena stages. For the latter purpose the seating is cleared from the centre, and a platform raised in its place, with rows of seats disposed appropriately on the stage perimeter. Lighting and scenery can be distributed freely throughout the hall, light being controlled from a cabin at the back of the house. This private theatre is closely related to the American type of experimental stage, but has little to do as yet with the every-day experience of the German theatre (see page 14).

A studio has been built at Ulm with modest technical resources—lift-and-lower platforms in the floor, attachable revolves, fixing points in the ceiling for spotlights and scenery. The minimum of technical equipment permits the maximum of dramatic opportunity, a real workshop-theatre (see page 175 et seq.).

There are two other houses with flexible forms of stage, namely the theatre and multi-purpose hall of the Academy of Art in Berlin, and the small house at Mannheim.

At the Academy a narrow stage extends obliquely through the hall, with the stalls rising gently on both sides. As there is no regular company and no theatre director to test this stage effectively, the opportunity which it offers is hardly being grasped (see page 180 et seq.).

The Mannheim stage is similarly adaptable. It can be drawn into the auditorium by dismantling the first rows of seats and, instead, providing other seats at the back of the stage (see page 118) and a few at the sides. A central bridge-like stage across the theatre was tried out by Piscator for the opening presentation of the 'Räuber' by Schiller and now, more than ten years later, has been tested again in Schiller's 'Fiesco'. In both performances the success was spontaneous, and it was clear that from an artistic viewpoint there was no objection to stages of this type. But the problems of internal management are greater. The stage cannot be reconstructed every day, and a public accustomed to a repertory programme refuses, within a few days, to patronize a piece played continuously. The house remains empty.

The stipulation of a conventional layout for the stage in many postwar new buildings is conditioned on the one hand by the artistic structure of the theatre, but the strong aversion towards any attempt to break new architectural ground has other causes, and is concerned with the style of performance. It was certainly not by chance that G. R. Sellner presented avant-garde theatre at the Orangerie in Darmstadt (even if generally on a conventional type of stage), that he made no special efforts to promote the building of a new theatre, and that now as Director of the Deutsche Oper in Berlin his productions are traditional in style. Economic recovery brought a desire for representative theatre, and for the most part convention very quickly stifled any attempts at innovation.

There have been exceptions. The Bremen company presents a challenging repertoire in a radically contemporary setting and expects an architecture and an audience to match it. They also perform traditional operetta in the same house for a very different public.

Another factor has a discouraging effect on the development of a modern theatre. There are a certain number of houses which have no (or almost no) company of their own. These have to rely on neighbouring theatres, and take their pick from what is offered. They therefore have to preserve a 'neutral' attitude and be prepared to tackle everything. This inevitably means that experiment is excluded from the outset.

Such theatres admittedly have an important social function. They lie as a rule in industrial areas, off the beaten track, but they cater for a definite section of the educated public, and have to offer something stimulating in order to compete with the large towns.

When, however, in a city like Ludwigshafen, no more than a ten-minute-ride from the Mannheim National Theatre, a house of this sort is built, one wonders what object there can be in this apart from the investment of money flowing into the town from industry. Surely there would have been a chance here to create a theatre of a special kind for a specific area comprising districts on both sides of the Rhine? However, instead, thirty-three million marks were paid out for a large and sumptuous theatre which enabled the people of Ludwigshafen to avoid visiting the one in Mannheim.

Flexibility of Proscenium Arch Zone

We have already mentioned that, for the nineteenth century, there was no ambiguity. The existing order of the theatre was not questioned. Semper (see page 11), like Fellner and Helmer—to name a few of the more prominent theatre architects—built balcony theatres (on occasions with boxes), the huge auditorium an obedient reflection of the social hierarchy, with the division between public and actors clearly emphasized by the proscenium arch of the picture-frame stage.

By the 1920s this form of theatre was no longer taken for granted—notably, by Piscator's productions for the Freie Volksbühne in Berlin—and a logical consequence of this was his invitation to Gropius to develop a radically new theatre (see page 17). The Second World War further undermined the structure of society and the traditional conception of the theatre. The many temporary stages broke with conventions. The protest was understood by the public, who accepted it.

At the same time there remained a longing for what used to be—the enchanting theatre of the past. As a result new buildings were planned everywhere, and immediately the situation was transformed. The temporary stages had made it possible to present Alban Berg's 'Wozzeck', but now the demand was revived for 'Palestrina' and 'The Meistersingers', and for operetta in all its glamour and glitter—today still the financial backbone of many (and not only of small) theatres. If, during the postwar period, the theatrical programme had been deliberately narrowed down to what was topical and possible, the entire repertoire would have now been reestablished. But, for all practical purposes, the experimental theatre was dead.

If today 'The Meistersingers' are presented, tomorrow the 'Merry Widow', and the day after a conventional play, not much can be done but adjust the set to the next piece. At times like this, since opera is being 'played' in the theatre, at least in the present instance, only one stage-audience situation is possible, that of strict opposites.

Thus the large new theatres have become no more than slightly modernized versions of nineteenth century houses, and all the ideological theses in the world cannot alter the fact that we are back once again with the picture-frame stage. The plush has been ripped out (not always to the benefit of the acoustics) and in its place modern art (or what passes for it) has been allowed to creep in. The costumes have been changed, and the boxes for the quality are absent, but in the basic structure of the theatre nothing whatever has been altered. We should have no illusions. All the innovations of recent years are simply improvements in detail of what has long been in existence.

Special attention has been directed in the 'mixed' houses to the boundary line between auditorium and stage, the proscenium opening and the forestage and orchestra area. The aim has been to make the separation as inconspicuous as possible and to achieve a smooth transition from picture-frame to open stage.

The first decisive step in this direction was taken in the playhouse at Bochum. When the reconstruction was tackled in 1951 (completed in 1953), the safety curtain was placed in front of the orchestra pit (which here, in a theatre predominantly devoted to plays, is comparatively small). However superficial and insignificant this change may seem, and trivial in practice, it set the pattern for all future schemes, for it released the forestage zone from its isolation. Had there been any desire in the nineteenth century to entice the actor out of his pasteboard setting and bring him on to the apron, it would have been found now, since scenery has changed and forms an integrated part of the production, so that the actor's detachment and isolation in front of the safety curtain on the forestage is a positive disadvantage. But by incorporating the forestage area in the stage-space protected by the curtain, it became completely 'playable'. The action could be carried right into the auditorium.

A second step has also been taken at Bochum with a proscenium opening which can be altered not only in height, but also in width. The stage can now be transformed without difficulty from a large set to an intimate 'picture', although the flexibility of the proscenium opening is often limited by the sightlines.

A further development is reflected in an increasing tendency towards an open stage and, on the other hand, to a combination of the forestage area with the technical equipment of the stage (light and scenery). The Gelsenkirchen municipal theatre formed an important landmark on this road. Here, for the first time, a double proscenium opening was built, and by this means the width could be varied even more. The design, however, contained a flaw, because the narrowest opening, when the width was reduced for intimate scenes, lay behind the second 'frame', and consequently a long way from the audience. Moreover the forestage area, while enclosed by the safety curtain, is difficult to reach with lights (most of the equipment being on the far side of the opening in the proscenium wings and on the bridge), and finally there is no mechanism for scene-changes. Thus the forestage is still a barrier between playgoer and player.

The next step was to design the opening as a single mobile system, i.e. able to be flown, and also moved back and forth horizontally as required. In this way the smaller proscenium 'frame', complete with its lighting installations, can be moved forward and the whole stage-set brought on to the apron, with no fear of reduced technical efficiency.

This contrivance was first put into operation in the municipal theatre of Bonn, and further improved at the Recklinghausen Festival theatre, where both openings are mobile, so that the entire acting area can become an open stage. Transition from auditorium to stage is effected by movable conversion elements and, in addition, the wagon of the revolve can be fitted to a front circular unit. Thus, even a revolving stage can be brought directly to the audience. Admittedly the whole fly-floor has to be emptied each time the proscenium openings are shifted and, when both are flown, the lighting apparatus has to be transferred to the bridge above the forestage. This naturally means a good deal of work, which may be feasible at festivals, but by no means always for the everyday production of repertory. In particular, the large prominent apron in front of the proscenium openings can only be lit from the bridge furthest to the front, which is sometimes not in use, so a light-vacuum is easy to occur. Two years earlier a variant of this form was realized in the Frankfurt playhouse, in which the sides open, after the proscenium arch is flown, leaving a space 75 ft wide. To avoid empty caverns, harmful to acoustics, on either side of the stage when it is enclosed, mobile partitions are suspended in the auditorium, adjustable to the proscenium opening.

The scheme carried out in the double-theatre at Darmstadt is the ultimate point so far reached in this type of development. The removal of the proscenium 'frames' to the back of the stage encounters certain difficulties in practice, and in both the Darmstadt houses these are so arranged that the proscenium wings can be inserted into side 'pockets', so that the stage may open to its full width. The wings, however, can be moved backwards or forwards, so that the whole of the orchestra space or part of it can be incorporated in the stage. At the sides extensions to the stage stretch into the auditorium. These can be entirely masked by panels, or opened in segments or to their full breadth, the panels being rotatable and designed to take scenery on their black reverse face. Behind the panels, on each side, are mobile lighting stands, for directing light on to the forestage. A curtain, hiding these front pockets, has also been added. The result provides considerable flexibility in the forestage area and a close unity between stage and audience, backed by technical facilities which, even in the routine of repertory, should not be too cumbersome to operate. The problem of versatility for the proscenium frame and forestage zone has been surmounted and thought out to the last detail. The confrontation remains, but a bridge of the most sympathetic character is established. In addition, with the proscenium zone tending to become architecturally more and more a part of the auditorium and emphasized as little as possible, an attempt has been made to do away with the dividing line. In Gelsenkirchen the architects went so far as to clothe the auditorium in black (in Nottingham, too, see page 35), although the effect of this is partly cancelled out by facing the balcony parapets with frosted aluminium, which acts as a reflector for the stage lighting and recreates a conspicuous spatial barrier. In fact, however, in the process of spiriting away the transition area, the frontier between the two zones has been obliterated in this instance, as far as is practicable within the framework of a conventional layout.

This situation—especially by architects—is often largely coloured by sociological overtones in talking of the all-embracing unity of actors and audience. But we ought—at least as far as actually built theatres are concerned—to start from the fundamental realities of dramatic art. The actor needs to be clearly heard; he must therefore be brought as close as possible to this public, but must not leave the theatrical context. This is why frontiers are tending to disappear, with the gap between stage and audience becoming narrower and the process of transition less abrupt.

Public Accommodation

Auditorium

The second design detail, which has seen a metamorphosis since the nineteenth century, is concerned with the auditorium. Here again the social aspects came first: a wish to tear down the barriers created by status and money, and to cure the obstructed sight-lines resulting from the balcony system. No more theatre seats for hearing only! So, in the 1930s, the arena-theatre (as it had been realized by Richard Wagner at Bayreuth) came to the fore. It is a striking fact that this was the only solution considered in the Kharkov competition (see page 13). The aim was to transform the public, with the help of the arena-plan, into an integrated social unit. But the abandonment of the balcony destroyed the great advantage of having all the audience close to the stage. In large theatres the distances were vastly increased, and even the finest acoustic conditions could not ensure a truly complete theatrical experience.

The prejudice against the balcony-type theatre has persisted in the oddest way, although it has no validity today, for modern reinforced concrete construction makes it possible to cantilever balconies without intermediate supports to block the view. And even for seats at the sides with a potentially poor view great improvements are now possible. Despite this, the arena-theatre is regarded nowadays as the genuine people's theatre, a fallacious attitude maintained with remarkable tenacity.

In many places a variant of the arena-theatre, of which the design by Adolf Loos of 1898 may be looked upon as typical (see page 12), has gained acceptance, namely the 'Parketttheater'. Here the stalls (Parkett) rise on a rectangular or wedge-shaped plan, but the rows do not form segments of a circle, nor is the forestage semicircular, but rather shaped in a shallow curve (Cologne, Frankfurt, Stuttgart).

Gerhard Weber took the most decisive step towards modernizing the balcony-theatre in the reconstruction of the Hamburger Staatsoper (1953–5). The side 'circle' (balcony) seats were transformed into sledge-like, slightly raked, balconies oriented towards the stage. (The Hanover opera house, which adopted the 'circle' type of balcony when reconstructed, is still struggling against unsatisfactory seating problems.) In the Cologne opera house, the feature of the sloping sledge became a basic design principle for balconies. Continuous rows were abandoned, and sledges project deep into the auditorium from folds in the containing walls, the distance to the stage being little more than ninety feet in a house with a capacity of 1350 seats.

The principle of the stepped side balcony has been followed in almost all balcony-theatres of the postwar period. It is applied at Münster, Gelsenkirchen, Kassel and Dortmund, where the sledges are carried on columns which do not obstruct the view. The balcony form, however, has been retained with virtually no exception in the so-called large houses, which are predominantly used for opera. The Stuttgart playhouse is without balconies, as is the one at Cologne (the latter in plan a rather inept concession to the overwhelming dominance of the opera house). At Kassel and Mannheim there are also no balconies. Wherever, therefore, a separation into two complete houses has been carried out, a 'Parkett' or arena theatre has been preferred to the more intimate playhouse. On the other hand, the Freie Volksbühne in Berlin, with 1043 seats, erected after the war, harks back to the balcony and even to the conventional form extending round the sides, although everywhere the view is excellent. The theatre architect Bornemann—he comes from a theatre family—has in this case dropped the 'Parkett' plan for the sake of more intimate dimensions (the greatest distance from the stage is not much more than eighty feet). In the new Darmstadt theatre scheme the playhouse will also have a balcony.

At Bonn a further variation of the balcony-theatre has been built, one which has previously been partly tried out in congress halls. The balcony sinks on one side into the stalls and is thus directly connected with them—a solution only feasible in comparatively small theatres. In this way a visual link is established between stalls and balcony. Sir Basil Spence has evolved an attractive variant at Southampton (see page 37), in which he continues the central balcony as a kind of raised flight of stalls, leaving the rows at the sides to embrace the stalls and 'hold them together'.

A feature of older theatres—the central gangway—has curiously enough not been perpetuated since the war. Although all the experts appreciate the obvious charm of this 'break' and the convenience of a passage through the rows for people finding their seats, there is an openly expressed fear of splitting the auditorium by a conspicuous central gangway. In postwar theatres there has been no more than a certain amount of grouping and separating on the higher levels—like the transposing of a few rows into 'upper' stalls—to give the stalls as a whole a more articulate form. In wide auditoria, like that of Cologne where a row has forty-six seats—the absence of a central gangway is a glaring defect.

Foyers

For foyers a specific type of layout has, as a general rule, emerged. On the ground floor, in front of the principal entrance or immediately behind it, is a group of rooms with box-office and waiting accommodation; and behind this, often placed underneath the slope of the stalls, are cloakrooms and staircases leading to the foyer serving the higher floors. The detailed design of the foyer clearly depends upon its precise location and the architect's personal taste.

The Münster team, who—minus Harald Deilmann—also worked at Gelsenkirchen, disposed the stairs round the drum-like core of the auditorium, at the same time exploiting them as a decorative and graphic element. A similar solution, if not so consistently worked-out, was attempted at Kassel.

In contrast, the stairs in the Cologne opera house are thrust outwards, resulting in attractive interrelationships between the various bridge-ways which give individual access to the 'sledge'-balconies. Bornemann, too, placed the staircases of the Deutsche Oper in Berlin adjacent to the outer sides of the foyer, using them as decorative elements for the onlooker outside, while creating inside—unlike Cologne—distinct, self-contained spatial groups.

The architects of the theatres at Bonn and Ingolstadt—to mention only two instances—sought the opposite effect. Their aim was to make the stairs counteract and enliven the pigeon-hole character of the spatial plan, exploiting them as the dominating and unifying factors in the foyer area. For his part, Gerhard Graubner, the only German architect to have built a whole series of theatres, has tried in several buildings to incorporate the slope of the stalls as an architectural element in the design of the foyer, which only reaches its full height along the glazed façades (Trier, Wuppertal).

The double-theatre of Mannheim represents a special case, in which the foyers of the two houses (on the ground floor) are combined. The cloakrooms are sited at the two narrow ends, round the respective cores of each under-stage (screened in a rather makeshift, temporary manner by curtains), with the large hall of the foyer between. The latter looks bleak and impersonal when one looks into it empty from the outside, but friendly and informal in the intervals. It is a place for meeting and talk, which invites lively discussion in the ebb and flow of constantly changing groups.

On the whole, however, it has been demonstrated that a large, roomy, but not too vast foyer proves best. If people have limited space and their movements restricted, groups stop circulating, and conversation flags and dies.

If, on the other hand, the space is over-generous and ramified, as at Dortmund, people cannot find each other and conversations never get started. The importance of such meeting-places should not be underestimated. Many objections can be raised against the social commentator, but it is essential for plays to be discussed, and for the public to be roused from its passive role to take part in the event. The foyer offers space for discussion, and a social meeting point. If there is no contact between members of the public, contact with the actor is all the harder to achieve.

In the past theatres shut themselves off from the outside world, but nowadays exactly the opposite happens. Every effort is now made to open the theatre to the town, to present life on the stage in an attractive light and, by exposing the theatre to public view, establish contact between it and the townspeople. Gerhard Weber was the first to adopt this policy for Hamburg; at Gelsenkirchen it was applied as a principal architectural feature. In Mies van der Rohe's design the transparent glazed elevations play a big part, and this influence can still be seen in the Mannheim theatre. In Frankfurt indeed the enveloping glass front became the unifying architectural motif, concealing behind it the diverse elements of different stages of construction.

Interior Design

Although, among an infinite variety of manifestations, certain uniform characteristics can be detected in the basic architectural conception, this is not possible for the decorative treatment of interiors (or indeed, as we shall see later, for the external form). White, gold and red plush used to be 'the' colours for the theatre, but today there is no such convention. One is tempted to say that there are as many preferences in taste as architects. The range varies from the austere and strictly practical to the psychodelic. Restraint and anonymity in one theatre are matched by the triumph of exuberant imagination in another.

An outstanding example of the way in which a good theatre atmosphere can be created with minimal means is the small house at Mannheim, where the red of the hollow brick partition-walls harmonizes well with the black of the plain wood seating. In Berlin Bornemann produced a similar effect of 'Prussian charm' by clear architectonic forms and walls faced with rare woods. In the foyer these big timber walls contrast with the carefully chosen works of art (which, unhappily, have not all been left in place). In Kassel, however, the ceiling of the theatre is enlivened with a wood inlay, and the walls are faced with decorative slate slabs, so that the effect is so strident and restless that it draws the attention from, rather than to, the stage.

At Ingolstadt the building material is left exposed. At Mannheim this is brick, at Ingolstadt board-marked concrete. The idiosyncratic handling of space and the discreet collaboration of a small number of talented artists afford proof that even 'béton brut' can radiate a certain air of festivity in a theatre.

In the Cologne opera house, where the walls are clad with a dark, almost black wood, acting as a foil to the white and bright blue of the ceiling and the 'sledges', the impression is one of serenity, which is in contrast to the light and cheerful welcome of the foyer. In the Gelsenkirchen theatre, which has a somewhat disproportionately large foyer for such a house, the large blue surfaces of Yves Klein give coherence to the room and an unmistakable quality of their own. But at Dortmund the pompous economic-miracle-luxury suppresses any inclination towards gaiety, and one feels weighed down by the extravagance.

These are simply a few examples, both in a positive and a negative sense, which could easily be multiplied, especially by those many pleasant but hardly exciting mediocrities which are unfortunately the majority.

The most difficult problem to solve is lighting. How simple it was for past centuries with their large central chandeliers and a few subdued fittings for the balconies and boxes respectively! Today the lighting has to be individually designed in each case and, at the same time, attuned to the acoustically modelled ceiling.

In this respect the theatre at Münster attracted much attention. Here the ceiling is completely taken apart and replaced by a large number of lamps of various sizes, with circular wire 'sleeves' above them, which also have an acoustic purpose. However unusual this solution may appear at first glance, it has the great disadvantage that the 'ceiling' is visually disturbing and, even in the dark, reflects too much light. At Bonn a similar lighting principle was later adopted in association with the painter Otto Piene. Here, too, there is a canopy of lights, but the units are smaller, graded in brightness and spread across the ceiling in broad 'Milky Ways', a satisfying arrangement. At Ingolstadt indirect lighting is used almost exclusively, as a continuous strip in the angle between ceiling and containing wall, and with a few single downlights recessed into the ceiling. In the foyer decorative lattice clusters have been suspended, conveying a particularly pleasing effect in their contrast to the austere interior design. At St. Gallen a similar lattice structure hangs like a chandelier in the auditorium, in this case a justifiable device.

The frontier between the felicitous and the tasteless in matters of this kind is easily crossed. The foyer lighting at Dortmund is obtrusive, while the constant endeavours to create effects with complex light fittings suspended in the auditorium always have an arty-crafty flavour. The more restrained the solution, as at Mannheim, where only single lights are hung in the auditorium, the more convincing the result.

The same applies to the handling of the ceiling, for which the acoustician almost invariably has the principal say. Many attempts have been made to incorporate the acoustic panels, with their complicated calculations, as decorative elements (Wuppertal, Solingen), but this always introduces a measure of restlessness into the house, which is somewhat distracting. In this context also, it has been proved again and again that the more restrained and unobtrusive the design, the better the consequences.

In the case of colour only one fundamental principle has emerged—too bright hues, by reflecting light from the stage, are a disturbing influence during the performance. The large house at Mannheim exemplifies this. Gelsenkirchen and Nottingham have turned to the other extreme by using black walls, the only indication of a spatial boundary being the reflecting surface of the balcony fronts. At Gelsenkirchen the colour scheme relies entirely on deep black and dark grey, but this apparent 'coolness' does not seem cold. At Ingolstadt the same colour tones are employed without detriment to the theatre. At Cologne, however, where the dark brown wood

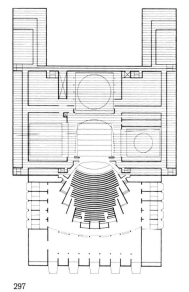

297

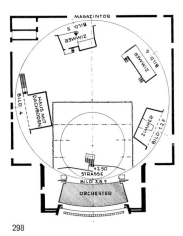

298

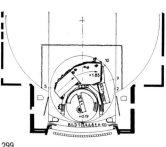

299

300

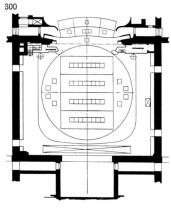

(which looks almost black) contrasts with light blue and white, the impression is a little frigid. Red still holds its own in many houses as a 'theatre colour', but if, as at Dortmund, it is combined with a conspicuous violet floor, the effect is merely modish and showy.

From all these comments it may be concluded that the auditorium as an end in itself and as a room designed for itself is gradually disappearing. Its subservient role is stressed much more and its air of costliness is created by rare woods rather than by other and gaudier decoration. In foyers, too—despite the money lavished upon them—restraint continues to demonstrate its worth. A few, carefully designed features are quite enough to produce a lively effect, especially if the rooms adequately reflect their inherent motivation (Ingolstadt, St. Gallen, Bonn, Cologne opera).

297
Opera House Cologne, floor plan at stage level

298—299
Opera House, Frankfurt am Main
Possible variations with large and small revolve ('Der Prozess' — Rennert/Maximowna, 'Die Räuber' — Buckwitz/Otto)

300
Burgtheater Vienna, floor-plan with revolving cylindrical stage

Stage Offices

Stage

As a rule, the theatre presents only its 'sunny side' to the public, where everything is directed towards the festive character of the occasion. It is easily forgotten, even by architects, that the theatre is a workshop, in which a complicated process of 'production' has to take place, and the first night is the 'product' of a long and hard job. People like to forget that the prerequisite for artistic creation, and for 'producing' something good, is to have suitable working conditions.

At the same time the proceedings on and about the actual stage on the evening of the performance must run as smoothly as on the days of preparatory work and at rehearsal; and, finally, the direction and supervision of all this complex apparatus have to function.

Unfortunately it has become increasingly noticeable that, even in large carefully organized competitions, it is precisely this work sequence which is insufficiently studied. In particular, architects who have not previously built theatres—and those who have built several are very few—simply provide the space required and pay no attention to the way in which it is allocated. In one case, the dressing-rooms are inconvenient for the stage; in another, the workshops disturb rehearsals. It may even happen that a thirty foot scene-store is built with heating pipes passing through it at a height of twenty feet, so that the room cannot be used for its intended purpose.

The trouble is generally due to a failure of communications between the two sides. The architect conceives his main task to be the design of the 'show-rooms', leaving the rest to his 'left hand' or, in the stage area, to a technician. The director, who often knows full well that he will not be in charge of the new house, is disinterested and, when his successor arrives, the position is irrevocable.

The competition conditions are not always helpful. As only very few theatre buildings are directly commissioned, the theatre director has to remain as neutral as possible in the preparation of preliminary plans so that none of the team is unduly influenced, and there is no real collaboration from the beginning. There are, of course, exceptions. The Mannheim theatre is one such. Here the director, Hans Schüler, had been working on the scheme for years and, with his technical chief, Hans Birr, was always at the architect's side. The result is a house which works, both technically and dramatically. The Düsseldorf playhouse is also an instance of joint development, to which the programming of Karl Heinz Stroux, the stage-manager of many years' standing, and his technical director, Willi Ehle, contributed decisively.

It remains to be seen whether the outcome will be to the benefit of the house. At Bochum, too, director Hans Schalla worked with Gerhard Graubner to fruitful effect. But this is a rarity and only possible in the few houses which have had the same director for a number of years. Stuttgart is another example

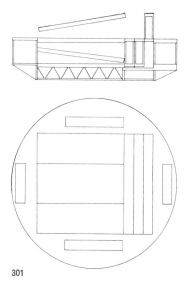

301

301 a

301–301 a
National Theatre, Mannheim
Plan of stage, steel framework of re-
volving cylindrical stage during assembly

of excellent workshop and rehearsal facilities. Whenever architect and director have come together it has been to the advantage of the operation. (One would never plan a factory without bringing in the managing director. What is a foregone conclusion in private industry is unhappily an exception in the theatre.)

The stage is the inextricable complement of the auditorium. We have already talked at length about the boundary separating them. Adolf Zotzmann, who has collaborated with many architects, has made a vital contribution to its technical development. As technical director for many years of the Ruhr Festival productions at Recklinghausen, he has long been involved in the actual work processes. His relationship with the stage is therefore not merely theoretical.

The close association of auditorium and stage has meant that a frontier, which in the modified picture-frame stage will never be completely erased, has been architecturally glossed over and underplayed. That this can never lead to satisfactory architectural solutions is obvious. If the technical stage-house and the auditorium are to be linked together, a compromise will always be inevitable. Two such diverse architectural entities cannot be fitted smoothly into each other, unless they are tackled from the beginning—as in the American theatres-in-the-round—as a single architectonic unit.

The most commonly used stage-type is the wagon-stage. The Cologne opera house—not the first of this form—can really be regarded as its prototype. The stage proper is connected to two wing stages, which have, as far as possible, the same shape and size as the main one. One of these side stages at Cologne is slightly constricted to accommodate two back-cloth stores. Although the back-stage is not the same height as the main stage, it has the same dimensions otherwise, so that a wagon with the revolve can travel forward on to it. Smaller wagons stand on the side stages and can be coupled to each other to make larger wagon 'complexes'. The main stage is separated on all sides by safety-curtains, so that the subsequent scenes may be assembled on the wing (side) stages.

The scene-stores for the current performance are in the external angles at the back. This is a practical layout, but wasteful of space. In theatres which are exclusively playhouses, at least one side stage is generally dispensed with. But, as a basic principle, the plan has been adopted for almost all postwar stages.

A completely different scheme has been devised in the Frankfurt opera house in collaboration with the director, Harry Buckwitz. Here a large revolving platform, one hundred and twenty-four feet in diameter, has been built into the stage-house, with a second revolve of fifty-two feet diameter inserted into it. On very rare occasions the large revolving stage is fully utilized for the evening performance; the back platform can carry the scenes for the second and third acts or the rehearsal sets for the

same and the next day can be left on it. With the aid of a crane installation, the scenery is transported straight into the back-stage main store. A number of practitioners prefer this arrangement to the wagon-stage, but it has not been adopted elsewhere, although it has turned up again in Helmut Bätzner's design for the Staatstheater at Karlsruhe. A special solution was developed for the Mannheim theatre, similar to that of the Burgtheater in Vienna. Both houses had space problems. In Vienna there were no wing-stages, and room had to be provided in the cellars. At Mannheim the cellars were obstructed by an air-raid shelter, and stage space had to be made on the floor above. Despite these different points of departure, the same system has been applied in each case, the main stage being constructed as a large cylindrical revolving drum. While in Vienna the scene-transportation gear is located centrally on the basement side-stages, at Mannheim machinery of extreme flexibility is mounted at main-stage and under-stage levels. Four podia are built into the cylindrical revolve, three lying parallel and one placed at right angles. These platforms can be lifted, sunk or inclined, so that slopes can be contrived mechanically in a few minutes and without elaborate construction. The transverse platform is tripartite with two tiers, and can be raised to eight feet. As the whole installation is assembled within the circumference of the revolve, the platforms can be moved into almost any corner of the stage. This equipment is justified and not only for complicated sets; the essential framework for rehearsals can also be supplied more rapidly and the work appreciably lightened. A similar scheme has been realized at Würzburg, but until now there have been few opportunities for exploiting it.

Two major elements have to be conveniently related to the stage: the dressing-rooms for soloists, chorus and ballet; the very important workshops. At Mannheim, where the workshops are in another building, the dressing-rooms flank the two stages along one side—a sensibly concentrated and handy position. In addition, the canteen has also been placed at stage-level, with a large and light glazed front. Those who know how much time has to be killed in the theatre will appreciate the importance in stage life of a good and friendly canteen, and will not consider it a secondary matter. It is far from a good idea to stick it, as at Dortmund, in some odd corner of the basement.

At Gelsenkirchen the dressing-room problem is solved in much the same way as at Mannheim. The dressing-rooms line one side of the house, with the director's room and administrative offices on the other.

Workshops

The workshop area must be as close as possible to the stage, so long as the latter and the soloists' rehearsal rooms are not disturbed by noise. Large transport installations inside the house are always costly. In this connection, too, Cologne shows the most logical arrangement, although once again it is very space-consuming. The big workshops are placed above the back-stage and wing-stages, namely the paint-shop, carpenter's shop and, in the middle, set-assembly. The machine-shop and other workshops are on the floors above in immediate proximity.

Such convenient arrangements are not always possible, especially if old buildings have to be reconstructed. For instance, in Frankfurt the workshops are very handsomely equipped, but no satisfactory transport facilities could be contrived because of the limitations imposed by the continued use of the former playhouse (in process of conversion to opera). In Berlin the Deutsche Oper has encountered similar difficulties resulting from piecemeal rebuilding. In Stuttgart—thanks to the astute initiative of an experienced director—the workshops for the playhouse are carefully and generously planned. The redevelopment has not only provided good conditions for the playhouse, but eased the workshop and rehearsal problems of the opera. To give one example, a rehearsal stage has been built, which has the same dimensions as the main stage and, in addition, a sunk orchestra-pit, so that genuine on-stage rehearsals can be held.

Lighting

Nowadays one of the most important items of equipment in a theatre is the lighting. There are a number of houses which forego mechanical aids—stage-wagons, revolve, traps, cyclorama—like the Freie Volksbühne in Berlin and the playhouse originated by Oskar Fritz Schuh in Cologne, but these have highly sophisticated lighting systems. The flexible character of the stage-opening has led at the same time to a further development of the lighting in this area, by elaborating the installation in such a way that the two (inner and outer) 'frames' are each fully equipped, and that out of these two lighting-bridges can be adapted a third, if both 'frames' are taken away and the stage opened to its maximum width. Often also one of the rear fly-galleries is designed as a travelling lighting-bridge. Schuh has used this system in Cologne, provision is made for it in the Frankfurt playhouse, and it is found as well in several other houses (Recklinghausen, Bonn). The most significant postwar change, however—besides the development of new apparatus—has taken place in lighting control. Modern electronics have made the old-fashioned switchboard redundant. Quicker and more frequent variations are now feasible. In particular the possibilities of storage, which make it possible to preselect a number of successive combinations, have simplified the task, both on the night

and at rehearsal. Münster was one of the first to introduce the system, which has subsequently been adopted in many theatres. In recent years it has been improved by a punched card technique, in which individual lights are no longer hand-fed, but selected by punched cards. It has been found that this system needs only a certain acclimatization period for the operators, and then works well. It was first installed in Frankfurt, and later at Bonn, Recklinghausen and Dortmund.

The siting of the lights-control point has also been altered. Previously this was located in most cases at the side in the proscenium wings, so that the operator would be within call and view of the stage. After the war experiments were made. For instance, in the Frankfurt opera house it was placed in the parapet of the orchestra-pit and below the rake of the stalls, while in Cologne, in the playhouse as well as the opera, it is in the wings. Other schemes put it in a 'pocket' between the orchestra stalls and the upper stalls. But in the meantime it has become accepted that the control point should be set back at the height of the first balcony (dress-circle) or above the highest tier of stalls. From here the operators have a good view of the stage without disturbing the audience with their work, and there are no problems of communication with the stage staff, thanks to modern radio methods.

Exterior Architecture

After the building, in recent years, of more than thirty theatres in the German-speaking regions alone and the reconstruction of a comparable number, has a particular 'theatre architecture' emerged? Is there a canon, a standard which has become an accepted model? The answer must be 'No'. There is no reliable convention, no distinctive type. Indeed the newer buildings appear as such direct descendants of the older that even the few frail indications of an incipient tradition seem to be in doubt.

At the turn of the century the temple of the muses was the determining basic form, varied no doubt in individual cases, but undisputed as a type. This by no means applies to postwar theatre architecture. The temple form was not original, but an adaptation of an historic motif, acknowledged none the less as obligatory. The building's mass rose by stages over the entrance portico and the auditorium dome behind to the dominating fly-tower. Today, with the disappearance of the pompous entrance, the handling of the fly-tower poses a big architectural problem. There had after all been a rule-of-thumb that it should be about twice the height of the profile of the stage. Now the first link in the chain—the portico—has gone, and it was all the more difficult to fit the high tower into the design as a whole.

At Münster, for example, an attempt was made to make it more pleasing by moulding the sharp lines into an oval. In this way the heavy tower would have an elegant air. In Cologne the aim was the opposite. On either side of the fly-tower, workshops and rehearsal rooms were piled into a massive, ungainly and singular structure, which immediately acquired nicknames like 'Aida's air-raid shelter' and 'the tomb of the unknown director'. Kassel followed tradition with a step-by-step rise from the entrance-hall and foyer to the auditorium and, finally, to the tower, but the unimaginative design hardly proved convincing. A high administration block is intended to counterbalance the mass of the fly-tower. The intention was similar at Dortmund. Here the tower is located in a giant office slab, which accommodates the administration and rehearsal rooms, and to which are connected on one side the three-pointed shell, with the auditorium, and on the other the somewhat ramified workshops. But these different architectural elements remain mutually isolated and fail to achieve a unified whole.

Weber found a clear solution for Mannheim. The stage-houses and foyers of both theatres have been combined into a straightforward, wedge-shaped structure, and above this rises, without any form of disguise, the rectangle of the fly-tower, simple and functional. The Gelsenkirchen theatre is also the product of the same basic thinking, the juxtaposition of individual forms according to their purpose. While all the spatial elements of the theatre are combined into a large cube, the oval drum of the auditorium and the rectangular fly-tower rise unembellished out of the massive block, their particular shape dictated by their function. More recent designs have turned against this practical objectiv-

ity. In his projects for Mannheim and Kassel, Scharoun tried to build up gradually towards the tower (see pages 16, 212 et seq.) the rather loosely associated, widely extending, constituent parts of the building, and this characteristic has been variously exploited by the younger generation. It was first seen at Bonn, where large tiered terraces climb up to the oblique silhouette of the fly-tower. However, the design is not consistently thought out and takes refuge in fashionable clichés. Ingolstadt displays a more successful version, everything being left in exposed concrete, with the intricate components of the theatre winding upward to the tower. The most logically organized solution, however, is the theatre at St. Gallen. The lively, varied, elevations, which avoid any show-side and even incorporate the so often perfunctorily treated back-view of the workshops, draw together all such diverse elements into a unified whole, so that none is left isolated. Here, for the first time, a theatre has been realized with an integrated architectural form of its own.

For those theatres which do not have their own repertory and rely on visiting companies, the task can be easier than it is for houses having complete workshop facilities—even if rather small in extent, as at St. Gallen. The former are able to concentrate upon the stage and auditorium, and do without extensive rehearsal, management, and workshop accommodation. Admittedly the 'Freie Volksbühne' is not of this type, but space is limited, and it was certainly no coincidence that this theatre and Ingolstadt can be counted among the best examples of postwar theatre architecture. The smaller mass of the building is easier to 'break down', and the fewer divergent spatial elements can be better combined. Nevertheless no distinctive stylistic principle has emerged for these smaller houses, which may reflect a given movement but do not conform to any particular pattern. An example abroad of especially unusual character should be mentioned, namely the students' theatre by Sir Basil Spence at Southampton (see page 37), in which auditorium and fly-tower are enclosed by two interlocking shells.

An idiosyncratic solution is in process of realization by Hans Scharoun at Wolfsburg. Here the low foyer and management offices are spread over the site like spiders' legs, while the stage-house and auditorium project high into the air, resembling gigantic pillars. The height of the stage-tower and its adjoining rooms is almost too pointedly emphasized.

Theatre architecture has shown no ability to create a style during the postwar period. It is one of the few remaining jobs offering the architect an opportunity for originality, and the chance has been so thoroughly exploited that every theatre has been exposed to the whims of its architect's peculiar genius. No new and compulsive interpretation of the programme has resulted. Of none of the executed schemes could it be said that this is the theatre of our time, the prototype which meets the requirements that we expect of the theatre today. And indeed it must once again be stressed that neither has the traditional form of the conventional theatre been satisfactorily developed, nor has a solution been found which responds to the possibilities of future forms. The chance has been missed—although this is not the place to inquire whether the company has been incapable of formulating the programme adequately or the architect has been unequal to the task.

In spite of the many individually noteworthy schemes, the outcome as a whole is negative. Diversity and unity are in this case incompatible. A host of details have not produced a recognizable portrait. So it is also scarcely surprising that theatre buildings play no significant role in the urban pattern. Theatres have been sited in places dictated by tradition or the local politics of land development, but nowhere have they been included as part of a larger comprehensive plan. They are built in more or less commanding positions in squares or important streets, or in isolation in parks, but they remain separate and aloof, their aura extending hardly at all beyond their own precinct. They are still states within the state and outside public life. All attempts to bring them into communication with the world around them—like those opened glass façades—are merely half-hearted gestures which do not alter the situation. The task of building theatres, set by the aftermath of war, appears to be largely completed. Only a few towns are still able to contemplate new buildings. But, although the stucco, the columns and the plush have gone, the twentieth century has not yet begun. The nineteenth continues to imprint its character on our present-day theatres.

List of Abbreviations Used on the Following Plans and Sections

Auditorium
A 1   Entrances
A 2   Entrance hall
A 3   Box-office
A 4   Cloakrooms
A 5   Staircase
A 6   Foyer/lobbies
A 7   Buffet/refreshments
A 8   Reception rooms
A 9   Auditorium/stalls
A 10   Upper stalls
A 11   1st balcony/boxes
A 12   2nd balcony/boxes
A 13   3rd balcony/boxes
A 14   Amphitheatre
A 15   Swivel-mounted partition
A 16   Sliding partition
A 17   Seat-wagon

Stage
B 1   (Main) stage
B 2   Right wing-space/side-stage
B 3   Left wing-space/side-stage
B 4   Back-stage
B 5   Under-stage
B 6   Orchestra podium/orchestra pit
B 7   Stage podium/floor
B 8   Stage-wagon
B 9   Revolve
B 10   Double podium
B 11   Trap
B 12   Travelling hoists/conveyors
B 13   Transport area
B 14   Prompter
B 15   Stage-manager's desk
B 16   Properties
B 17   Projection room
B 18   Sound studio
B 19   Service boxes
B 20   Fly-tower
B 21   Fire-proof curtain/safety curtain
B 22   Front curtain
B 23   Proscenium roof
B 24   Stage opening/proscenium opening
B 25   Light control-board/switchboard
B 26   Light-bridge/light-batten
B 27   Gallery/fly-floor
B 28   Grid
B 29   Smoke vent
B 30   Cyclorama
B 31   Curtain set
B 32   Lantern lines
B 33   Cyclorama lights
B 34   Curtain and scenery lines
B 35   Spotblock lines
B 36   Electrically operated lines
B 37   Hand-worked lines
B 38   Flying machinery
B 39   Control desk for under-stage machinery
B 40   Control desk for above-stage machinery
B 41   Ceiling elements
B 42   Projection recess

Direction/Management/Technical Supervision
C 1   Director
C 2   Offices of director's staff
C 3   Library
C 4   Musical director
C 5   Administrative director
C 6   Administration offices
C 7   Technical director
C 8   Offices of technical staff
C 9   Stage door
C 10   Porter/janitor

Rehearsal Rooms
D 1   Rehearsal stage
D 2   Orchestra rehearsal room
D 3   Chorus rehearsal room
D 4   Ballet rehearsal room
D 5   Ensemble/company rehearsal rooms
D 6   Soloists' rehearsal room
D 7   Musicians' practice room

Dressing-rooms
E 1   Soloists' dressing-rooms
E 2   Green room
E 3   Washrooms/showers
E 4   Make-up
E 5   Dressing-rooms for chorus
E 6   Extras' dressing-rooms
E 7   Ballet soloists' dressing-rooms
E 8   Ballet dressing-rooms
E 9   Children's ballet
E 10   Dressing-rooms for orchestra

Store-rooms
F 1   Scenery store
F 2   Freight-lift
F 3   Back-cloth store
F 4   Back-cloth lift
F 5   Wardrobe/costumes
F 6   Lighting store
F 7   Furniture store
F 8   Properties
F 9   Armoury
F 10   Wigs
F 11   Materials store
F 12   Scenery-wagon
F 13   Instruments store

Workshops
G 1   Paint-shop
G 2   Scenery assembly
G 3   Carpenter's shop
G 4   Smith/mechanic
G 5   Scenic construction
G 6   Electrician
G 7   Tailor/dressmaker/fitting-room
G 8   Shoemaker
G 9   Make-up studio
G 10   Armourer
G 11   Upholsterer
G 12   Scenery-sewing
G 13   Properties workshop

Staff Rooms
H 1   Caretaker's flat
H 2   Sitting-rooms
H 3   Kitchen/service rooms
H 4   Canteen
H 5   Restaurant
H 6   Doctor
H 10   Public utilities

Miscellaneous
J 1   Light well
J 2   Garden court/courtyard
J 3   Garages
J 4   Garage access
J 5   Theatre forecourt
J 6   Terrace
J 7   Roof
J 8   Ruins
J 9   Shops
J 10   Old building
J 11   Conference room
L   Void

All plans and sections on the following pages drawn to a scale of 1:1000

Notes on Technical Data

For purposes of comparison and in the interests of clarity, a similar arrangement has been followed for each theatre in presenting technical data. The information has been checked and supplemented by the architects and technical directors concerned. When particulars of a scheme (e.g., wing-spaces, stage-wagons, etc.) are not given, it may be assumed that the relevant elements are not provided in the theatre.

Cost (overall)
Space enclosed
Number of seats
Stalls
1st balcony
2nd balcony
Distance between rows
Seat width
Position of fire curtain
Maximum auditorium width   clear (unobstructed) width
Maximum auditorium depth   clear (unobstructed) depth from proscenium opening
Greatest distance from stage   The cardinal factor in seating is the distance from the proscenium opening (not the fire curtain).

Stalls
1st balcony
2nd balcony
Dimensions of (main) stage   width by depth (to the proscenium opening, once again)
Dimensions of right wing-space   (side-stage)
Dimensions of left wing-space
Backstage dimensions
Number of proscenium openings
Maximum (proscenium) opening   width by height
Minimum opening
Height of grid
Orchestra space
Lighting control system
Number of levers (dimmers)
Number of circuits
Number of pre-set possibilities
Number of line-sets
Electrically operated lines
Manual (hand-worked) lines
Counterweight lines
Stage-wagons   width by depth
Right wing-space
Left wing-space
Backstage
Revolve
Dimensions of stage-podia   platform-elevators, plateau-elevators, etc.
Limits of travel
Cyclorama or substitute

proscenium opening

maximum auditorium depth

greatest distance from stalls to stage

1m

main stage

main stage ( )

main stage ( ) with orchestra-pit covered

● reference point = front edge of proscenium opening

State Theatre of Niedersachsen, Hanover — Opera

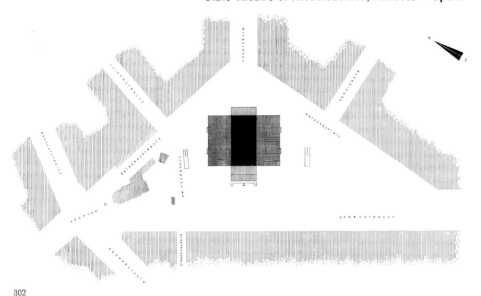

The state theatre in Hanover may reasonably stand as the representative example of the countless theatres of the Federal Republic which have been reconstructed.

The classical building by Georg Ludwig Friedrich Laves sited in the centre of the city and, with its disciplined proportions, still an impressive structure, was not restored in strict accordance with the original design. During an operation lasting fifteen years, architect Werner Kallmorgen tried to blend the old with the new, and has successfully harmonized the classical forms with his own 'North-German' rigid objectivity.

While the circular auditorium with three embracing balconies (already needing thorough renovation thanks to inadequate funds for the initial decorations) still relies strongly on convention, good results have been obtained in the foyer, buffets and staircase areas by contrasting and juxtaposing old

302

303

302
Site plan

303
Entrance hall

304

and new; e. g., the entrance hall, where the rough exposed brick of the ceiling acts as a foil to the white plastered walls; or the classical niches introduced into the plain barrel-vaulted foyer; or the buffet, with its discreet exploitation of the orders. If one may have reservations over many details, there is no denying that the architect strove conscientiously to bring new life to tradition and was able to build a bridge between the past and the present. In face of so many unimaginative reconstructions this theatre, which was among the first to be restored deserves particular credit.

304—305
Staircase, auditorium view

306—307
Foyer, buffet

308—310
First floor, ground-floor, section

305

310

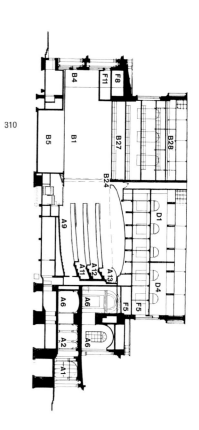

State Theatre of Niedersachsen, Hanover — Opera

306

307

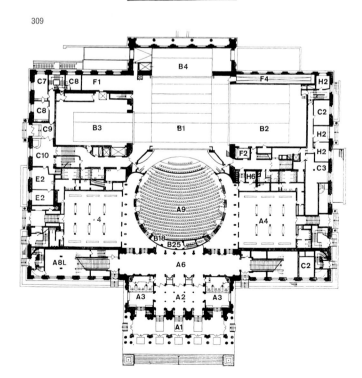

308

309

Client	City of Hanover
Artistic categories	opera, operetta, ballet, plays, concerts
	for concerts: orchestra 'shell' on stage
Competition	1949
Period of building	1949–1965 in five stages
Opening	first stage December 1950
Architects	Werner Kallmorgen, Klaus Hoffmann
Stage technical consultant	Adolf Zotzmann
Structural engineers	Peters — Windels
Acoustics	Heinrich Keilholz
Tests (structure)	Alkar Rudelt
Cost	DM 21,625,000
Space enclosed	135,000 m³
Number of seats	1500
	stalls 772, 3 orchestra rows with 57 seats
	1st balcony 267 (281)
	2nd balcony 228
	3rd balcony 224
Distance between rows	90 cm
Seat width	55 cm
Fire curtain behind orchestra	
Maximum auditorium width	c. 23.50 m
Maximum auditorium depth	c. 25 m
Greatest distance from stage	stalls c. 23 m
	1st balcony c. 24.40 m
	2nd balcony c. 25.20 m
	3rd balcony c. 27.20 m
Dimensions of main stage	25.95 x 20.20 m
Dimensions of right wing-space (stage)	20.70 x 16.45 m
Dimensions of left wing-space	20.70 x 13.75 m
Dimensions of backstage	17.30 x 7.80 m
Number of proscenium openings	1
Maximum opening	14 x 11.60 m
Minimum opening	8.50 x ± 0 m
Height of grid	25.80 m
Orchestra space	currently 100 m², ultimately 140 m²
Lighting control system	currently Siemens-Bordoni
Number of levers (dimmers)	108
Number of circuits	130 circuits with switchboard interconnection
Number of lines (sets)	46 back-cloth lines
Hydraulic	6 pan-cloth lines
Manual	23 spot-lines
Counterweight	3 flood-lines
Stage-wagon dimensions	
Right wing-space	3 x 16 x 5.08 m
Left wing-space	1 x 16 x 5.08 m + 1 x 16 x 2.53 m
Backstage	1 x 16 x 5.08 m + 1 x 16 x 2.53 m
Dimensions of stage-podia (elevators)	1 x 16 x 5.08 m + 4 x 16 x 2.53 m
Limits of travel	podium 1 + 0.75 to — 5.50 m
	podium 2–4 + 3 to — 3 m
	podium 5 + 3 to — 5.50 m
Traps	2

Municipal Theatres, Frankfurt am Main

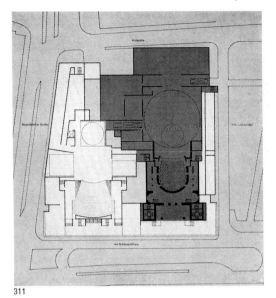

311

312

313

The Frankfurt theatres form a heterogeneous group. The opera house was built in the ruins of the former playhouse, a new playhouse being added twelve years later. Concurrently the two houses have been given a common foyer in front, while at the side an administration and dressing-room wing has been so disguised that the building presents new 'show-case' elevations on three frontages.

Such a structure, of course, is not to be judged by the standards of a completely new building. The auditorium of the opera has adopted the traditional balcony plan, but the spacious stage has been equipped, according to the ideas of Harry Buckwitz, the experienced director, with a giant revolve which extends as far as the conventional back-stage area. It serves for scene-changes, instead of the normally preferred wagons.

As well as the addition of a new playhouse to the older complex, the workshops were in part extended. This has resulted in an extremely intricate arrangement, accentuated by the confined site, and one not always convenient.

The playhouse, a simple amphitheatre with wide lateral access platforms which can also be used for actors' entrances, is designed as a wagon-stage with three subsidiary stages. Great care has been taken with the area of the stage opening. The 'arch' can be flown and the stage opened to its full width, with the auditorium walls bordering the wings drawn back. Unfortunately the side pockets formed when a picture-frame stage is in use produce acoustic problems. The Frankfurt playhouse was one of the first to introduce the punched-card system for stage-lighting.

The lack of space proved especially awkward in locating the foyer, which could only be handled as a narrow passage extending in front of both houses. In order to provide air in at least one direction, it was raised to a height of some thirty feet, the effect of this being mitigated by the free-hanging 'clouds' of Zoltan Kemeny—a much discussed, but certainly quite satisfactory solution to a thorny architectural problem.

The small studio theatre, entered at the back of the group, is delightful. The steeply raked seating, as in a lecture-room, modestly decorated in grey and black, gives the hall a special atmosphere, equally suited to classical works and modern experiments.

311
Site plan

312–313
Entrance front, foyer

314–315
Auditorium and stage: opera house and playhouse

314

315

316

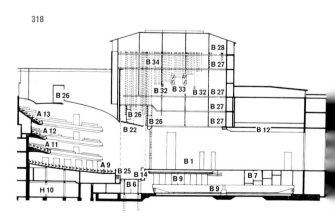

317

316
Auditorium of small theatre

317—318
Section through playhouse, section through opera house

319—321
Upper storey, foyer floor, ground-floor

319

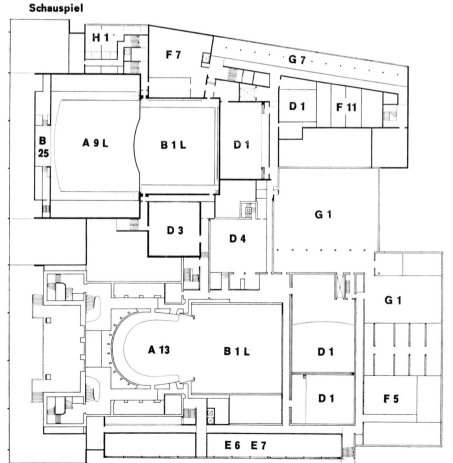

Schauspiel

Oper

318

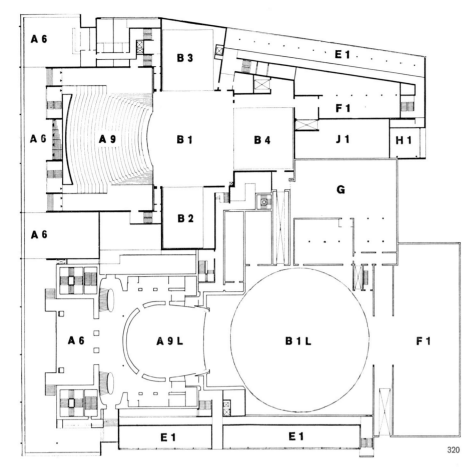

320

321

Schauspiel

99

Municipal Theatres, Frankfurt am Main

Client	City of Frankfurt
Artistic categories	opera, operetta, ballet
Period of building	1949–1951
	(reconstruction of former play-house with new stage)
Opening	23. 12. 1951
Architects	architectural partnership of Apel, Letocha, Rohrer
Theatre consultant	Paul Kuhnert
Stage technical consultant	Adolf Linnebach
Structural engineer	Petry
Acoustics	Albrecht Eisenberg
Extensions	1962–1963
Cost	1951: DM 12,000,000
+ scene-store building	1955: DM 2,000,000
+ foyer and dressing-rooms	1963: DM 6,000,000
Space enclosed	171,000 m³
Number of seats	1430
	stalls 692
	1st balcony 232
	2nd balcony 209
	3rd balcony 297
Distance between rows	83 cm
Seat width	55 cm
Fire curtain in front of orchestra	
Maximum auditorium width	19 m
Maximum auditorium depth	31 m
Greatest distance from stage	stalls 28.50 m
	1st balcony 29 m
	2nd balcony 29 m
	3rd balcony 34 m
Dimensions of main stage	23.50 x 19.50 m
Dimensions of whole stage area	40 x 40 m
	(This area—with wing-spaces and backstage—has a built-in scene-shift revolve of 38 m diameter.)
Number of proscenium openings	2 (first in front of orchestra-pit, second behind orchestra-pit)
1 maximum opening	15 x 11 m
minimum opening	10 x 3 m
2 maximum opening	13 x 9 m
minimum opening	10 x 3 m
Height of grid	26 m
Orchestra space	99 m²
Lighting control system	Siemens-Bordoni voltage transformer
Number of levers (dimmers)	240
Number of circuits	260
Number of lines (sets)	82
Electrically operated	2
Hydraulic	35
Manual	45
Revolve	The 38 m scene-shift revolve contains a 16 m revolving-stage.
Dimensions of stage-podia (elevators)	4 x 16 x 2.25 m

Municipal Theatres, Frankfurt am Main

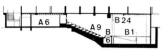

322

Schauspiel

Kammerspiele

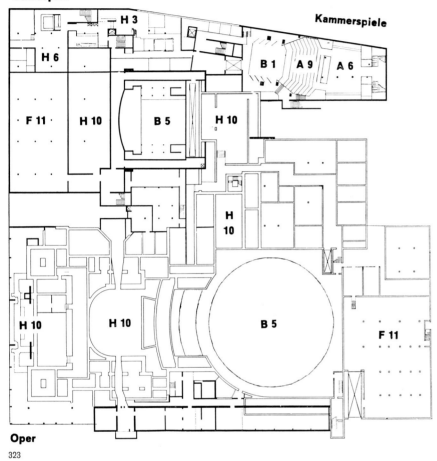

Oper

323

322–323
Section through small theatre, basement

Client	City of Frankfurt
Artistic categories	plays, musicals
Plan	1956
Period of building	1960–1963
Opening	21. 12. 1963
Architects	Otto Apel, Hansgeorg Beckert, Gilbert Becker
Sculptor	Zoltan Kemeny
Painter	Marc Chagall
Theatre consultant	Walter Huneke
Stage technical consultant	Paul Kuhnert
Structural engineer	von Ohlnhausen
Acoustics	Karl Hans Weisse
Tests (structure)	Beck
Cost	DM 23,000,000 (playhouse and studio)
Space enclosed	109,500 m³

Playhouse

Number of seats	911
Distance between rows	90 cm
Seat width	53 cm
Fire curtain in front of orchestra	
Maximum auditorium width	28 m (38 m)
Maximum auditorium depth	25 m
Greatest distance from stage	25 m
Dimensions of main stage	25 x 22 m
Dimensions of left wing-space	16 x 14 m
Dimensions of right wing-space	16 x 14 m
Dimensions of backstage	20 x 17 m
Number of proscenium openings	1 (The whole arch can be flown.)
Maximum opening	14 x 8 m
Minimum opening	9 x 3 m
Opening for arena-stage	24 x 8 m
Height of grid	26 m
Orchestra space	40 to 72 m²
Lighting control system	Siemens magnetic-amplifier
Number of levers (dimmers)	220 + 40 master-panel
Number of circuits	410, partly interchangeable
Number of pre-set possibilities	4 + unlimited with punched cards
Number of lines (sets)	54
Electrically operated	4
Hydraulic	50
Stage-wagon dimensions	
Left wing-space	2 x 2 m to 3 x 4 m free-moving
Right wing-space	1 x 16 x 2.50 m
	3 x 16 x 3 m
Backstage	16 x 16 m
Revolve	15.70 m diameter in backstage wagon
Dimensions of stage-podia (elevators)	
Segmental podium	14.30 x 1.75 m
1st two-tier rostrum	14.30 x 2.25 m
2nd two-tier rostrum	16 x 2 m
Traps	10 x 2 m
Limits of travel	+ 0.66 to — 4.50 m

Studio theatre

Number of seats	200
Distance between rows	90–97 cm
Seat width	53 cm
Maximum auditorium width	15.50 m
Maximum auditorium depth	11 m
Greatest distance from stage	12 m
Dimensions of main stage	16 x 11 m
Number of proscenium openings	1
Maximum opening	10 x 4.20 m
Minimum opening	8 x 4.20 m
Height of grid	5 m
Orchestra space	16 m²
Lighting control system	AEG transistor-semiconductor
Number of levers (dimmers)	60 (double panel)
Number of circuits	60
Number of pre-set possibilities	2 x 20
Number of lines (sets)	78 electrically driven spot-lines
Manual	2
Dimensions of stage-podia (elevators)	10 x 6 m
	adjustable to + 1 m slant

Combined Municipal Theatres, Krefeld

324

The town theatres of Krefeld were built in two phases. The planning of the first structure began in 1949 and was in the hands of Eugen Bertrand. At the same time, however, a project by the Swiss architects, A.P. von Laban and E. Stoecklin (see page 17), and one by the Hamburg team of Werner Kallmorgen and Adolf Zotzmann were under consideration. In the end the design by the Krefeld architect Bertrand was chosen, because it could be carried out in stages.

This building, opened in 1952, was thus from the beginning only one part. Moreover it emerged, when there was a move towards completing the scheme—Bertrand had in the meantime died during the execution of the first stage—that a simple expansion of the original plan was not feasible. So in 1956 a new competition was held, which led to the commission going to Gerhard Graubner, who retained the nucleus of the original building and did not completely remodel it. From this first phase was preserved the rather shallow, but remarkably wide, stage with its 'Cinerama'-type opening, while in front space was provided for the audience and, at the back, for rehearsals and management which before had received only makeshift attention.

The result is a house with 'all the trimmings' and, bearing in mind the difficulties of the situation, not unskilfully handled, but without clear lines and the conviction characterizing an integrated concept.

325

326

324–326
General view, view of auditorium from stage, foyer

327
Site plan

327

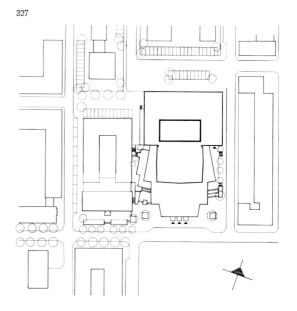

Combined Municipal Theatres, Krefeld

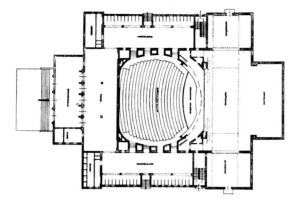

328

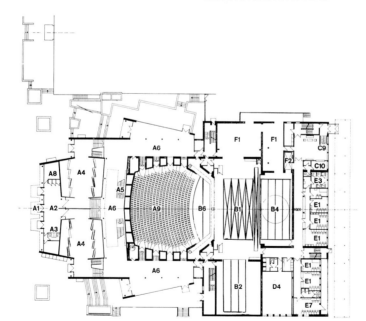

329

330

331

102

Client	Municipality of Krefeld
Artistic categories	opera, operetta, ballet, plays

First stage

Period of building	1951–1952
Opening	October 1952
Architects	Eugen Bertrand, Heinrich Stickelbrocks

Second stage

Competition	1956
Commissioned	1960
Period of building	1901–1903
Opening	12. 1. 1963
Architect	Gerhard Graubner
Painter	Fernand Leger
Tapestries	Juan Miró
Stage technical consultant	Adolf Zotzmann
Cost	DM 11,800,000
Number of seats	832
	stalls 652
	1st balcony 180
Distance between rows	stalls 87.5 cm, balcony 90 cm
Seat width	56 cm
Fire curtain behind orchestra	
Maximum auditorium width	22.70 cm
Maximum auditorium depth	23 m
Greatest distance from stage	stalls 23 m
	balcony 23.75 m
Dimensions of main stage	26.50 x 11.30 m
Dimensions of right wing-space	14 x 12 m
Backstage dimensions	19.30 x 8.60 m
Number of proscenium openings	1
Maximum opening	16 x 6.50 m
Minimum opening	11 x 4 m
Height of grid	20.50 m
Orchestra space	c. 100 m²
Lighting control system	Siemens
Number of levers (dimmers)	140
Number of circuits	127
Number of lines (sets)	26 + 4 pan-cloth lines
Electrically operated	30
Manual (with winch)	
Backstage	5
Stage-wagon dimensions	
Right wing-space	3 x 14 x 2 m
Backstage	8 x 16 x 2 m
Revolve	7.50 m diameter
Dimensions of stage-podia (elevators)	4 x 16 x 2 m
Limits of travel	—2 to + 2 m
Cyclorama	available

328
Ground-floor of first stage of building

329–331
Second stage: first floor, ground-floor, section

Bochum Theatre — Playhouse

332–334
Aerial view, view of playhouse auditorium, view of small theatre stage and auditorium

335
Site plan

332

The theatre at Bochum is not really a new building, but a thorough reconstruction in conventional forms. It earns a place here by reason of its importance to the development of the proscenium area. At Bochum the fireproof curtain was placed for the first time in front of the orchestra-pit in a convex curve, so that for plays the entirc forestage zone can be used for acting and scenery.

The stage is of the wagon-type with two subsidiary stages.

In 1966 a studio-theatre was added to the large house. It is laid out as an amphitheatre, with a stage equipped with a minimum of machinery (no grid, no wagons, no traps). Yet it is not to be regarded as particularly experimental, for it can only be used in a traditional manner. The forestage alone is variable. The discreet, unpretentious décor lends a certain distinction to the theatre.

333

334

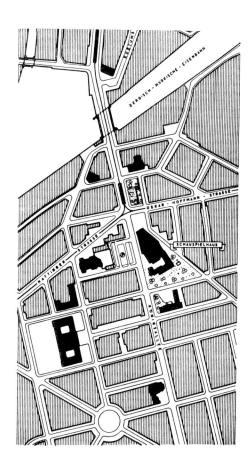

335

Bochum Theatre – Playhouse

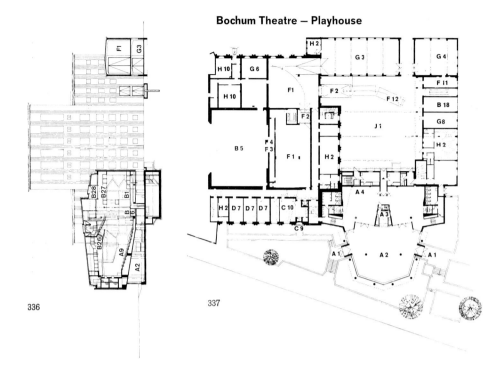

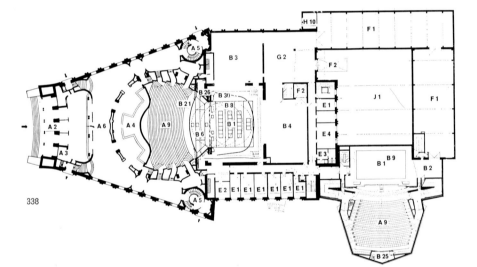

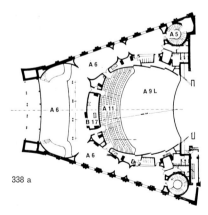

336

337

338

338 a

336
Section through small theatre

337–338 a
Playhouse: basement, principal floor, balcony floor

Playhouse

Client	Municipality of Bochum
Artistic category	plays
Period of building	1951–1953
Opening	23. 11. 1953
Architect	Gerhard Graubner
Stage technical consultant	Walther Unruh
Structural engineer	Bruno Kohlhaas
Acoustics	Karl F. Darmer
Cost	no information
Number of seats	916
	1st rows stalls 241, boxes 31
	2nd rows stalls 304
	3rd rows stalls 161
	1st balcony 179
Distance between rows	84 cm
Seat width	55 cm
Fire curtain in front of orchestra	in a convex line to the auditorium
Maximum auditorium width	15.50 m
Maximum auditorium depth	24 m
Greatest distance from stage	25.50 m
	1st rows stalls 7.50 m
	2nd rows stalls 18 m
Dimensions of main stage	15 x 20 m
Dimensions of left wing-space	13.70 x 13.10 m
Backstage dimensions	10.70 x 16.40 m
Number of proscenium openings	1
Maximum opening	12 x 8 m
Minimum opening	7.50 x 4 m
Height of grid	22.35 m
Orchestra space	72 m²
Lighting control system	Siemens-Bordoni
Number of dimmers	160
Number of circuits	200
Number of lines (sets)	
Manual	45
Counterweight	1
Revolve	13.30 m diameter
Dimensions of stage-podia (elevators)	12 x 2.50 m
Limits of travel	— 3 to + 3 m

Studio theatre

Client	Municipality of Bochum
Artistic category	plays
Opening	13. 10. 1966
Architect	Gerhard Graubner
Stage technical consultant	Adolf Zotzmann
Cost	no information
Number of seats	401
	1st rows stalls 161
	2nd rows stalls 171
	3rd rows stalls 69
Distance between rows	80 cm
Seat width	50 cm
Maximum auditorium width	19.30 m
Maximum auditorium depth	12.40 m
Greatest distance from stage	15 m
Dimensions of main stage	12 x 16.30 m
Dimensions of right wing-space	4 x 8 m
Number of proscenium openings	1
Maximum opening	13 x 5 m
Minimum opening	9 x 3.50 m
Height of grid	9 m
Lighting control system	Siemens-Thyristoren
Number of levers (dimmers)	75
Number of pre-set possibilities	4 appliances
Number of circuits	75
Number of lines (sets)	18 manual
	2 plan-cloth
	4 electrical winch
	500 kg load
	24 hand-spot
	1 flood

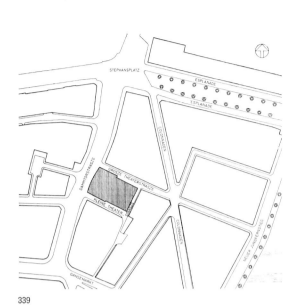

339

340

The state opera in Hamburg is a combination of the new and the restored. The stage-house, with the dressing-rooms and stage-offices, has been largely preserved, but the auditorium was destroyed. A new auditorium was erected in front of the reconstructed stage. This meant that it was necessary to adhere to the old site; hence the restricted conditions in the foyer and the inconvenient access facilities for cars. Nevertheless, the Hamburg state opera has become the model for many subsequent buildings. For the first time the street-and-foyer front was designed as a large glazed façade, partly as a visual extension of the foyer, and partly to avoid segregating the theatre from the city. A still more important development was the introduction of 'sledges', instead of the prolongation of the balconies round the sides. In both box and balcony theatres there is always the handicap of an extremely limited view from the side-seats. Here the balcony is split up into separate sledge-like parts and all the audience sit facing the stage directly, without mutual interference. This device has made the balcony-theatre a practical possibility once again. The obstructed sight-lines from balconies brought the arena-theatre into prominence in the nineteenth and early twentieth centuries, but now the advantages of the balcony theatre, which include short distances from the stage, can be combined with a uniformly good view. The Hamburg stage is wagon-type, with three subsidiary stages; the revolve is built into the back-stage wagon, and the podia of the stage proper are two-tiered and capable of being raised to more than thirty feet.

339
Site plan

340–341
View from the Dammtorstrasse, view from the stalls of the side sledge-type boxes

341

342

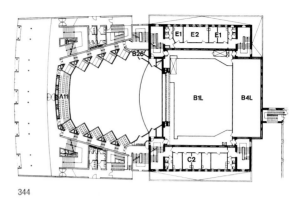

344

343

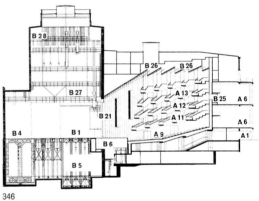

345

346

342–343
Second balcony foyer, view of auditorium from stage

344–346
Floor plans: first balcony, stalls, section

Client	City of Hamburg Senate
Artistic categories	opera, operetta, ballet
Period of building	reconstruction 1953–1955
Opening	15. 10. 1955
Architects	Gerhard Weber, W. Lux, H. Ebert, U. Gastreich
Colour consultant	F. Kronenberg
Stage technical consultant	State Opera Technical Bureau
Structural engineers	W. Bültmann, F. Grebner
Acoustics	Albrecht Eisenberg
Cost	no information
Number of seats	1679
	stalls 856
	1st balcony 285
	2nd balcony 230
	3rd balcony 172 + 16 standing
	4th balcony 112 + 8 listening
Distance between rows	90 cm
Seat width	55 cm
Fire curtain behind orchestra	
Maximum auditorium width	27.50 m
Maximum auditorium depth	28.50 m
Greatest distance from stage	stalls 30 m
	4th balcony 36.50 m

Dimensions of main stage	15 x 16.50 m (18 m)
Dimensions of right wing-space	11 x 7.50 m
Dimensions of left wing-space	11 x 7.50 m
Backstage dimensions	15 x 7.50 m
Number of proscenium openings	1
Maximum opening	12 x 8.20 m
Minimum opening	9 x 4 m
Height of grid	29 m
Orchestra space	129 m²
Lighting control system	Thyratron
Number of levers (dimmers)	240
Number of circuits	240
Number of lines (sets)	60, including 3 grid-lines
Counterweight lines	1 manual
Stage-wagon dimensions	3 x 15 x 2.50 m
Right wing-space	3 x 11 x 2.50 m
Left wing-space	3 x 11 x 2.50 m
Backstage	15 x 7.50 m
Revolve	14.80 m diameter
Dimensions of stage-podia (elevators)	15 x 2.50 m
Limits of travel	+ 10 m
Cyclorama	available

Park Theatre, Grenchen/Switzerland

The park theatre, by Ernst Gisel, erected at Grenchen in 1954—5, exemplifies admirably a situation which occurs today in many industrial areas, where people want to participate in cultural functions, where musical and theatrical guest-performances are expected to take place with appropriate pomp and circumstance, and where facilities are needed for social and community occasions, and also for conferences and small congresses.

Such buildings are often described as multi-purpose halls, the ambiguity of the programme generally imparting a slightly derogatory sense to the term—especially as the effort to provide for the spatial needs of a variety of functions leads in most cases to unhappy architectural results.

Gisel designed a composite structure, in which the principal room is primarily a theatre, but which can also be used for other purposes.

The design of the exterior, with the gentle slope of the fly-tower, usually the bugbear of theatre architecture, reflected in the deliberately contrasting roof angles of the hall and gallery wing—is both subtle and architecturally satisfying. In the interior also the strictly formal treatment and the clear objective restraint with which the individual rooms are designed for their particular functions and interrelated bear witness to the thoroughness with which an exacting task has been approached—and guided to a convincing solution. Abrupt divisions, where these are inevitable, are not disguised, and the construction is exposed. The way in which the theatre has been adapted to the discipline of a public square on one side and to the freedom of an old park on the other is particularly creditable.

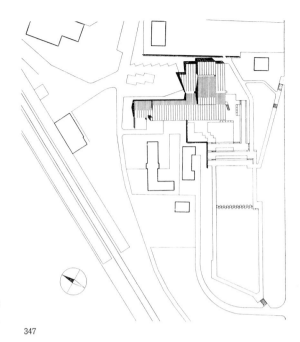

347

347
Site plan

348
View from north

348

Park Theatre, Grenchen/Switzerland

349

350

Client	Municipality of Grenchen
Artistic categories	opera, operetta, plays, cabaret, etc.
Competition	1949
Period of building	1953–1955
Opening	1955
Architect	Ernst Gisel
Sculptor	Max Bill
Painter	Hans Fischer
Glass	Otto Staiger
Tapestry	Elsi Giauque
Theatre consultants	Theo Otto, Ferdinand Lange
Stage technical consultant	Albert Isler
Structural engineers	Emch + Salzmann
Acoustics	Furrer
Cost	Sw. fr. 3,896,000
Space enclosed	17,152 m³
Number of seats	stalls (demountable) 420
	side gallery c. 200
	balcony (fixed seating) 180
Distance between rows	90 cm
Seat width	53 cm
Fire curtain behind orchestra	
Maximum auditorium width	12.60 m (without side gallery)
	side gallery 6.60 m
Maximum auditorium depth	21 m
Greatest distance from stage	stalls 21 m
	balcony 23.20 m
Dimensions of main stage	12.60 x 8.30 m (11.90 m)
Dimensions of left wing-space	7.40 x 8.40 m
Number of proscenium openings	1
Maximum opening	10.70 x 4.40 m
Minimum opening	6.60 x 2.90 m
Height of grid	13.50 m
Orchestra space	17.25–29.40 m²
Lighting control system	Grandmaster
Number of levers (dimmers)	48 double levers (extensible to 60)
Number of circuits	48
Number of lines (sets)	22 manual

349–351
View from south, views of auditorium

352
Ground-floor

351

352

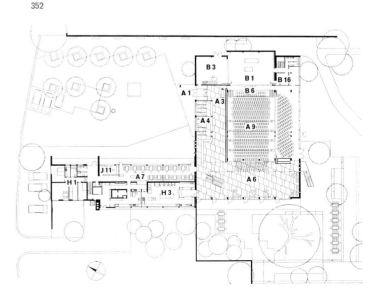

Municipal Theatre, Münster

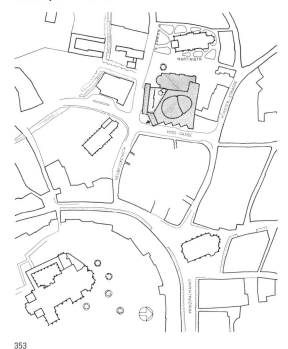

353

354

355

356

The position of the theatre at Münster is a special one in an urbanistic sense. The classical façade of the old town house of the Rombergs was still there and—in view of the destruction of so many important old buildings—had to be preserved. In consequence the possibility of marking effective use of the available site for a theatre was extremely slight. The executed design of the young team of Harald Deilmann, Max von Hausen, Ortwin Rave and Werner Ruhnau (united in protest against uninspiring competition entries) is not only the best for the particular situation, but one of the most imaginative in German postwar theatre architecture.

To take full advantage of the depth of the site, the building is placed diagonally. The façade of the Romberg palace rises on a terrace in front of the foyer like free-standing sculpture and makes a telling contrast to the modern structure.

The theatre is simply a playhouse with some storage-accommodation, which has to make do with the old building for other essential space. Unfortunately the completed plans for the small house will not be realized within the foreseeable future (see page 206 et seq.). The distinctive architectural feature of this building is the arrangement of the staircases as 'free ornament' around the core of the auditorium. The interior of the latter is impaired by the third balcony, which does not fit very happily into the relatively small dimensions of the theatre. The ceiling of lamps, behind which a system of acoustic

Municipal Theatre, Münster

357–360
Balcony storey, upper storey, ground-
floor, section through fly-tower

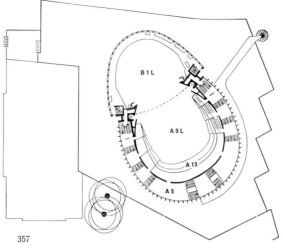

357

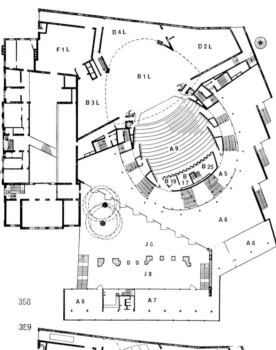

358

359

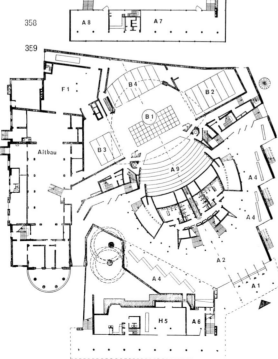

360

tricks is concealed, is a visual delight, but is somewhat distracting to the normal business of the
house.

The stage is modestly equipped, and the left-hand
wing-stage will not be built until the next phase of
construction. The oblique lines of the bow-shaped
fly-tower are at times disturbingly conspicuous, but
in criticizing we should not forget the constricting
nature of the site.

Client	Municipality of Münster
Artistic categories	opera, operetta, ballet, plays
Competition	1953
Period of building	1955–1956
Opening	4. 2. 1956
Architects	Harald Deilmann, Max v. Hausen, Ortwin Rave, Werner Ruhnau
Sculptor	Norbert Kricke
Stage technical consultant	Adolf Zotzmann
Structural engineer	E. Knoche
Acoustics	Erwin Meyer
Tests (structure)	H. Beaucamp
Second phase planning	Max v. Hausen, Ortwin Rave, Werner Ruhnau
Cost	no information
Space enclosed	48,470 m³
Number of seats	955
	stalls 495
	1st balcony ⎫
	2nd balcony ⎬ 460
	3rd balcony ⎭
Distance between rows	100 cm
Seat width	52 cm
Fire curtain behind orchestra	
Maximum auditorium width	21.50 m
Maximum auditorium depth	23 m
Greatest distance from stage	stalls 18.50 m
	1st balcony 22 m
	2nd balcony 24 m
	3rd balcony 26 m
Dimensions of main stage	19 x 13 m (max. 18.50 m)
Dimensions of left wing-space	storage area only
Dimensions of right wing-space	15 x 8 m
Backstage dimensions	14 x max. 9 m (irregular shape)
Number of proscenium openings	1
Maximum opening	13 x 10 m
Minimum opening	10 x 3 m
Height of grid	24.80 m
Orchestra space	65 m²
Lighting control system	Thyratron
Number of levers (dimmers)	2 x 120
Number of circuits	120
Number of pre-set possibilities	8
Number of lines (sets)	
Electrically operated	1
Manual	29
Stage-wagon dimensions	
Right wing-space	6 x 2 x 7 m
Left wing-space	3 x 2 x 7 m
Backstage	7 x 2 x 7–5.50 m
Revolve	rotatable element
Cyclorama	available

Municipal Theatre, Münster

361

362

363

364

364
View of opera house from north-east

365
Site plan

366—368
Opera house: views of auditorium, foyer

369—371
Playhouse: entrance front, staircase, view of auditorium and stage

The Cologne 'double-house', erected with an interval of five years by Wilhelm Riphahn, is the largest theatre scheme to be realized in West Germany since the war. The huge mass of the opera house embraces the entire workshop and rehearsal-room system, as well as the management's offices. Its vast and curious form, rising gradually in two dominant slopes on either side of the fly-tower, gives the building an impressive monumentality. In contrast, the low building of the playhouse appears sympathetic and unassuming, the disposition of the entrance court being particularly successful.

The foyer with the enveloping gallery-balcony and 'bridges' leading to the staircases is extraordinarily felicitous. In the strikingly wide sweep of the auditorium the alternating pattern of the balcony 'sledges' is a characteristic feature, lending a very distinctive air to the great room, although the effect of the bright blue and black against the dark brown background is a little chilly.

In the layout of the playhouse, the lack of space (only a studio-theatre was contemplated in the first place) is exceedingly noticeable. In comparison with the congenial entrance-hall the foyer seems narrow and compressed, and the long attenuated auditorium with its segregated upper stalls has little of the intimate atmosphere conducive to acting. It may be argued that a somewhat higher building with a tier of balcony seats would have achieved a better proportioned interior.

While the opera house stage has been generously equipped technically as a wagon-stage, the playhouse—at the express wish of the director at the time, Oskar Fritz Schuh—has few mechanical aids, except for its lavish lighting installation. The spacious stage and narrow auditorium of the playhouse have produced acoustic difficulties.

365

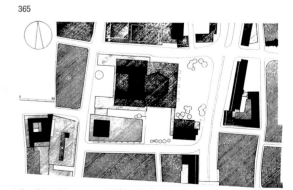

366

367

368

369

370

371

City of Cologne Theatres

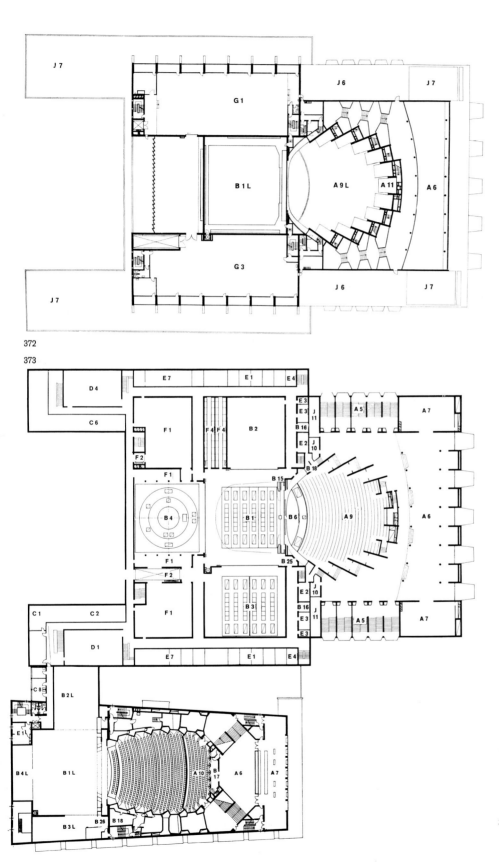

372

373

Client	City of Cologne
Artistic categories	opera, operetta, ballet
Competition	stage 1, 1946
	stage 2, 1952
Period of building	1954–1957
Opening	18. 5. 1957
Architects	Wilhelm Riphahn, Hans Menne
Sculptor	Freundlich
Colour consultant	Joseph Fassbender
Theatre consultants	Members' Committee of the
	Theatres
Stage technical consultant	Walther Unruh
Structural engineer	Merkle
Acoustics	Werner Gabler
Tests (structure)	Molz
Cost	DM 14,000,000
Space enclosed	175,000 m³
Number of seats	1346
	stalls 899
	1st balcony (sledge-boxes) 222
	2nd balcony (sledge-boxes) 225
Distance between rows	90 cm
Seat width	55 cm
Fire curtain behind orchestra	
Maximum auditorium width	30 m (1st balcony)
Maximum auditorium depth	30 m
Greatest distance from stage	stalls 28 m
	1st balcony 30.50 m
	2nd balcony 32.10 m
Dimensions of main stage	25.50 x 22 m (max. 28 m)
Dimensions of right wing-space	19 x 15.50 m
Dimensions of left wing-space	19 x 22 m
Backstage dimensions	18.50 x 19 m
Number of proscenium openings	1
Maximum opening	13 x 19 m
Minimum opening	9 x 0.50 m
Height of grid	26 m
Orchestra space	100 m²
Lighting control system	magnetic-amplifier
Number of levers (dimmers)	200
Number of circuits	224, of which 24 not variable
Number of lines (sets)	66 manual in grid
Stage-wagon dimensions	
Right wing-space	18 x 12.50 m
Left wing-space	2 x 18.20 x 7.50 m
Backstage	17 x 18 m
Revolve	16 m diameter
Dimensions of stage-podia	
(elevators)	6 x 18 x 2.50 m
Cyclorama	available

372–376

Opera house: upper storey. Opera and playhouse: floor plan, level 7.25 m. Opera and playhouse: floor plan, level 3.65 m. Playhouse: floor plan, level 0.20 m. Section

City of Cologne Theatres

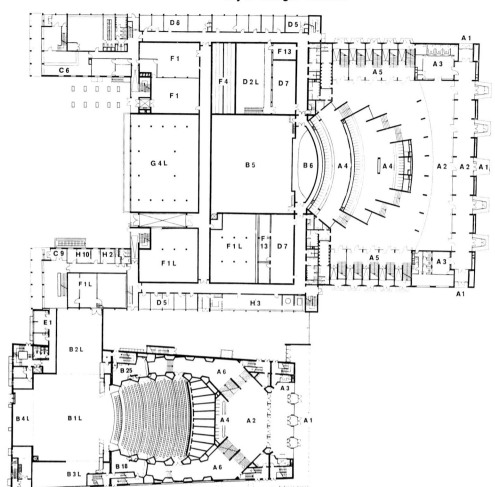

Playhouse

Client	City of Cologne
Artistic categories	plays
Period of building	1960–1962
Opening	8. 9. 1962
Architects	Wilhelm Riphahn, Bonvenuto Bausch
Colour consultant	Chargesheimer
Theatre consultants	Schuh, Neher
Stage technical consultant	Adolf Zotzmann
Structural engineers	Pechuel, Loesche
Acoustics	Keilholz, Zeller
Tests (structure)	Wolter
Cost	DM 8,625,000
Space enclosed	55,500 m³
Number of seats	920
	stalls 920 (upper stalls 183)
Rise of stalls	5.80 m
Distance between rows	90 cm
Seat width	43 cm
Fire curtain behind orchestra	
Maximum auditorium width	23 m
Maximum auditorium depth	28 m
Greatest distance from stage	stalls 28.30 m
Dimensions of main stage	23 x 20.50 m (max. 24 m)
Dimensions of right wing-space	17.30 x 11.80 m
Dimensions of left wing-space	6.50 x 14.50 m (18 m) (irregular)
Backstage dimensions	15 x 5.50 m
Number of proscenium openings	1
Maximum opening	15 x 6 m
Minimum opening	9 x 4.50 m
Height of grid	22.25 m
Orchestra space	60 m², when not in use can accommodate 43 seats for public
Lighting control system	Siemens-Bordoni
Number of levers (dimmers)	160
Number of circuits	20, not variable
Number of lines (sets)	44 manual

374

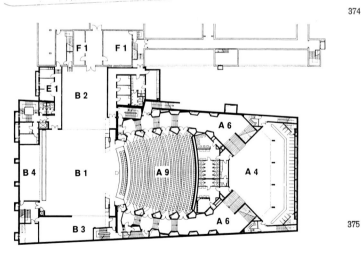

375

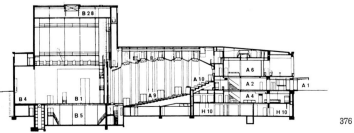

376

National Theatre, Mannheim

377

378

379

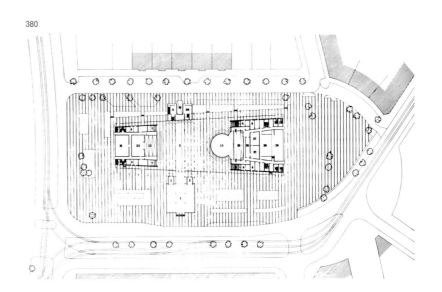

380

Mannheim's two houses are (for Germany) a special case, to the extent that both are devoted to the presentation of plays. Workshops, management, and most of the rehearsal rooms are accommodated in another group of buildings not far from the theatre.

The plan is unusual. Since a large air-raid shelter under the site could not be shifted, the stages are at first-floor level. The large vacant space on the ground floor between the two stage nuclei serves as foyer for both houses. The attraction of this large central meeting-place is obvious during intervals. The two foyers at either entrance front are scarcely used. Admittedly, however, the rather inadequately screened cloak-rooms of the main foyer are unsatisfactory.

On the first floor the two stages stand back to back, separated only by a common transport passage across. The large house is designed as a steeply raked amphitheatre, with a principal central balcony and small stepped balconies at the sides, very bright and light in colour. Facing the audience is an unusually wide and deep stage, which is difficult to reduce for intimate scenes. The layout of the stage, evolving out of the particular local situation, deviates from the traditional type: a large revolve, with built-in 'slopable' podia and an additional group of two-tier podia (rostra), and a cylindrical revolving stage (see page 87).

The small house, with no balcony, exemplifies how an outstanding theatre can be created at minimal expense. Materials: warm red hollow brick, black wood seating and plain parquet. The full width of the stage can be used by the players, and the side rostra can also be used for entrances. The house can be adapted to an arena-stage.

The clear, disciplined, cubic form with the starkly prominent fly-tower is basically adopted from a Mies van der Rohe prototype (see page 22). The diminishing effect of the trapezium shape is not visually successful.

National Theatre, Mannheim

381

382

383

377—379
View from south-west. Large house: view
of auditorium, one of the two principal
ways up (with stairs to boxes)

380
Site plan

381—383
Large house: auditorium; foyer, looking
towards main entrance. Small house:
view of the auditorium from the stage

National Theatre, Mannheim

384

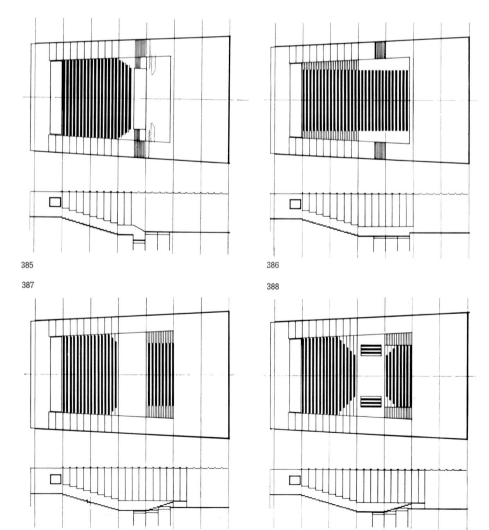

385

386

387

388

Client	City of Mannheim
Artistic categories	opera, operetta, ballet, plays
Competition	1953
Period of building	1955–1957
Opening	13. 1. 1957
Architects	Gerhard Weber, H. W. Hämer, H. Fischer
Colour consultant	P. Meyer-Speer
Theatre consultants	Schüler, Pape, Walter
Stage technical consultant	Birr, Mechanical Engineer's Office of the City of Mannheim
Structural engineer	F. Grebner
Acoustics	Albrecht Eisenberg
Cost	no information
Space enclosed	130,060 m³ (both theatres)
Large house	
Number of seats	1201
Distance between rows	90 cm
Seat width	43 cm
Fire curtain behind orchestra	
Maximum auditorium width	26 m
Maximum auditorium depth	29 m (balcony)
Greatest distance from stage	stalls 27 m
	1st balcony 30 m
Dimensions of main stage	30 x 23 m (25 m)
Dimensions of left wing-space	11 x 14 m
Backstage dimensions	25 x 14 m
Number of proscenium openings	1
Maximum opening	20 x 10 m
Minimum opening	10.50 x 4 m
Height of grid	25 m
Orchestra space	100 m²
Lighting control system	magnetic-amplifier
Number of levers (dimmers)	200
Number of circuits	200
Number of pre-set possibilities	8
Number of lines (sets)	
Electrically operated	8
Manual	58
Back-cloth	1
Stage-wagon dimensions	assembled as required
Revolve	17 m diameter, can be tilted
Dimensions of stage-podia (elevators)	2 x 3 x 9 m
	1 x 4 x 9 m
Limits of travel	—2 to +2.50 m
	3 x two-tier, each 1 x 10 m
	± 0 to +2.50 m
Cyclorama	available
Small house	
Number of seats	stalls 580–805 (can be varied)
Distance between rows	90 cm
Seat width	43 cm
Maximum auditorium width	29 m
Maximum auditorium depth	27 m
Greatest distance from stage	stalls 18 m
Dimensions of main stage	29 x 21 m
Dimensions of right wing-space	7–12 x 13 m (trapeziform)
Backstage dimensions	21 x 6 m
Number of proscenium openings	2
Extent of openings	limited by wing-floods, freely variable
Height of grid	9.40 m
Orchestra space	45 m²
Lighting control system	magnetic-amplifier
Number of levers (dimmers)	120
Number of circuits	120
Number of pre-set possibilities	8
Number of lines (sets)	
Electrically operated	1
Manual	24, distributed between stage and house
Stage-wagon dimensions	variable, assembled as needed
Revolve	can be fitted, diameter 7 m + 9 m
Dimensions of stage-podia (elevators)	3 x 15 x 3 m, can be tilted + 1 m and raised ± 0 to 4.50 m

National Theatre, Mannheim

384
Small house: Erwin Piscator's staging of 'Die Räuber'

385–388
Possible stage variations:
Playhouse stage with orchestra–506 seats
Lecture room and concert hall – 775 to 871 seats
Arena-stage, two-sided – c. 680 seats
Arena-stage, all round – c. 674 seats

389–393
Second floor, first floor plans; ground-floor, level – 4.55 m. Sections, small and large house

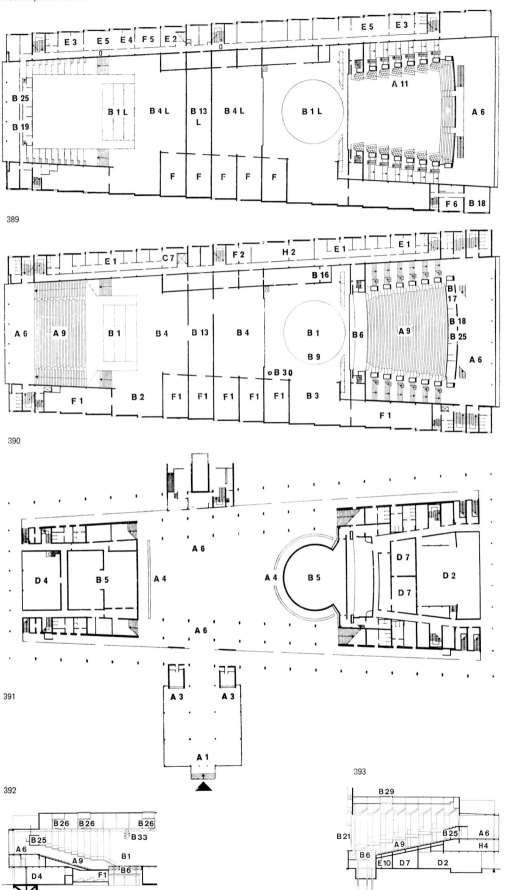

Landestheater, Linz/Austria — Intimate Theatre

394

395

396

Clemens Holzmeister's intimate theatre at Linz is often quoted as the model for the Salzburg Festival theatre. As always with such comparisons, this is only true in a limited sense, but both theatres bear witness to a disciplined vitality of line.

At the same time the Linz theatre—there will ultimately be two—is essentially more intimate, and indeed in the foyer area extraordinarily unpretentious, in part no doubt because of the confined site. But a certain insipidity in the interior design and a tendency towards monumentality cannot be overlooked.

The house is noteworthy for its marked simplicity, although a measure of gaiety has been achieved by the careful choice of fine woods for cladding the internal walls.

The stage area is limited to a large main stage with little wing space—a solution determined by the situation of the building, but quite adequate for the intimate type of performance proposed here. The forestage—the safety-curtain hangs behind the orchestra—can be used in two segments simultaneously.

394—396
View from south-west, cloak-rooms and access ways, auditorium

Landestheater, Linz/Austria — Intimate Theatre

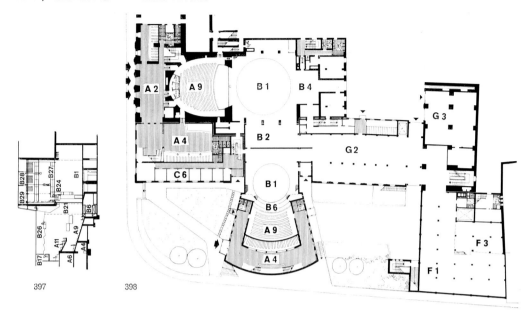

397   398

Client	Provincial Authority of Upper Austria
Artistic categories	opera, operetta, ballet, plays
Period of building	1955–1957
Opening	28. 9. 1957
Architect	Clemens Holzmeister
Sculptor	Rudolf Hoflehner
Painters	Franz Zülow, Rudolf Steinbüchler, Vilma Ecki
Theatre consultant	Walther Unruh
Stage technical consultant	Walther Unruh
Acoustics	Schweiger
Cost	no information
Number of seats	391
	stalls 228
	1st balcony 163 + 30 standing
Distance between rows	75 cm
Seat width	50 cm
Fire curtain behind orchestra	
Maximum auditorium width	16.50 m
Maximum auditorium depth	16.50 m
Greatest distance from stage	stalls 14 m
	1st balcony 16.50 m
Dimensions of main stage	13.50 x 11 m
Backstage dimensions	10 x 3 m
Number of proscenium openings	1
Size of opening	fixed, 6 m high, 7.60 m wide
Height of grid	13.50 m
Orchestra space	45 m²
Lighting control system	Siemens magnetic-amplifier
Number of levers (dimmers)	90
Number of lines (sets)	27, 3 backstage
Electrically operated	1 flood, and 2 proscenium arch
Manual	27
Counterweight	1 flood, and 2 proscenium arch
Revolve	9.60 m diameter
Dimensions of stage-podia (elevators)	built-in trap 3 x 1 m
Limits of travel	± 0 to — 2.60 m

Municipal Theatre, Gelsenkirchen

399
View from south-east

400
Site plan

399

The municipal theatre of Gelsenkirchen—opened in 1959—may well stand as the happiest and most thoroughly integrated example to emerge during the first decade of postwar theatre-building. It is generously planned and completely new, with a studio-theatre projecting from one side. The same team as for Münster worked on the scheme, although Harald Deilmann dropped out during the course of the work.

The unusual conception of a staircase disposed round the core of the auditorium is imposingly realized. The opening of the theatre to the town—a typical coal-and-steel place, where the theatre has to assert its prestige—is an almost exhibitionist performance, exploited to the limit and extending the whole width of the main façade. The extremely spacious foyers are given coherence by the coloured murals of Yves Klein. Active consultations took place with painters and plastic artists during the design process, and this early collaboration is reflected in the quality of the building.

The auditorium is almost austere, with black-painted wood slats as panelling; anodised aluminium for the balcony fronts, and dull grey seating. The room, however, has a certain restrained gaiety of its own. The proscenium-opening was, for the first time, designed to be flexible—a result of close co-operation with Adolf Zotzmann; the stage is entirely of the wagon type, with three large subsidiary stages.

400

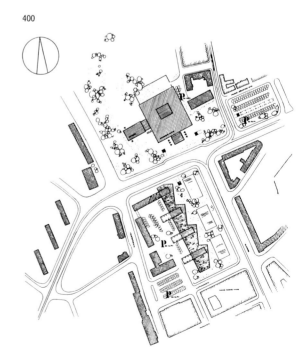

122

Municipal Theatre, Gelsenkirchen

401–402
Large house: foyer

401

402

404

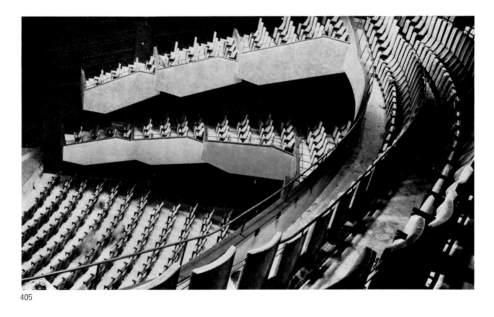

405

403

403
Possible variations of proscenium
opening

404—405
Large house: auditorium views

The studio, originally planned for experimental productions, appears in strange contrast to the large house and, indeed, to its own particular purpose with its far more costly wood panelling. It is certainly no accident that this very attractive house was promptly adopted as an 'intimate' theatre and has become entirely strange to its role as an experimental studio (see page 79).

A particular merit of the Gelsenkirchen theatre is its clearly defined architectural silhouette. Although all the elements of functionalism are back again here, there can be no doubt that a theatre has been created which is in all respects convincing.

406

408

407

406–407
Small house: possible variations of stage
and auditorium

408
View of stage and auditorium

Client	Municipality of Gelsenkirchen	
Artistic categories	opera, operetta, ballet, plays	
Competition	1954	
Period of building	1956–1959	
Opening	15. 12. 1959	
Architects	Max von Hausen, Ortwin Rave, Werner Ruhnau	
Sculptors	Robert Adams, Paul Dierkes, Norbert Kricke	
Painters	Yves Klein, Jean Tinguely	
Theatre consultant	Werner Kallmorgen	
Stage technical consultant	Adolf Zotzmann	
Structural engineer	Guido Schoen	
Acoustics	Erwin Meyer	
Tests (structure)	W. Ziehm	
Cost	DM 18,600,000	
Space enclosed	135,000 m³	

Large house

Number of seats	1018
	stalls 537
	1st balcony 277
	2nd balcony 204
Distance between rows	85 cm
Seat width	55 cm
Fire curtain in front of orchestra	
Maximum auditorium width	22 m (stalls)
Maximum auditorium depth	23 m (1st balcony)
Greatest distance from stage	stalls 19.80 m
	1st balcony 24.50 m
	2nd balcony 26.50 m
Dimensions of main stage	24 x 19 m (max. 22.50 m)
Dimensions of right wing-space	16.50 x 13.50 m
Dimensions of left wing-space	16.50 x 16.50 m
Backstage dimensions	16 x 14 m
Number of proscenium openings	2
Maximum opening	15.50 x 9.30 m
Minimum opening	12 x 4.75 m
Height of grid	24.12 m
Orchestra space	105 m² (extensible of 165 m²)
Lighting control system	ASEA (Brüdgam-Zotzmann)
Number of levers (dimmers)	120 x 6
Number of circuits	120 x 60 independent circuits
Number of pre-set possibilities	6
Number of lines (sets)	
Electrically operated	5
Manual	35
Winch	4 + 3
Pan-cloth	4
Stage-wagon dimensions	
Left wing-space	3 x 15 x 4 m
Backstage	1 x 15 x 13 m
Revolve	11 m diameter in backstage wagon
Dimensions of stage-podia (elevators)	
Podium 1	18 x 3 m, curved, — 3.20 to + 0.20 m
Podium 2	16.50 x 2.35 m, trapeziform, — 3.20 to + 0.20 m
Podium 3	15 x 2.35 m, trapeziform, — 0.80 to + 3.20 m, with two tiers — 3 m
Podium 4	15 x 4 m, — 1 to + 3 m, with two tiers — 3 m
Podium 5	15 x 4 m, — 2.18 to + 2 m
Podium 6	15 x 4 m, — 2.18 to + 2 m
Cyclorama	available

Municipal Theatre, Gelsenkirchen

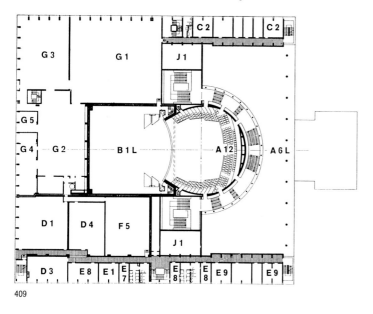

409

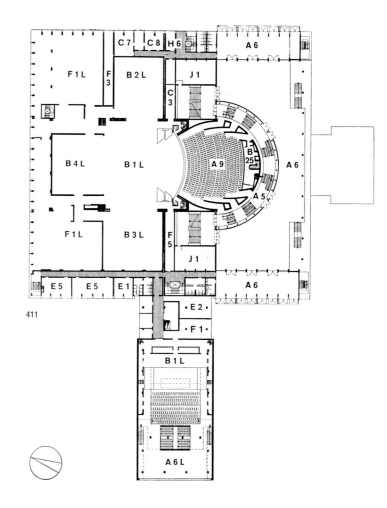

411

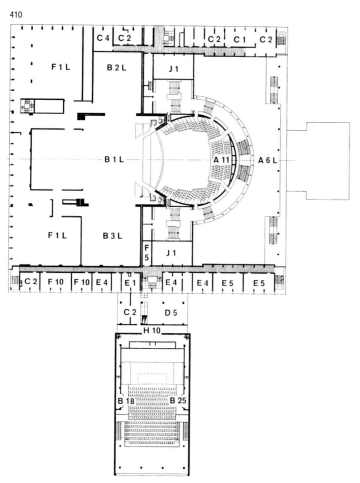

410

409–411
Floor plans: second balcony, first balcony, main foyer

412–414
Mezzanine, entrance floor, section

126

Municipal Theatre, Gelsenkirchen

Small house (Studio)

Number of seats	353
	1st balcony 233
	2nd balcony 120
Seat width	55 cm
Safety curtain behind orchestra	
Maximum auditorium width	19.50 m (1st balcony)
Maximum auditorium depth	25 or 18 m
Greatest distance from stage	stalls 12.50 m
	1st balcony 20 m
Dimensions of main stage	17 x 1 m to 17 x 7.75 m
Number of proscenium openings	1, movable
Maximum opening	11 x 3.75 m
Height of grid	8.50 m
Orchestra space	14 x 3.25 m
Lighting control system	ASEA (Brüdgam-Zotzmann)
Number of circuits	60 x 40 independent circuits
Number of levers (dimmers)	60
Number of pre-set possibilities	2
Number of lines (sets)	
Manual	8
Winch	7

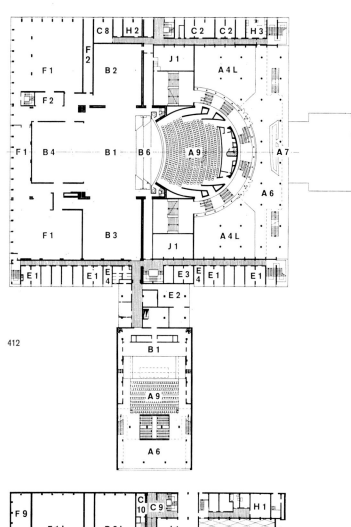

412

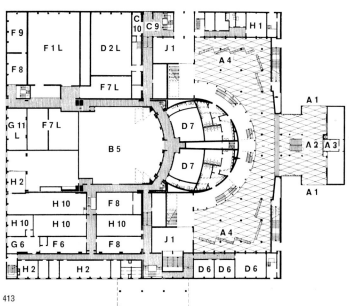

413

414

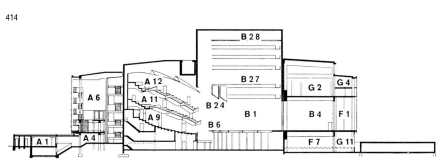

127

State Theatre, Kassel

The history of the competition for the state theatre at Kassel is one of the least pleasant episodes of postwar German architecture. The winner was Hans Scharoun, and we publish his design in our projects section (see page 212 et seq.).

In the end the commission was given by the authorities of the State of Hessen and the City of Kassel to the architects Paul Bode and Ernst Brundig. Unhappily the resultant building by no means vindicates the clients' decision.

Today the Kassel theatre, little more than a decade after its opening, reveals traces of age, which are inexcusable and cannot be satisfactorily explained by economies made in course of construction.

The décor of the foyer and especially of the auditorium proves how detrimental to a theatre art misapplied to architecture can be. The restless pattern of the ceiling, the 'wood wall elements composed of encaustic, gold-leaf and incised motifs' (thus the description of the building) and the 'balcony-fronts carved, coloured and pierced' distract the audience from events on the stage rather than serve their needs. The room, not ill-proportioned in its basic plan, irritates the playgoer, instead of concentrating his attention on the performance.

The stage, with a particularly wide opening, is equipped as a complete wagon-stage. As at Mannheim, the stages of the large and small houses stand back to back, but the small house is one floor lower and somewhat off-centre. The natural fall of the land has been followed in the plan, without however really exploiting the architectural possibilities of an incomparable site—the theatre at Kassel is built on the heights above the Karlsaue.

The small house is plain, with a minimum of machinery, and the effect is more attractive than that of the lavish large theatre, if a little dull.

415

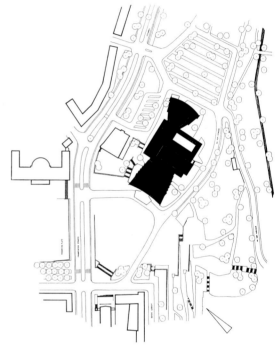

416

415
View from south

416
Site plan

State Theatre, Kassel

417–418
Large house auditorium, small house auditorium and stage

417

418

Clients	large house – Province of Hessen	Maximum auditorium width	23.40 m
	small house – City of Kassel	Maximum auditorium depth	31.25 m
Artistic categories	opera, operetta, ballet, plays	Greatest distance from stage	stalls 30 m
Period of building	1956–1959		1st balcony 30.50 m
Opening	12. 9. 1959	Dimensions of main stage	25 x 16 m
Architects	Paul Bode, Ernst Brundig	Dimensions of right wing-space	15.75 x 15 m
Sculptor	Blasius Spreng	Dimensions of left wing-space	15.75 x 15 m
Painters	Werner & Son	Backstage dimensions	15 x 12 m
Theatre consultant	Walther Unruh	Number of proscenium openings	1
Stage technical consultant	Walther Unruh	Maximum opening	16 x 7.50 m
Structural engineer	Hellmuth Bickenbach	Minimum opening	8 x 0.50 m
Acoustics	Werner Gabler	Height of grid	24.80 m
Tests (structure)	A. Mehmel	Orchestra space	70 m²
Cost	DM 3,500,000	Lighting control system	magnetic-amplifier
	(large house DM 18,500,000)	Number of levers (dimmers)	160
Space enclosed	92,000 m³ (complete scheme)	Number of pre-set possibilities	4
		Number of lines (sets)	
Large house		Electrically operated	42
Number of seats	945	Manual	33
	stalls 676	Stage-wagon dimensions	
	1st balcony 269	Right wing-space	15 x 9 m
Distance between rows	90 cm	Left wing-space	15 x 9 m
Seat width	55 cm	Backstage	14 x 11 m
Fire curtain in front of orchestra		Revolve	12 m diameter, can be fitted

State Theatre, Kassel

Dimensions of stage-podia (elevators)	3 x 15 x 3 m
	1 x 15 x 2 m
Limits of travel	—3 to + 3 m
Cyclorama	available

Small house

Number of seats	stalls 540–580
Distance between rows	90 cm
Seat width	55 cm
Fire curtain behind orchestra	
Maximum auditorium width	21.50 m
Maximum auditorium depth	23.50 m
Greatest distance from stage	stalls 23 m
Dimensions of main stage	17.70 x 15.25 m
Dimensions of left wing-space	14.90 x 7.10 m
Number of proscenium openings	1
Maximum width of opening	10 m
Minimum width of opening	7 m
Height of grid	11.90 m
Orchestra space	28 m²
Lighting control system	magnetic-amplifier
Number of levers (dimmers)	100
Number of lines (sets)	23 manual
Stage-wagon dimensions	2 x 4 x 2 m
Revolve	12 m diameter, can be fitted in both large and small houses
Dimensions of stage-podia (elevators)	10 x 10 m, can be tilted

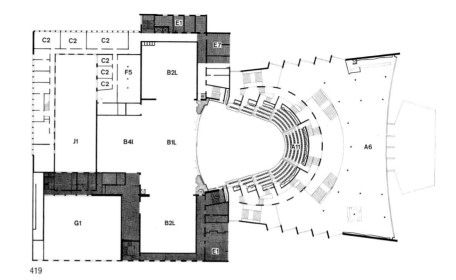

419

420

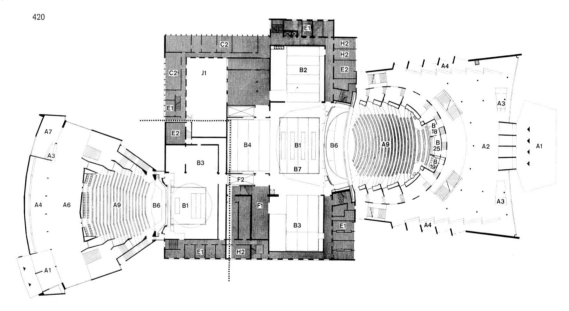

421

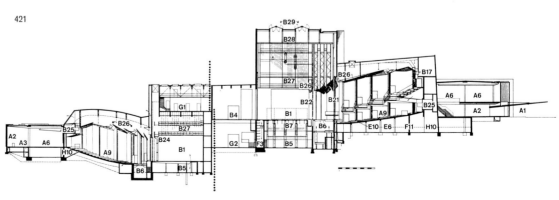

419–421
Upper floor (large house), ground-floor, section

130

Salzburg Festival Theatre

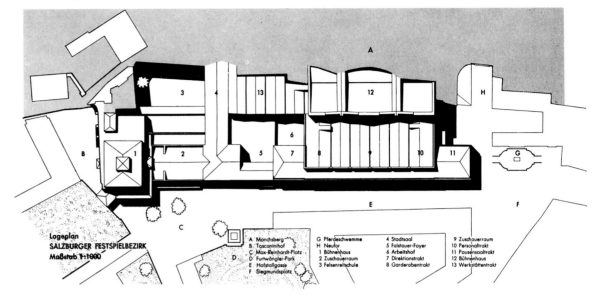

422

423

424

The ground-plan of the Festival 'domain' was determined by the topographical conditions: the mountain behind, the Hofstallgasse in front. The external walls of the old stable buildings had to be preserved under all circumstances. Thus the present Festival complex embraces the Felsenreitschule (riding-school) and the small and large Festival theatres. The site for the large house had partly to be blasted out of the solid rock at the back. The location indeed made it inevitable that space could only be increased in width, and not in depth.

Clemens Holzmeister, who had been associated with the Festival buildings since the twenties, undertook the new construction. His style has a tendency towards heaviness and monumentality, giving the rooms, which could not always be freely extended in any direction, a feeling of constriction. The narrow lobbies in front of the auditorium and the ponderous foyers ranged at the side fail to capture the lightness of the charming Baroque town. The great auditorium, however, with its capacity of more than two thousand seats, does not seem excessively large despite its vast size. On the other hand, the stage, with its pronounced 'Cinerama' character, produces great problems. It was the character of this house which almost defied Karajan's Easter festival with Wagner's works. Mozart, whose spirit dominates the place, is extraordinarily difficult to perform in this setting, and even the 'Rosenkavalier' of Strauss encountered difficulties on the first night.

The stage is equipped with many technical aids, and in this process the back-stage has been dispensed with for the sake of a large main stage; but, with two subsidiary stages placed respectively on either side, ample room is provided for the preparation of individual scenes.

423–424
View from south-east, entrance hall

Salzburg Festival Theatre

425

426

427

Clients	Federal government, province, city
Artistic categories	opera, plays
Period of building	1956–1960
Opening	26. 7. 1960
Architect	Clemens Holzmeister
Stage technical consultant	Walther Unruh
Structural engineer	Ernst Mühlberg
Acoustics	H. Keilholz, G. A. Schwaiger
Cost	c. Aus. S 210,000,000
Spaced enclosed	c. 200,000 m³
Number of seats	2300
	stalls 1400 + 150 (over orchestra)
	1st balcony 750
Distance between rows	90 cm
Seat width	54 cm
Fire curtain behind orchestra	
Maximum auditorium width	35 m
Maximum auditorium depth	36 m
Greatest distance from stage	stalls 30 m
	1st balcony 36 m
Dimensions of main stage	43 x 25 m
Dimensions of right wing-space	18 x 15 m + 11 x 14 m
Dimensions of left wing-space	18 x 15 m + 11 x 14 m
Number of proscenium openings	1
Maximum opening	30 x 9 m
Minimum opening	14 x 0 m
Height of grid	27.80 m
Orchestra space	114 m²
Lighting control system	Siemens magnetic-amplifier
Number of levers (dimmers)	300
Number of circuits	350
Number of pre-set possibilities	4
Number of lines (sets)	77 manual
Stage-wagon dimensions	
Right wing-space	6 x 6 x 3 m
Left wing-space	9 x 6 x 3 m
Dimensions of stage-podia (elevators)	
	4 x 24 x 3 m
	1 x 18 x 3 m
	— 3 to + 3 m
Cyclorama	2

Salzburg Festival Theatre

425–427
View of auditorium from the stage, stage with safety curtain, upper foyer

428–431
Upper storey, level 11.00 m; floor-plan, stalls and box-foyer, level 2.40 m; floor-plan, street level – 4.00 m. Section

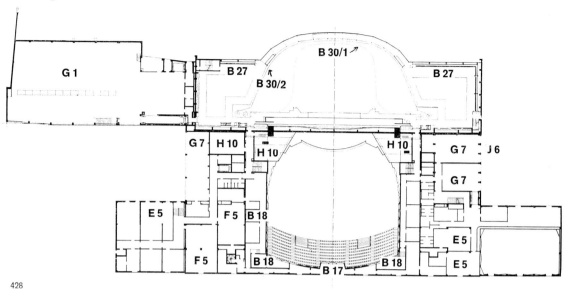

428

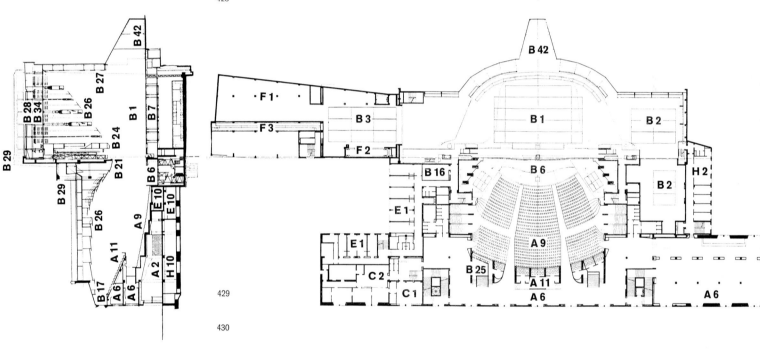

429

430

431

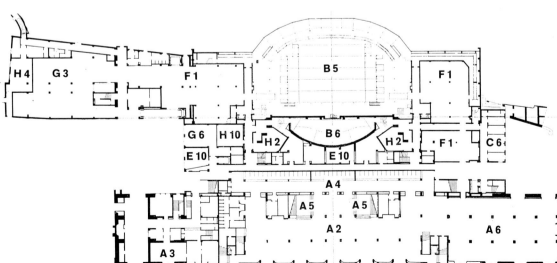

Deutsche Oper, Berlin

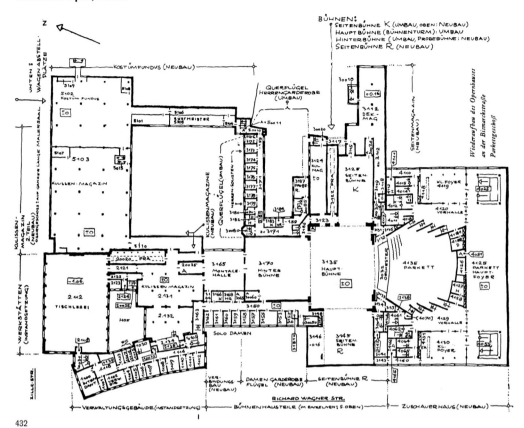

The Deutsche Oper in Berlin is the result of a phased reconstruction of the destroyed Charlottenburg opera house. Following a two-stage competition, Fritz Bornemann was entrusted with the comprehensive task of designing the auditorium complex and certain additions to the stage-house.

The main problem of the brief lay in the site's lack of depth and the busy-street frontage. Bornemann therefore closed the theatre to the Bismarckstrasse with a solid concrete-slab curtain, throwing the building open at the sides and placing—in order to exploit the full depth for the auditorium and foyers— the staircases just inside these open side-façades.

The plain dark panelling of the foyers has an unusually engrossing effect and, during the inaugural season, a few cleverly chosen works of art supplied a lively counterpoise. (Unfortunately not all of them were subsequently acquired for the theatre.)

The auditorium shows the same disciplined and clear articulation as the entrance-halls and foyers. The impression, however, is not stiff or unfriendly. Those attending the opening spoke, not unfairly, of the 'Prussian charm' of the building.

The house is designed as single-tiered theatre, with two balconies, the lower one stepped downward at the sides, the upper range terminating in 'sledges'.

There is nothing modernistic about this Berlin theatre, which evolves logically from traditional precedents, but with no jarring echoes from the past and without rejecting the present.

Deutsche Oper, Berlin

433/434
View from south-west, view of auditorium
from stage

433

434

135

Deutsche Oper, Berlin

435

436

437

Client	Senate of Berlin
Artistic categories	opera, ballet
Competition	1st stage 1953
	2nd stage 1955
Period of building	1956–1961
Opening	24. 9. 1961
Architects	Fritz Bornemann (auditorium)
	Senate Building and Housing
	Dept. (stage, storage, etc.)
Sculptor	Hans Uhlmann
Painter	Ernst Nay
Theatre consultant	Walther Unruh
Stage technical consultants	Walther Unruh, Willi Ulmer
Acoustics	Ludwig Cremer, Werner Gabler
Structural engineer	Werner Thiedge, Werner Torge
Tests (structure)	Hellmuth Bickenbach
Cost	DM 27,400,000
Space enclosed	230,000 m³
Number of seats	1900
	stalls 1200
	1st balcony 365
	2nd balcony 335
Distance between rows	85 cm
Seat width	54 cm
Fire curtain behind orchestra	
Maximum auditorium width	27.60 m
Maximum auditorium depth	32 m
Greatest distance from stage	stalls 28 m
	1st balcony 31 m
	2nd balcony 32 m
Dimensions of main stage	27 x 21 m
	(18 x 18 m playing area)
Dimensions of right wing-space	22.50 x 12 m
Dimensions of left wing-space	18 x 19.50 m
Backstage dimensions	22.50 x 23 m
Number of proscenium openings	1
Maximum opening	14.60 x 8 m
Minimum opening	11 m
Height of grid	27.50 m
Orchestra space	136 m²
Lighting control system	magnetic-amplifier
Number of levers (dimmers)	240
Number of circuits	240
Number of pre-set possibilities	4
Number of lines (sets)	
Electrically operated	30
Manual	26
Electrically operated spot	6
Stage-wagon dimensions	
Right wing-space	3 x 18 x 3 m
Left wing-space	1 x 18 x 9 m
	1 x 18 x 3 m
	1 x 18 x 2 m
Backstage	18 x 18 m
Revolve	17.50 m diameter
Dimensions of stage-podia	
(elevators)	18 x 3 m
Limits of travel	−3 to + 3 m
Cyclorama	available

Deutsche Oper, Berlin

435–437
Foyer (two views), auditorium

438–442
Section. Floor plans: first balcony level,
upper stalls, stalls, entrance floor

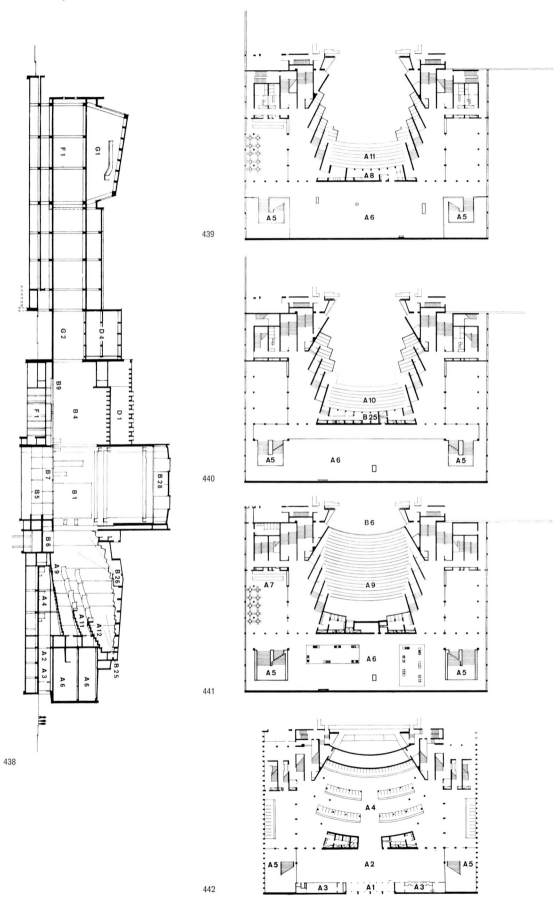

438

439

440

441

442

443

443
Entrance front

444
Site plan

444

Of Max Littmann's original two-theatre group in Stuttgart only the playhouse was destroyed. The opera survived and was later modernized, to satisfy the purists. (A more recent reconstruction has since been planned.)

The new playhouse is the product of two competitions, of which the second involved three stages. But a happy blending of the old and the new has not been achieved. The shining white marble-clad octagon of the auditorium building ill-accords with the warm yellow sandstone of the earlier construction.

Broad ribbon windows extending round the top of the auditorium block overlook the surrounding Schlossgarten. The foyer is fixed to the outside wall like a continuous balcony, leaving the freestanding structure of the auditorium in the middle, but exposing the cloakrooms below to the public gaze. Access is by bridging-stairs and small platforms, not always architecturally convincing as a method.

The interior of the auditorium, comprising 841 seats, is pleasantly intimate. The house is designed as a pure amphitheatre, with only the production boxes and two associated service boxes suspended at the back. The tent-like folded ceiling introduces—as at Kassel—an element of restlessness.

445

446

The stage is of the wagon-type, with two wing-stages and a small back-stage.

Outstanding, both in its layout and strictly practical execution, is the scene-store and workshop wing at the back of the stage-house. Here for once a scheme was worked out—and, alas, this is rarely the case—with an experienced director, Dr. Walter Erich Schäfer, expert in the manifold needs of theatre management.

447

445—447
Fly-tower, auditorium, upper foyer

State Theatre of Württemberg, Stuttgart — Playhouse

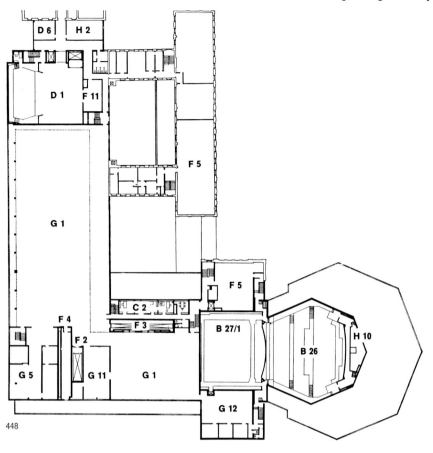

448

449

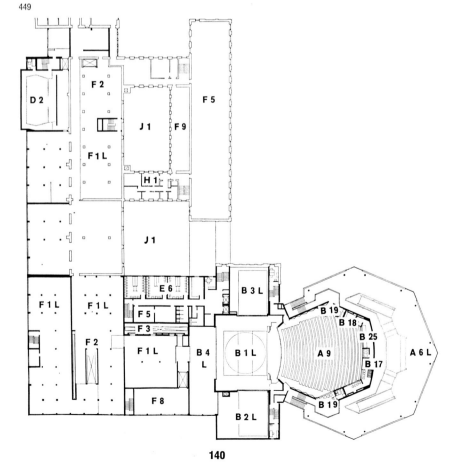

Client	Province of Baden-Württemberg
Artistic categories	plays
Competition	1st competition 1953
	2nd competition
	1st stage 1957, 2nd stage 1958,
	3rd stage 1958
Period of building	1958–1962
Opening	5. 10. 1962
Architects	Hans Volkart, Kurt Pläcking,
	Bert Perlia
Sculptor	Wander Bertoni
Theatre consultants	Thomas Münter, Rudolf Biste
Stage technical consultants	Thomas Münter, Rudolf Biste
Structural engineers	Kani, Holzapfel
Acoustics	Oskar Gerber
Tests (structure)	Building Test Station, Stuttgart
Cost	no information
Space enclosed	140,000 m³ (including workshops)
Number of seats	stalls 841
Rise of stalls	3.53 m
Distance between rows	90 cm
Seat width	54 cm
Fire curtain in front of orchestra	
Maximum auditorium width	27 m
Maximum auditorium depth	24.50 m
Greatest distance from stage	stalls 24 m
Dimensions of main stage	20.50 x 15 m (maximum 18 m)
Dimensions of right wing-space	13 x 10.50 m
Dimensions of left wing-space	13 x 14.50 m
Backstage dimensions	23.50 x 7.50 m
Number of proscenium openings	1
Maximum opening	12 x 7 m
Minimum opening	9 x 0.50 m
Height of grid	21 m
Orchestra space	38 m²
Lighting control system	Siemens magnetic-amplifier
Number of levers (dimmers)	200
Number of circuits	166
Number of pre-set possibilities	8
Number of lines (sets)	43
Electrically operated	5
Manual	38
Stage-wagon dimensions	
Right wing-space	1 x 12 x 8 m
Left wing-space	2 x 12 x 4 m
Revolve	11.70 m diameter
Dimensions of stage-podia	
(elevators)	3 x 12 x 4 m
Limits of travel	—2 to + 2 m

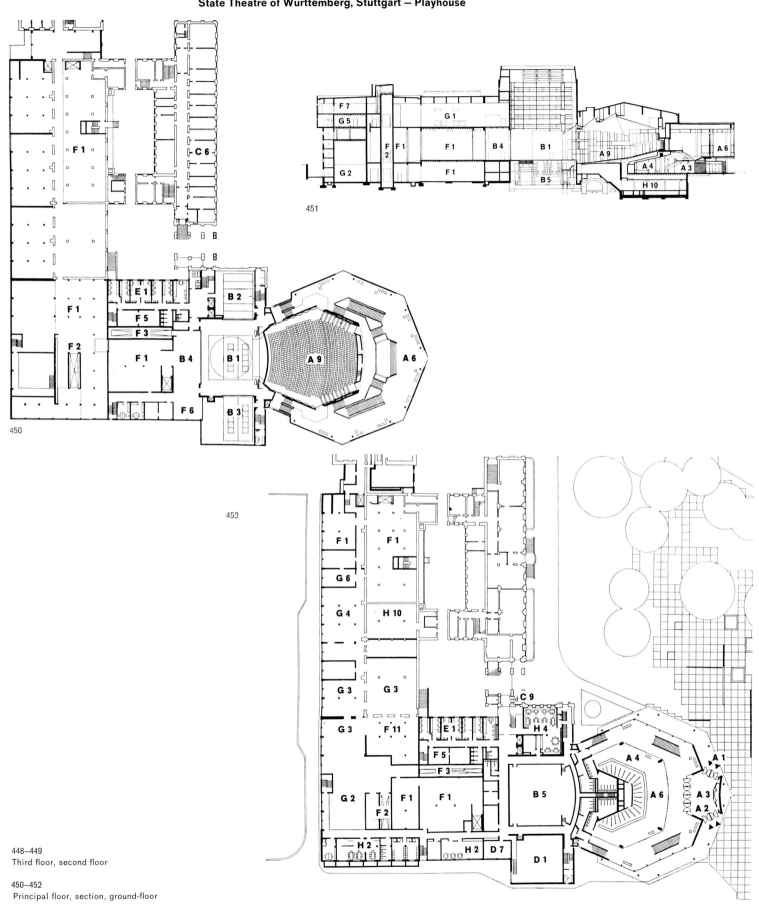

451

450

452

448–449
Third floor, second floor

450–452
Principal floor, section, ground-floor

453—454
Entrance side; auditorium, looking towards stage

453

454

Freie Volksbühne, Berlin

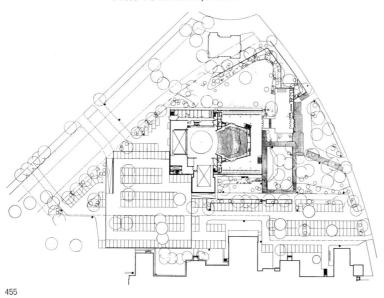

455

456

In discussing the characteristics of the new building for the Freie Volksbühne in Berlin, two things should be mentioned at once:

1. The theatre—auditorium, stage-house, and management and cloakroom accommodation—was built at minimal expense. The building costs amounted to 9.3 million marks (1961—3).

2. It was built by a theatre specialist. Fritz Bornemann, the architect, comes from a theatrical family. His father was in charge of the stage workshops of the Prussian state theatres.

It is a house in which the playgoer feels immediately at home, and which is equally popular with actors. The dimensions suggest an intimate theatre, but one does not feel cramped or confined. The acoustics are excellent and the sight-lines good. Although built as a traditional balcony theatre, it is unconventional. The spacious balcony holds nearly three hundred people, and one forgets in the auditorium that the house, with more than a thousand seats, is in a higher capacity bracket than is nowadays considered suitable for playhouses.

The foyers have been very adroitly handled, with large glazed fronts open to the old park forming the site, while ingenious lighting effects avoid any sense of separation due to the reflection of glass surfaces. The use of the large box-office hall as a smoke-room is a far from haphazard solution.

The dimensions of the stage are generous, but not gigantic. In agreement with the owner at the time, Erwin Piscator, machinery is restricted to a minimum. The stage floor cannot be sunk and is not trapped throughout. Lighting and above-stage machinery are of the standard type. The house has no modernistic gimmicks, and in architectural conception is the best integrated and, at the same time, theatrically the most positive building of the postwar period.

457

455
Site plan

456—457
Auditorium and stage, one of two ways up to the balcony foyer

Freie Volksbühne Berlin

458–460
Balcony floor, ground-floor, section

Client	Freie Volksbühne Berlin e. V.
Artistic category	plays
Period of building	1961–1963
Opening	30. 4. 1963
Architect	Fritz Bornemann
Sculptor	Volkmar Haase
Theatre consultants	Thomas Münter, Rudolf Biste
Stage technical consultants	Hema, Gossen, Märkische
	Maschinenfabrik, Franke
Structural engineer	Werner Torge
Acoustics	Werner Gabler, Lothar Cremer
Tests (structure)	Hans Schröder
Cost	DM 9,500,000
Space enclosed	50,842 m³
Number of seats	stalls + 1st balcony 1047
Distance between rows	86–90 cm
Seat width	53 cm
Fire curtain in front of orchestra	
Maximum auditorium width	24 m
Maximum auditorium depth	21.60 m (1st balcony)
Greatest distance from stage	stalls 23 m
	1st balcony 26 m
Dimensions of main stage	21 x 16 m (max. 20 m)
Dimensions of left wing-space	22.50 x 13 m (+ storage pockets)
Backstage dimensions	16.30 x 12 m
Number of proscenium openings	1
Maximum opening	12.80 x 8 m
Minimum opening	9 x 0.50 m
Height of grid	18.50 m
Orchestra space	28.25 m²
Number of levers (dimmers)	140
Number of lines (sets)	42
Electrically operated	10
Manual	32
	1 spot-line installation with
	12 cable drums of 1000 kg
	capacity
Stage-wagon dimensions	
Left wing-space	1 x 14 x 5 m
	2 x 14 x 2 m
	1 x 4 x 5 m
	2 x 4 x 2 m
Revolve	15 m diameter
Cyclorama	available

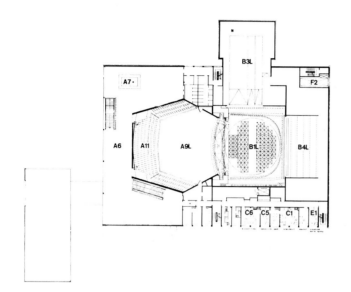

458

459

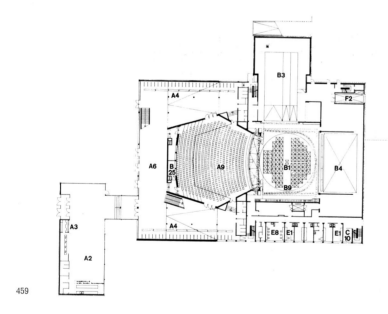

460

461–463
View from west, foyer, view of auditorium and stage

464
Site plan
Municipal theatre, second construction stage, public buildings,
proposed green spaces

461

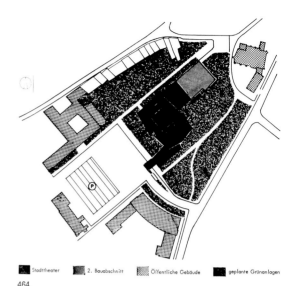

464

Stadttheater | 2. Bauabschnitt | Öffentliche Gebäude | geplante Grünanlagen

462

463

The building of the municipal theatre at Trier was at first a source of controversy. Originally the intention had been to build it over the Roman baths, but such strong objections were raised that the scheme, slightly modified, was transferred to another site close to the city hall. The first prize in the competition held in 1959 went to Gustav Hassenpflug, but the design of the fifth prize-winner, Gerhard Graubner, was the one executed, in collaboration with the Trier architect Hans Schneider.

The resultant building is a tidily planned package for the various essential functions, dependable in every respect—Graubner is one of the few architects to have built quite a number of theatres—a house which, despite a few modernistic adjuncts, remains firmly grounded in tradition.

The auditorium, asymmetrical in plan, has no balcony, but a separated section of 'upper' stalls, which contrives a subdivison of the 'audience mass'.

Great care has been taken—and this is where the significance of the building lies in historical evolution—with the area of the proscenium opening as the boundary between auditorium and stage. At Bochum Graubner had placed the safety-curtain in front of the orchestra pit. At Trier he moved one step further, in order to make the forestage fully 'playable'. The ceiling can be opened out and fly-lines are provided, while the wings can be varied by movable partitions and stands; finally, the proscenium border can be flown, so that the picture-frame is removed and the house exposed in its entire width to the stage.

The stage itself is constructed as a horizontal wagon-stage, with one side-stage and back-stage. A large number of scene-stores and workshops will not be built until a later date.

Municipal Theatre, Trier

Client	City of Trier
Artistic categories	opera, operetta, plays
Competition	1959
Period of building	1962–1964
Opening	27. 9. 1964
Architects	Gerhard Graubner, Hans Schneider
Theatre consultant	Meyer
Stage technical consultant	Adolf Zotzmann
Structural engineers	Bruno Kohlhaas, Eberhard Lippke
Acoustics	Karl F. Darmer
Tests (structure)	Reiter
Cost	DM 8,750,000 (1st stage)
Space enclosed	42,000 m³
Number of seats	stalls 622
Distance between rows	90 cm
Seat width	50 cm
Fire curtain in front of orchestra	
Maximum auditorium width	27.50 m
Maximum auditorium depth	24.50 m
Greatest distance from stage	upper stalls 24 m
Dimensions of main stage	20 x 13.50 m (max. 19 m)
Dimensions of right wing-space	15 x 14 m
Backstage dimensions	14 x 14.50 m
Number of proscenium openings	1
Maximum opening	15.50 x 7.10 m
Minimum opening	9 x 4.50 m
Height of grid	20.20 m
Orchestra space	78 m²
Lighting control system	Siemens four-colour
Number of levers (dimmers)	96
Number of circuits	96
Number of lines (sets)	
Manual	32
Counterweight	4
Stage-wagon dimensions	
Right wing-space	3 x 13 x 4 m
Backstage	13 x 13 m
Revolve	11.40 m diameter
Dimensions of stage-podia (elevators)	3 x 13 x 4 m
Limits of travel	—2 to + 2.40 m

465–467
Stage floor, ground-floor (including second construction stage — paint shop, scene-store, etc.), section

465

planned   executed

466

467

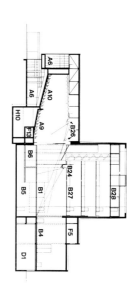

Municipal Theatre, Bonn

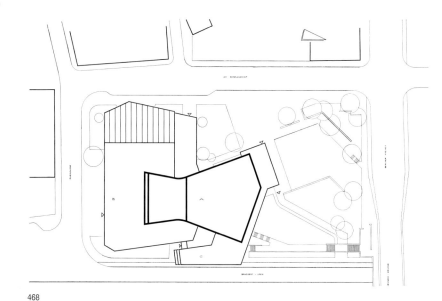

468
Site plan

469—470
Entrance front, store and workshop side

468

469

470

The theatre at Bonn exemplifies how good individual ideas can be stifled by fashionable clichés, and how the building has strayed from its purpose of bringing out the special quality implied by theatre.

In describing the exterior one should begin, oddly enough, with the scene-store and workshop block at the back which, with its sober, clearly defined, functionalism and calculated simplicity, fits splendidly into the street-scene. In the auditorium section, however, where the showy architecture is in evidence, the flaws appear, whether in the unhappy junction of fly-tower and auditorium, or the projecting foyer terraces, which are so domineeringly obtrusive that they lose their connection with the building as a whole.

Far more successful are the different foyers with their varied recesses and bays, their changing views and Otto Piene's globes of light. The Bonn theatre is one of the few buildings in which artists were invited to collaborate from the beginning—not merely as supernumerary decorators. Piene was responsible for lighting design, HAP Grieshaber for the treatment of the containing screen-wall of the smoking-foyer, and Lothar Quinte for accentuating features of the auditorium (the least persuasive).

The auditorium is conceived as a balcony-theatre with shallow-raked stalls, the balcony drawn on one side so far down to the latter that they are linked by a short flight of steps. As a result, the space under the balcony is very low.

The mechanical aids are extraordinarily lavish for a theatre of this size (a conflict no doubt between the 'provincial town' and the 'capital city'): punched-card control system; two proscenium openings, both of which can be flown; large wagon-stage, with one wing-stage and back-stage. Here mechanization—brilliantly applied in details (Adolf Zotzmann)—takes undue command. The workshops, however, have not been sacrificed to the stage-machinery. They are as spaciously and generously equipped as could be desired for smooth technical operation.

147

Municipal Theatre, Bonn

471

472

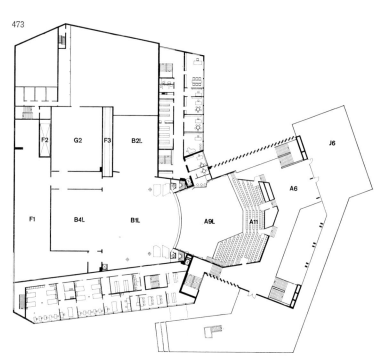

473

148

Municipal Theatre, Bonn

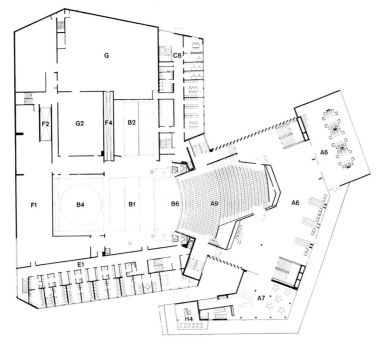

Client	City of Bonn
Artistic categories	opera, operetta, ballet, plays
Competition	1960
Period of building	1961–1965
Opening	5. 5. 1965
Architects	Klaus Gessler, Wilfrid Beck-Erlang, Peter Frohne
Sculptors	Kurt Frank, HAP Grieshaber, Erich Hauser
Painter	Lothar Quinte
Foyer and auditorium lighting	Otto Piene
Stage technical consultant	Adolf Zotzmann
Structural engineer	Eugen Pirlet
Acoustics	Erwin Meyer
Tests (structure)	S. Thomass, P. Dahmen
Cost	DM 23,200,000
Space enclosed	95,340 m³
Superficial area	5,800 m²
Number of seats	896
	stalls 603
	upper stalls 71
	balcony 222
Distance between rows	91–93 cm
Seat width	53 cm
Fire curtain in front of orchestra	
Maximum auditorium width	23 m
Maximum auditorium depth	23.80 m
Greatest distance from stage	stalls 24.50 m
	balcony 26 m
Dimensions of main stage	18 x 21 m (max. 25 m)
Dimensions of right wing-space	16 x 14 m
Backstage dimensions	16 x 14 m, 8 m high
Number of proscenium openings	2
Extent of openings	1st 13.25 x 7.50 m (invariable)
	2nd 12.25 x 7 m max.
	11 x 4.50 m min.
	Both are mobile.
Widest opening without proscenium arch	14.50 x 8.50 m
Height of grid	23.70 m
Orchestra space (podia 1–3)	92 m²
Lighting control system	Siemens magnetic-amplifier
Number of circuits	120
Number of pre-set possibilities	4
	programming with automatic equipment for 200 punched cards
Number of lines (sets)	
Electrically operated	6
Manual	38
Stage-wagon dimensions	
Backstage	14 x 12 m, can be lowered in area of podia
Revolve	10.50 m diameter, built into backstage wagon
Dimensions of stage-podia (elevators)	14 x 4 m
Limits of travel	
Podium 1 (orchestra) and 2	each — 3.20 to + 0.20 m
Podium 3 and 4 (both two-tier)	each — 1 to + 3.20 m
Podium 5 and 6	each — 3.20 to + 2.50 m

474–476
Floor plans: stalls, ground-floor. Section

Ruhr Festival Theatre, Recklinghausen

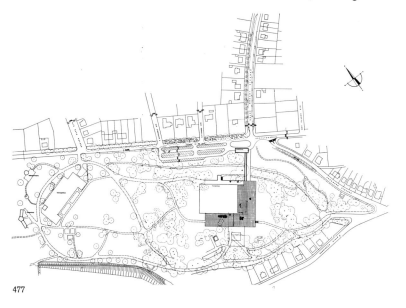

477

478

479

This building is one of the greatest disappointments of Federal German postwar theatre-building. From an institution—the German Trade-union Federation (DGB)—which, in association with the mining town of Recklinghausen, has for years been arranging in makeshift accommodation noteworthy theatrical performances of a progressive kind and modern art exhibitions of international calibre, one expected a festival theatre of similar quality.

The competition proved disillusioning. With few convincing designs to choose from, the jury plumped for the most conventional. There are indeed no postwar theatres whose mistaken monumentality so dismally recalls the architecture of the Third Reich, which the DGB had bitterly striven to oppose.

The building, however, is interesting for the mechanical equipment of the stage. Adolf Zotzmann, long technical director of the Ruhr Festival, has been able to exploit to the full his ideas on the flexibility of the forestage area: two openings, which can be flown to expose the entire extent of the stage; a revolve fitting into the segment of the proscenium, and thus brought close up to the ramp; a smooth transition from auditorium to stage by successive mobile partitions and platforms. No expense in machinery has been spared (and in a festival house this may well be justifiable); and if one wants a theatre which, while preserving the fundamental status-quo of audience-and-actor confrontation, responds to the greatest possible number of forms of repertory, this is certainly to date the best solution. However, this has nothing to do with the architecture of the theatre, which is a separate issue.

477
Site plan

478—479
View from south, south-east front

480
Auditorium

481—483
Stage and foyer floor, entrance floor, section

Ruhr Festival Theatre, Recklinghausen

480

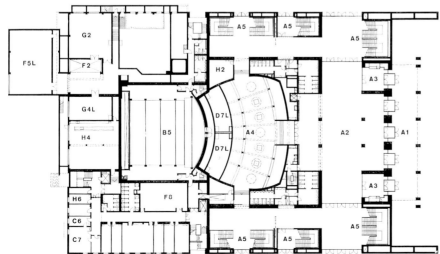

481

482

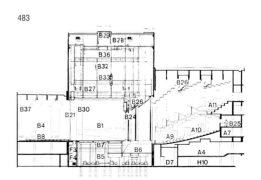

483

Clients	Municipality of Recklinghausen, German Federation of Trade Unions
Artistic categories	plays (opera and operetta)
Competition	1956
Period of building	1960—1965
Opening	11. 6. 1965
Architects	Felix Ganteführer, Fritz Hannes
Sculptor	Henry Moore
Painter	Hans Werdehausen
Stage technical consultant	Adolf Zotzmann
Structural engineer	Guido Schoen
Acoustics	Erwin Meyer
Tests (structure)	P. Walter
Cost	DM 23,000,000
Space enclosed	130,490 m³
Number of seats	1061
	stalls 723
	balcony 338
Fire curtain in front of orchestra	
Maximum auditorium width	28.60 m
Maximum auditorium depth	25.20 m
Greatest distance from stage	stalls 25 m
	balcony 30 m
Dimensions of main stage	25 x 18.70 m (max. 23 m)
Dimensions of right wing-space	18.60 x 18 m
Dimensions of left wing-space	7.50 x 12.50 m
Backstage dimensions	19 x 14 m
Number of proscenium openings	2
Maximum opening	14.50 x 8.50 m
Minimum opening	10 x 4.50 m
Height of grid	24.19 m
Orchestra space	118 m²
Lighting control system	punched cards, semiconductor
Number of levers (dimmers)	200
Number of pre-set possibilities	unlimited (punched cards)
Number of lines (sets)	36
Electrically operated	12
Stage-wagon dimensions	
Right wing-space	1 x 17 x 2.40 m
	3 x 17 x 4 m
Backstage	17 x 12 m
Revolve	11 m diameter
Dimensions of stage-podia (elevators)	1 x 18 x 2 m
	1 x 17 x 2.40 m
	3 x 17 x 4 m
Limits of travel	—3.25 to + 2.75 m
Cyclorama	planned

Municipal Theatres, Dortmund

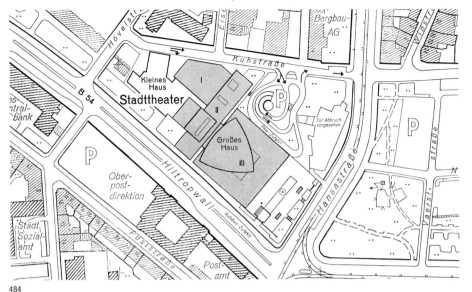

484

484
Site plan

485
View from south-east

There can hardly be a more striking proof that every town gets the architecture which reflects its particular character than the opera house at Dortmund—a building which came close to costing forty million marks, and on which no expense was spared. But it also shows that financial strength—conspicuously available at the time—and architectural inspiration are not complementary. Art is not an integral part of these industrial towns. Growing prosperity has stimulated the artistic interests of certain sections, but these are really of limited influence.

The social situation is mirrored in the theatre. A large and modern shell structure has been erected, but its American provenance has been misinterpreted and the logical meaning of the architecture has been lost. A technical instrument has been created, concentrated in a massive multi-storey block and immediately exposing its want of proportion. The building is equipped with every expensive item, but the result is a caricature of the economic miracle and not a vehicle for presenting dramatic art.

The stage is organized as a technically complete wagon-stage, with ample wing-spaces and backstage. But the fire-proof curtain—due to the shell construction of the auditorium, which links far from smoothly with the stage-house—is set so far back that problems of acoustics and acting-technique occur. Indeed the proposed staging of grand spectacular pieces seems an almost utopian dream.

485

486—488
Foyer, views of auditorium

Municipal Theatres, Dortmund

All the same, the workshops are arranged on a scale to match the amplitude of the remaining accommodation, so that there is at least a chance that this theatrical colossus will operate with mechanical proficiency.

486

487

488

Municipal Theatres, Dortmund

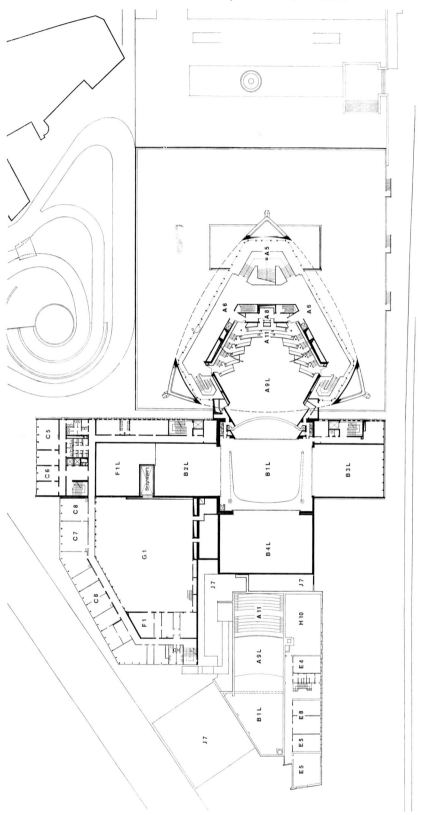

Client	Municipality of Dortmund
Artistic categories	opera, operetta, ballet, plays
Competition	1955
Period of building	1958–1966
Opening	3. 3. 1966
Architects	Heinrich Rosskotten, Edgar Tritthart, Josef Clemens
Sculptors	Fritz Kühn, Hugo Kückelhaus, Ferdinand Ris, Rudolf Hoflehner
Tapestries	Elisabeth Kadow, Hubert Berke, Harry Fränkel
Stage technical consultant	Walther Unruh
Structural engineers	Kurt Wüst, Wolfgang Zerna
Acoustics	Albrecht Eisenberg
Tests (structure)	Gerhard Caspers, Wilhelm Kähling
Cost	DM 37,375,000
Space enclosed	139,200 m³
Number of seats	1160
	stalls 816
	1st balcony 158
	2nd balcony 186
Distance between rows	90–94 cm
Seat width	54–58 cm
Fire curtain behind orchestra	
Maximum auditorium width	29.50 m
Maximum auditorium depth	31 m
Greatest distance from stage	stalls 32 m
	1st balcony 32.50 m
	2nd balcony 34 m
Dimensions of main stage	25.45 x 18 m (max. 24.60 m)
Dimensions of right wing-space	16.86 x 13.85 m
Dimensions of left wing-space	19.12 x 13.85 m
Backstage dimensions	25.45 x 15.10 m
Number of proscenium openings	1
Maximum opening	15 x 8 m
Minimum opening	11.50 x 5.50 m
Height of grid	25 m
Orchestra space	108 m²
Lighting control system	semiconductor transistor
Number of levers (dimmers)	200
Number of circuits	624
Number of pre-set possibilities	2 (and unlimited by punched cards)
Number of lines (sets)	57
Electrically operated	42
Manual	10
Counterweight	5
Stage-wagon dimensions	
Right wing-space	3 x 16 x 2.50 m
Left wing-space	1 x 16 x 7.50 m
	2 x 8 x 5 m
	4 x 4 x 2.50 m
Backstage	16 x 15 m
Revolve	14.60 m diameter (backstage wagon)
Dimensions of stage-podia (elevators)	6 x 16 x 2.50 m
Limits of travel	—3 to +3 m
Cyclorama	available

489

489
Balcony floor

490–491
Main floor, section

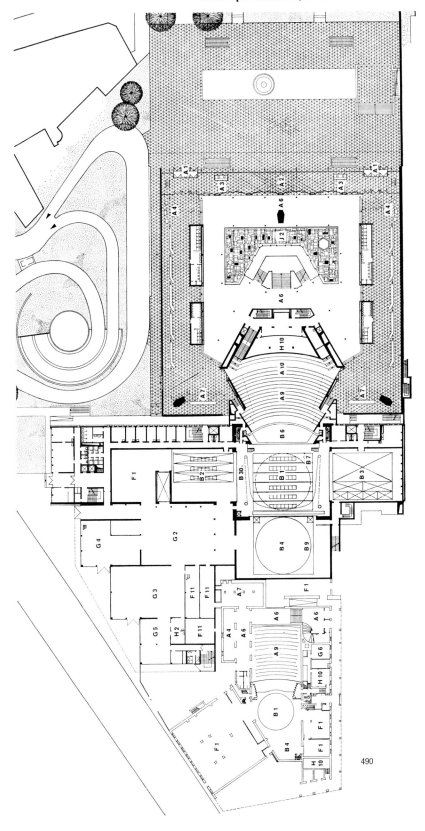

490

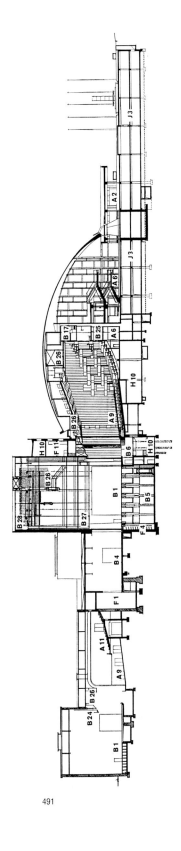

491

Wuppertal Theatres — Playhouse

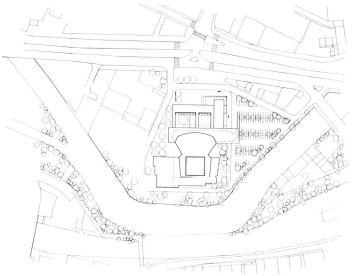

492

493
494
495

As though in defiance of the gloomy grey of the industrial town on the Wupper, the playhouse stands dazzling white in a bend of the river. It is a plain, self-contained, structure open to the outside (and to internal courts) solely by means of narrow ribbon windows—the house had to be screened against the antiquated and noisy elevated railway, a Wuppertal feature, clattering over the near-by river.

The building shows once again how rare it is nowadays for a theatre to be treated architecturally as an integrated whole. While the main front is impressively provided, the back part, normally hidden from the visitor, presents undisciplined confusion. Here the resultant building mass has simply been rendered—there is nothing against such a finish, but after a short time one cannot already help noticing 'behind the scenes' how quickly the theatre will age.

The house itself is designed as a large single-tiered theatre, divided rather perfunctorily into lower and upper stalls by a modest parapet. The great width makes the distances to the stage short, but does not always guarantee a faultless view from seats at the side. The generously planned foyer is enlarged by two Japanese gardens placed at the front, which divide the cloakroom and box-office wing from the main building and also light the foyer indirectly.

The stage was planned as a wagon-stage, with a trapped principal stage (only one wing-space has been built). Completion is delayed until a later stage.

The house is built purely for plays, with scene-stores but no workshops.

492
Site plan

493—496
Three views, auditorium

496

Wuppertal Theatres — Playhouse

Client	Municipality of Wuppertal
Artistic category	plays
Period of building	1964—1966
Opening	24. 9. 1966
Architect	Gerhard Graubner
Garden design	Akira Sato, Kuro Kaneko
Stage technical consultant	Adolf Zotzmann
Structural engineers	A. Koch, K. L. Fricke
Acoustics	Karl F. Darmer
Tests (structure)	W. Bonekämper
Cost	DM 12,500,000
Space enclosed	43,527 m³
Number of seats	750
Rise of stalls	3.35 m
Distance between rows	90 cm
Seat width	55 cm
Fire curtain in front of orchestra	
Maximum auditorium width	40.80 m
Maximum auditorium depth	28 m
Greatest distance from stage	stalls 23 m
Dimensions of main stage	19 x 14 m (max. 17.80 m)
Dimensions of right wing-space	13.70 x 13 m
Backstage dimensions	13.50 x 11 m (storage area)
Number of proscenium openings	1, completely retractable, including wing elements
Maximum opening	12.60 x 7 m
Minimum opening	9 x 4.90 m
Height of grid	18.80 m
Lighting control system	magnetic-amplifier
Number of circuits	120
Number of lines (sets)	42
Manual	38
Counterweight	3 winch (backstage) 2 winch (wing-space)
Stage-wagon dimensions	
Right wing-space	2 x 12 x 4 m
Backstage	13 x 10 m
Dimensions of stage-podia (elevators)	1 x 12 x 2 m
Limits of travel	—2.60 to + 2 m

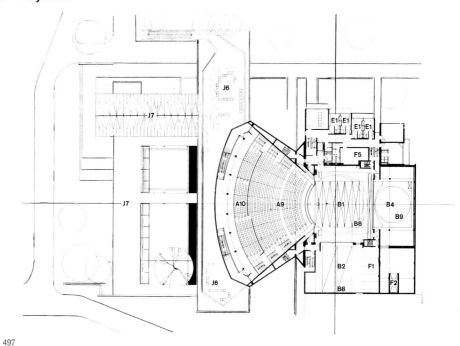

497

497—499
First floor (stalls), ground-floor, section

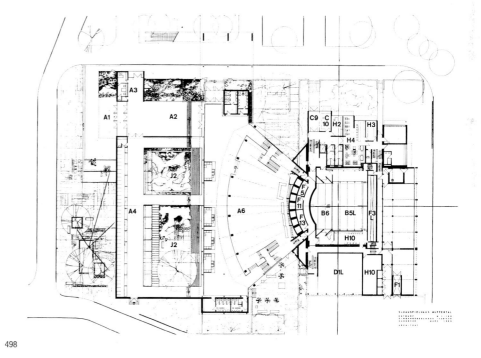

498

499

Municipal Theatre, Ingolstadt

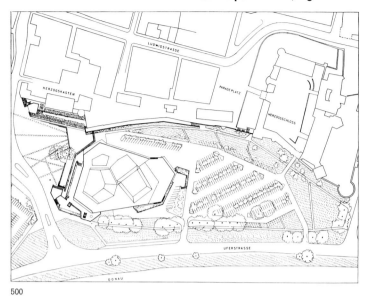

500

501

502

Arriving at Ingolstadt, with its medieval buildings and neo-medieval restorations and large factories and refineries in front of the gates, one wonders how such a place ever fathered this interesting and unusual modern theatre. The solid building spreads across a handsome open 'square', which faces the town gates and extends along the bank of the Danube; and it remains to be seen whether this stranger is destined to remain unique or, in the course of time, to be assimilated—in the best sense of the word—into the townscape.

Ingolstadt is the antithesis of Münster and Gelsenkirchen, which in both cases represent the beginning of a building phase. Ingolstadt stands almost at the end. It is not the most recent theatre to be built, but the time of the big new houses is past. Ingolstadt reveals the image of the next generation.

The right angle is rejected, wherever feasible, in this building which splays out and over the open square, and rises step by step to the fly-tower. The board-marked concrete is left exposed, and is certainly exploited at times as an end in itself, but with the vitality and enthusiasm of youth which knows what it wants.

The complex includes a hall for congresses and public meetings, as well as a theatre, intended principally for plays, but also for occasional guest performances of opera and operetta. Management accommodation has been kept to a minimum. The stalls of the theatre rise sharply, framed by side ramps converging at the back in a 'balcony' which houses technical and service booths. The foyer is generously planned, varied and spacious, and opens on to the 'square' through wide window-walls.

The stage is relatively well equipped as a wagon-stage with one pre-set wing-space, and traps and podia of adjustable rake on the main stage. But as the safety-curtain is behind the orchestra area, the deep-projecting forestage is only of limited use.

Municipal Theatre, Ingolstadt

500
Site plan

501–502
West and north-west views

503–505
Views of auditorium and foyer

503

504

505

Municipal Theatre, Ingolstadt

506–507
Main floor, section

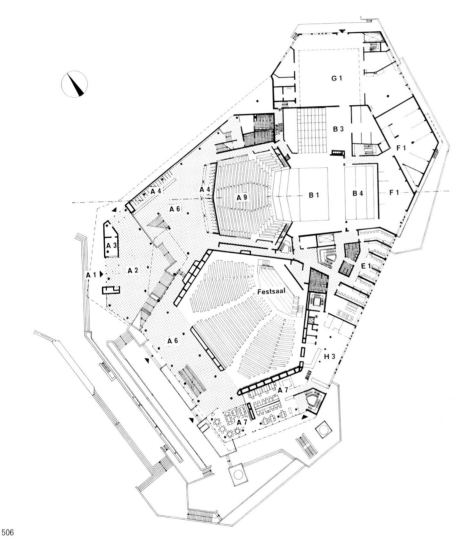

Client	Municipality of Ingolstadt
Artistic categories	plays (own company); opera, operetta, musicals as guest performances
Competition	1959
Period of building	1962–1966
Opening	21. 1. 1966
Architects	Hardt-Waltherr Hämer and Marie-B. Hämer-Buro, Klaus Meyer-Rogge, Norbert Weber
Sculptor	Hans Aeschbacher
Colour consultant	Heinrich Eichmann
Painters	Heinrich Eichmann, Lieselotte Spreng
Restaurant furnishings and foyer lighting	Robert Haussmann
Theatre consultant	Hardt-Waltherr Hämer
Stage technical consultants	Thomas Münter, Rudolf Biste
Structural engineers	Obermeyer, Konstruktionsbüro der 'Arbeitsgemeinschaft Theaterneubau Ingolstadt', Sager & Woerner, Eisenried & Spreng
Tests (structure)	Knittel, Brunner, Landes
Acoustics	Gabler, Spandöck
External layout	Walter Rossow, G. Gollwitzer
Cost	DM 21,500,000
Space enclosed	95,000 m³
Number of seats	stalls with side galleries 650–734 (The balcony is used for technical purposes and has a stage-direction 'box'.)
Distance between rows	87.50–95 cm
Seat width	52–54 cm
Fire curtain behind orchestra	
Maximum auditorium width	28 m
Maximum auditorium depth	25 m
Greatest distance from stage	stalls 25 m balcony – stage-direction box 25 m
Dimensions of main stage	21 x 13.50 m
Dimensions of left wing-space	12.30 x 18.70 m (with transport area)
Backstage dimensions	17.10 x 9 m
Number of proscenium openings	1
Maximum opening without arch	16.50 x 7.70 m
Maximum opening with arch	14 x 7.70 m
Minimum opening	10 x 5 m
Height of grid	18.50 m
Orchestra space	56–80 m² = orchestra-podia, 1 two-tier-podium
Lighting control system	AEG
Number of levers (dimmers)	2 x 120
Number of circuits	120
Number of lines (sets)	
Electrically operated	85 spot, every 4–5 between the hand-worked 42 front-of-house spot
Manual (hand-worked)	16
Stage-wagon dimensions	
Left wing-space	44 x 1 x 2 m 8 x 1 x 1 m
Backstage	2 x 14 x 3 m 1 x 14 x 2 m
Dimensions of stage-podia (elevators)	14 x 8 m main-podium
Limits of travel	— 2 to + 1.50 m (also tiltable)
Cyclorama	provision for flying pan-cloth

506

507

160

Municipal Theatre, Würzburg

508

509

510

508–510
View from south-west, auditorium, foyer

The town theatre at Würzburg is an entirely new building, with complete workshop facilities and its own garage. The narrow and rather long site, not far from the Residenz, with three street frontages, is not propitious, and the ponderous massive building has not converted the disadvantage of the location into an asset.

A building like this shows how, from among the large number of new theatres, definite conventions have frequently emerged which ensure a certain solidity in the design. Würzburg adheres to such a convention and, since no attempt has been made to break with it, the result is unexciting.

The house is conceived as a balcony theatre with stalls of fan-shape plan, which none the less offer adequate sight-lines.

The machinery is unusual. The Viennese principle of the cylindrical revolve has been adopted (here combined, however, with spacious wing- and back-stages), the slope of the in-built podia being adjustable, as at Mannheim.

The experiment has been tried of extending the open forecourt into the entrance-hall by retaining the external paving and introducing an internal court. But as the room is screened from the outside by solid masonry, the sense of continuity is lost. Only the foyer at first-floor level is open wide and welcoming to the little Theaterplatz, but the massive box-office building in front of the entrance hall has a distancing effect.

Client	City of Würzburg
Artistic categories	opera, operetta, plays
Competition	yes
Period of building	1963–1966
Opening	4. 12. 1966
Architect	Hans Joachim Budeit
Sculptors and painters	entrance doors: Müller sculpture, cloak-room hall: Zech
Stage technical consultants	Emmerlich and Schneider
Structural engineer	Kröncke
Acoustics	Werner Gabler
Tests (structure)	Gewerbeanstalt Würzburg
Cost	DM 18,000,000
Space enclosed	61,000 m³
Number of seats	756
	stalls 568
	balcony 164
	boxes 24
Distance between rows	90 cm
Seat width	55 cm
Fire curtain behind orchestra	
Maximum auditorium width	27 m
Maximum auditorium depth	21.80 m

Greatest distance from stage	stalls 22 m
	balcony 22.40 m
Dimensions of main stage	18.50 x 14.50 (16.50), (20.60) m
Dimensions of right wing-space	12.88 x 10.25 m
Backstage dimensions	13.04 x 14.10 m
Number of proscenium openings	1 (hydraulically driven)
Maximum opening	12 x 6.50 m
Minimum opening	9 m x height to 0
Height of grid	18.50 m
Orchestra space	89.25 m²
Lighting control system	Siemens transistor with punched cards
Number of levers (dimmers)	140
Number of circuits	140
Number of lines (sets)	40 back-cloth
	3 heavy back-cloth
	3 lighting
	10 spot
	11 heavy back-cloth backstage
Stage-wagon dimensions	small wagons coupled as needed
Right wing-space	small wagons coupled as needed
Backstage	small wagons coupled as needed
Revolve	two-tier, 12.60 m diameter, invariable
Stage-wagon dimensions	lift-, sink-, and tilt-able up and down + 1.85 to — 1.85 m
	4 hydraulic podia 2 x 8 m, limits of travel — 3 to + 2 m, built into revolve
Cyclorama	curved pan-cloth type

Municipal Theatre, Würzburg

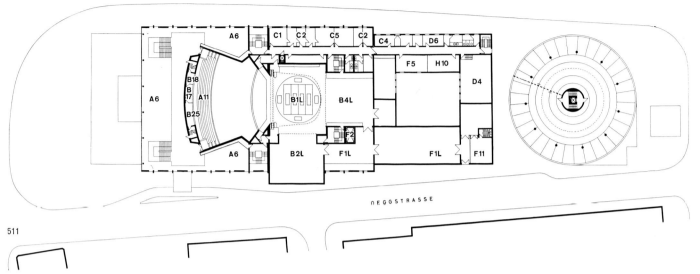

511

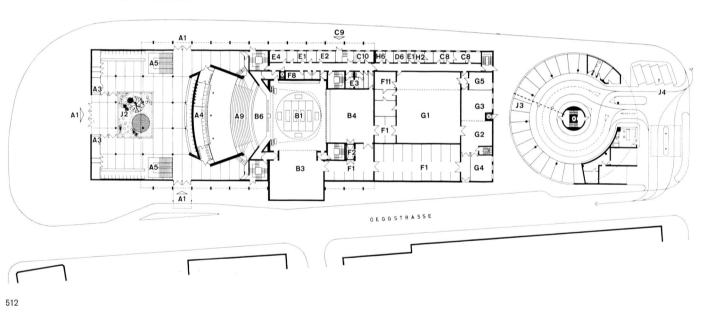

512

511–513
Upper floor, ground-floor, section

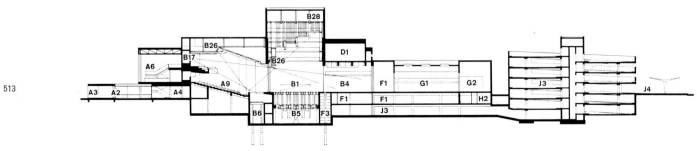

513

Tiroler Landestheater, Innsbruck

514

The Landestheater at Innsbruck is a reconstruction which has been enlarged by a grandiose extension. Of the old building only the classical façade and the outside walls remain, while the whole interior has been reorganized.

The Innsbruck theatre is the only postwar house to have been rebuilt on the box principle, which survives as a far more vigorous tradition in Austria, where few theatres were destroyed and the new ones—with the exception of the Staatsoper in Vienna—are straightforward restorations of existing buildings. Visually, however, the boxes have been disguised as large balconies by continuous parapet-fronts.

An ample new structure for the stage has been added to the old building, so that the back-stage could be extended and a spacious wing-stage attached. A trapped revolve is built into the main stage.

514–515
Entrance front, view of auditorium from stage

515

Clients	Province of Tirol and provincial capital of Innsbruck
Artistic categories	opera, operetta, ballet, plays
Competition	first, for rebuilding auditorium second, for artistic design
Period of building	1962–1967
Opening	17. 11. 1967
Architects	Erich Boltenstern, Provincial Building Authority
Sculptors	bronze panels, foyer: Franz Pöhacker auditorium ceiling and balcony fronts: Hilde Schmidt-Jesser
Painters	mosaics, hall: Kurt Fischer fire curtain: Max Weiler
Stage technical consultants	Waagner-Biro
Structural engineer	Walter Passer
Acoustics	Edmund Hirschwehr
Cost	Aus. S 122,200,000
Space enclosed	89,500 m³
Number of seats	881
	stalls 428 + 58 with orchestra-pit covered
	1st balcony 107
	2nd balcony 107
	gallery 181
Distance between rows	80 cm
Seat width	53 cm
Fire curtain behind orchestra	
Maximum auditorium width	19.20 m
Maximum auditorium depth	23.50 m

Tiroler Landestheater, Innsbruck

516–518
Balcony floor, stage floor, section

Greatest distance from stage	stalls 18.50 m
	1st balcony 21.20 m
	2nd balcony 22.20 m
	gallery 26 m
Dimensions of main stage	25 x 16.50 m
With backstage as part of acting area	25 x 25 m
With backstage and covered orchestra pit	25 x 30.60 m
Dimensions of left wing-space	18.50 x 25 m
Backstage dimensions	15.50 x 8.50 m
Number of proscenium openings	1
Maximum opening	10.30 x 8 m
Minimum opening	4 x 1 m
Height of grid	20.20 m
Orchestra space	70 m²
Lighting control system	Siemens punched-card pro-gramming equipment and 1 pre-set panel
Number of levers (dimmers)	168 + 25 on the master-console
Number of circuits	160 + 8 for auditorium
Number of lines (sets)	
Electrically operated	3 + 4 spot-lines in front of fire curtain
Manual	57 + 4 pan-cloth + 2 spot in front of fire curtain
Counterweight	4 (with winches) backstage
Stage-wagon dimensions	4 x 4 m
Revolve	14 m diameter
Dimensions of stage-podia (elevators)	1 x 4 x 8 m
	5 x 1 x 1 m
Limits of travel	—3.66 to + 2.84 m
Cyclorama	available

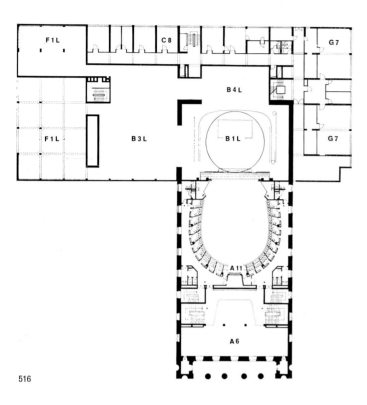

516

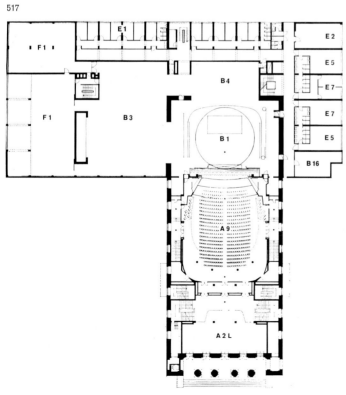

517

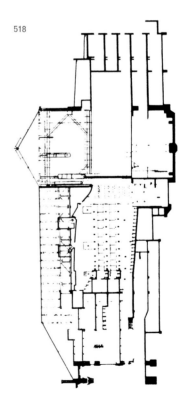

518

164

519

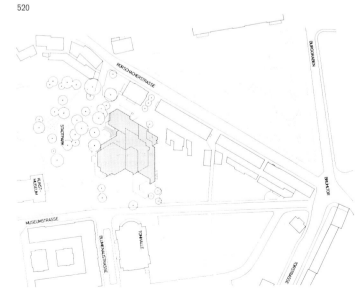

520

519
View from east

520
Site plan

While in the Federal Republic the wave of new theatre buildings is declining, in Switzerland a series of important new houses is now rising: Basle, Winterthur, Zürich (opera and playhouse). A small provincial theatre marked the prelude: St. Gallen. And what a prelude!

At a modest cost of thirteen million Swiss francs, a building has resulted which fears comparison with no metropolitan theatre. A first glance at the plan may make one doubt whether the architect's apparently obsessive delight in the hexagon will be successful. But in practice one is astonished to find how rare are the difficulties, how smoothly everything dovetails and how animated and gay this far from extravagant little theatre turns out to be.

It is one of the very few theatres designed to be 'circumambulated' completely. Although there is no 'show' front—the house stands in a fine old park—the entire external face is intended to be seen. Each

521–523
Views of foyer, auditorium

521

522

side, indeed, has its particular character, without being architecturally obtrusive.

The foyer extends spaciously round the nucleus of the under-stage and soars upward about the auditorium. It is remarkable what impressive effects can be achieved in a relatively small 'room'. The auditorium—gently rising stalls with one balcony—is asymmetrical, perhaps the first example of successful asymmetry not conceived as a deliberate gimmick. The auditorium lighting, a modern version of the chandelier—a surface of light, is very dexterous. It is suspended in the angle in front of the technical service-rooms and flown when the performance begins.

The stage, also designed as a hexagon, is 'intimate' in size. The safety-curtain hangs behind the orchestra pit; but, as this is set rather far back, the wide forestage is difficult to use. The main stage, however, can be extended to almost the full depth of the back-stage, and the side-stage, too, is roomy and offers ample pre-set space.

The technical installations have been economized until a later date, but all workshops and other subsidiary accommodation are included in the contract price.

523

Municipal Theatre, St. Gallen

524–526
Section, main floor, ground-floor

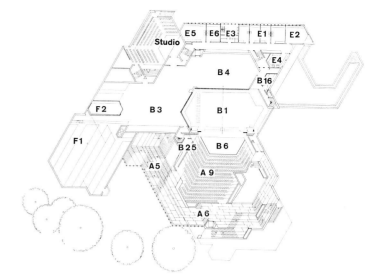

525

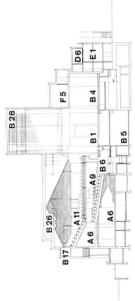

524

526

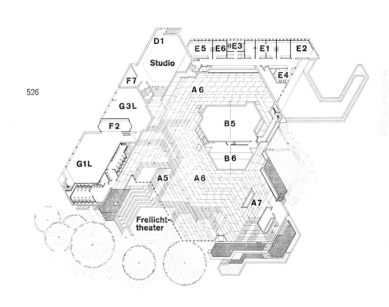

Client	St. Gallen Town Theatre Corporation
Artistic categories	opera, operetta, ballet, plays
Competition	1961
Period of building	1964–1968
Opening	15. 3. 1968
Architects	Claude Paillard (Atelier CJP), Hansjörg Gügler
Stage technical consultant	Adolf Zotzmann
Structural engineers	Zähner & Wenk
Acoustics	A. Lauber, W. Furrer, Max Adam
Cost	Sw. fr. 13,200,000
Space enclosed	52,400 m³
Number of seats	stalls 397
	balcony 374
	orchestra-pit seats 84
	total: for opera 771;
	for plays 855
Distance between rows	90 cm
Seat width	52 cm
Fire curtain behind orchestra	
Maximum auditorium width	29.10 m
Maximum auditorium depth	26.90 m

Greatest distance from stage	stalls 18.50 m
	balcony 27.80 m
Dimensions of main stage	20 x 11.10 m (max. 12.70 m, including forestage) (max. 17.20 m, including orchestra-pit)
Dimensions of left wing-space	15 x 9 m
Backstage dimensions	17 x 9.10 m
Number of proscenium openings	1
Maximum opening	13 x 7.50 m
Minimum opening	9 x 5 m
Height of grid	22 m
Orchestra space	73 m²
Lighting control system	Thyristor equipment
Number of levers (dimmers)	80 (extensible to 100)
Number of circuits	80
Number of lines (sets)	36
Manual	27 (including 3 forestage)
Counterweight	3

167

Düsseldorf Playhouse

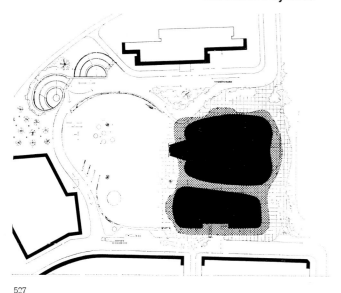

527

The triple-slab skyscraper of the Thyssen concern was already standing when the competition for the playhouse was held. The theatre (opened 1969) had thus to contend from the beginning with the immediate proximity of the towering office complex, and it was thought that this could best be done with a flamboyant piece of serpentine 'architectural sculpture' to act as counterpoint. It can be seen from the plan how difficult it proved to fit the rectangular rooms of the stage area into this undulating contour; and, in another respect, one forms the impression that the architecture is not quite happily related to its intended purpose, the auditorium (1036 seats) being carried on a gigantic mushroom column, from which the load-bearing construction radiates. This system, moreover, looks so ponderous and massive that the effect is not only visually obstructive, but crushing, so that a far from small foyer seems cramped.

The one thousand strong audience is accommodated in a single tier of stalls, covered by an arched wood ceiling, which gives the room despite its size an almost intimate character.

On the other hand, the stage (supplemented by three large subsidiary stages) has opera-house dimensions, and one doubts whether the players can hold their own upon it. It seems as if the maximum programme had slipped past the building committee with no allowance made for reductions.

The small house is organized as a studio-theatre with three hundred seats, but here the relationship of the various spatial functions is technically so simple and logical that one has every hope that the multifarious possibilities of the theatre can be effectively exploited.

The two houses are separated on the ground-floor by a passage, which links the Jan-Wellem-Platz and the Hofgarten. A theatre-café built within the framework of the small theatre is intended as a social meeting-point on the edge of the Hofgarten.

528

529

527
Site plan

528–529
Views from the 'Hofgarten' and Theaterplatz

530–533
Foyer, two views of auditorium. Studio: auditorium and stage

168

Düsseldorf Playhouse

530

531

532

533

Clients	Cultural Office, provincial capital of Düsseldorf
Artistic category	plays
Competition	1st stage 1959
	2nd stage 1961
Period of building	1965–1969
Opening	November 1969
Architect	Bernhard M. Pfau
Theatre consultant	Willi Ehle
Stage technical consultant	Willi Ehle
Structural engineers	Haesaerts, Bruno Kohlhaas, Kina
Acoustics	H. Graner
Tests (structure)	Landesprüfamt für Baustatik (LPA)
Cost	c. DM 36,000,000
	large and small houses
Space enclosed	c. 124,930 m^3

Large house

Number of seats	stalls max. 1008
Distance between rows	90 cm
Seat width	55 cm

Fire curtain, straight, in front of technical (proscenium) opening

169

Düsseldorf Playhouse

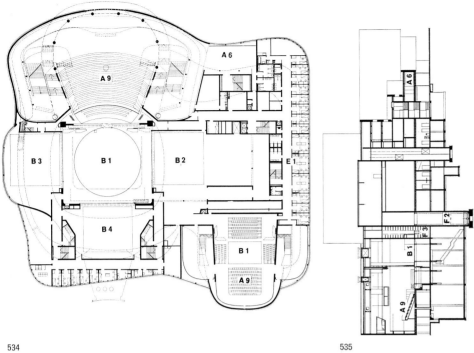

534

535

536

537

Maximum auditorium width	28 m
Maximum auditorium depth	30 m
Greatest distance from stage	stalls 29 m
Dimensions of main stage	24.30 x 21.50 m
Dimensions of right wing-space	16 x 15 m
Dimensions of left wing-space	32 x 15 m
Backstage dimensions	15 x 15 m
Number of proscenium openings	**1**
Maximum opening	15.50 x 8.50 m
Minimum opening	11 x 0.50 m
Height of grid	24 m (rolling system)
Orchestra space	c. 64 m²
Lighting control system	completely electric, with programming (Siemens)
Number of levers (dimmers)	240 variable
Number of circuits	240 variable
Number of pre-set possibilities	4 x 240
Number of lines (sets)	
Electrically operated	62
Manual	35
Electric counterweight	27
Spot	14
Stage-wagon dimensions	
Right wing-space	4 x 14 x 3 m
Left wing-space	4 x 14 x 3 m
Backstage	4 x 14 x 3 m
Revolve	19.30 cm cylindrical
Dimensions of stage-podia (elevators)	4 x 14 x 3 m
Limits of travel	—3 to + 3 m, tiltable (1:10)

Small house

Number of seats	stalls max. 309 (arena)
Distance between rows	82 cm
Seat width	55 cm
Fire curtain: flexible safety curtain in front of technical (proscenium) opening	
Maximum auditorium width	16 m
Maximum auditorium depth	17 m
Greatest distance from stage	stalls 14 m
Dimensions of main stage	9 x 7 m
Number of proscenium openings	**1**
Maximum opening	15.50 x 6.75 m
Minimum opening	9 x 1 m (swivel-mounted)
Height of grid	12.50 m (rolling system)
Lighting control system	(cf. large house)
Number of levers (dimmers)	72 variable
Number of circuits	72 variable
Number of pre-set possibilities	4 x 72
Number of lines (sets)	33
Electrically operated	25
Spot	8
Stage-wagon dimensions	9 x 7 m, 9 x 6 m
Limits of travel	—1.20 to + 2 m

534—537
Floor-plans ± 0 and —4.25 m; sections,
studio and large house

Landestheater, Darmstadt

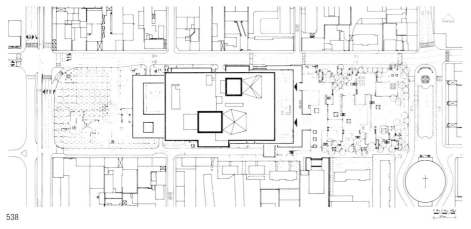

538

The Provincial Theatre at Darmstadt will not be opened until 1972, so that a description of the building cannot be complete. But the plans, which are largely concluded—the carcass is already well advanced—show so many interesting details that we were eager to include the scheme in the documentary section.

The site allocated for the two-theatre complex is favourably placed. Confronted, however, by this narrow, elongated, plot, it would be easy to lose courage.

The foreground of the theatre is undermined by a large subterranean car-park, in which the problems of access and exit for cars and buses are extremely well solved.

From the forecourt the theatre rises gradually over the box-office, foyer and auditorium to the fly-tower and stands as open as possible to the city.

The advantage of the elongated site is its size, which enables a large architectural mass to be accommodated. The workshops are arranged with unusual spaciousness, in very convenient relation to the two stages, and on the same level. The artists' dressing-rooms are disposed underneath the auditorium—also at stage-level—so that, since both houses are designed for opera and plays, the artists' paths to the stage are kept as short as possible. The dressing-rooms are conceived purely as places to work in (artificial light and artificial ventilation). For this reason the green-rooms and restrooms have been put above the auditorium, and enjoy splendid views of the town and plain of the Rhine.

The technical organization of the proscenium area has already been discussed (see page 82). It is the same for both houses. Ideas first tentatively applied in the Frankfurt playhouse and Recklinghausen Festival theatre have been further developed here. The opening can be expanded to the full width of the stage (over sixty feet); the proscenium wings are separate from the border and can also be moved backwards, so that any opening is feasible, both behind and in front of the orchestra pit. Front and acoustic curtains, carried in the wings, contain the stage.

On either side of the front rows of seats, the platform of the stage extends into the auditorium. Partitions, which can be moved or folded, enclose the room, so that this area is completely flexible. They can also be rotated to reveal their black reverse sides, on which scenery can be mounted. A mobile lighting stand, which can be concealed by a partition, lights the forestage. In front of this part of the stage and of the orchestra-pit is a curtain, which is lowered vertically from the roof.

The house has not yet been put to the test, but in the hands of skilled producers promises to be a versatile and flexible instrument.

538
Site plan

539–540
Photos of models: view from east-south-east, auditorium

539

540

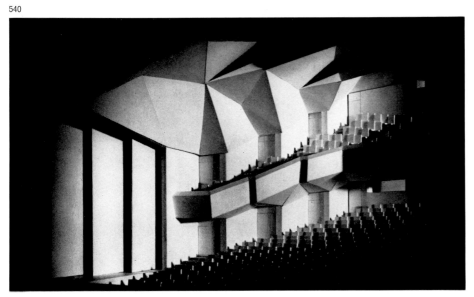

Landestheater, Darmstadt

Clients	large house – Province of Hessen
	small house – City of Darmstadt
Artistic categories	opera, operetta, ballet, plays
Competition	1963
Period of building	under construction
Opening	early in 1972/73 season
Architect	Rolf Prange
Stage technical consultant	Adolf Zotzmann
Structural engineers	Beck, F. W. Gravert,
	K. H. Schneider
Acoustics	Karlhans Weisse
Tests (structure)	Hessische Landesprüfstelle für
	Baustatik
Cost	c. DM 56,000,000
Space enclosed	217,000 m³

Large house

Number of seats	950
	stalls 715
	balcony 235
Distance between rows	95 cm
Seat width	55 cm
Fire curtain in front of orchestra	
Maximum auditorium width	c. 23 m
Maximum auditorium depth	c. 25.35 m
Greatest distance from stage	stalls 24.90 m
	balcony 26.90 m
Dimensions of main stage	200 centrally controlled,
Dimensions of right wing-space	24 x 24.90 m (max. 28.50 m)
Dimensions of left wing-space	16.60 x 15.70 m
Backstage dimensions	22.87 x 16 m
Number of proscenium openings	17 x 16 m
Maximum opening	1
Minimum opening	19 x 8.50 m
Height of grid	10 x 5 m
Orchestra space	25.71 m
Lighting control system	130.40 m²
Number of levers (dimmers)	Siemens
Number of circuits	200
	+ 40 independent
Number of lines (sets)	
Electrically operated	25 back-cloth
	2 pan-cloth
Manual	28
	2 pan-cloth
Counterweight	5 electrically operated,
	each 1000 kg
	2 hand-worked-forestage

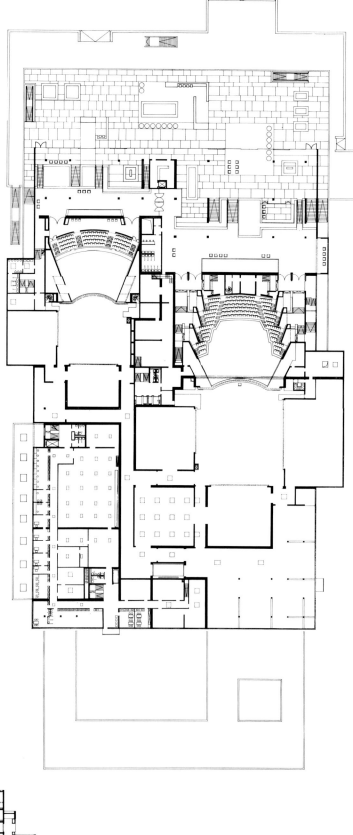

541

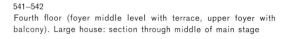

541–542
Fourth floor (foyer middle level with terrace, upper foyer with balcony). Large house: section through middle of main stage

542

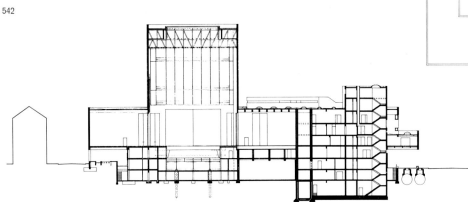

172

Landestheater, Darmstadt

Stage-wagon dimensions
Right wing-space   2 x 14.50 x 5 m
Left wing-space   3 x 14.50 x 5 m
   1 x 14.50 x 2.50 m
Backstage   15 x 14.50 m
Revolve   14 m diameter
Dimensions of stage-podia
(elevators)   3 x 14.50 x 5 m
   1 x 14.50 x 2.50 m
Orchestra-podia   14.50 x 2.75 m
   14.50 x 2.50 m
Limits of travel   —3 to + 3 m, depending upon
   the level of the stage

Small house
Number of seats   470
   stalls 360
   balcony 110
Distance between rows   95 cm
Seat width   55 cm
Fire curtain in front of orchestra
Maximum auditorium width   c. 23 m
Maximum auditorium depth   c. 20.05 m
Greatest distance from stage   stalls 17.90 m
   balcony 20.80 m
Dimensions of main stage   20 x 15.30 m (max. 18.75 m)
Dimensions of right wing-space   14 x 13.50 m
Backstage dimensions   14 x 11 m
Number of proscenium openings   1
Maximum opening   15.50 x 7 m
Minimum opening   8 x 4.50 m
Height of grid   21.97 m
Orchestra space   52.70 m²
Lighting control system   Siemens
Number of levers (dimmers)   120
Number of circuits   120 centrally controlled
   + 30 independent
Number of lines (sets)   32 hand-worked
   4 pan-cloth
   2 forestage
   3 electrically operated winch,
   each 1000 kg
Right wing-space   3 x 12 x 2.50 m
Backstage   12 x 10 m
Revolve   9.50 m diameter
Dimensions of stage-podia
(elevators)   5 x 12 x 2.50 m
   1 x 12 x 2 m
   (orchestra-podium 1)
Limits of travel   —3 to + 3 m

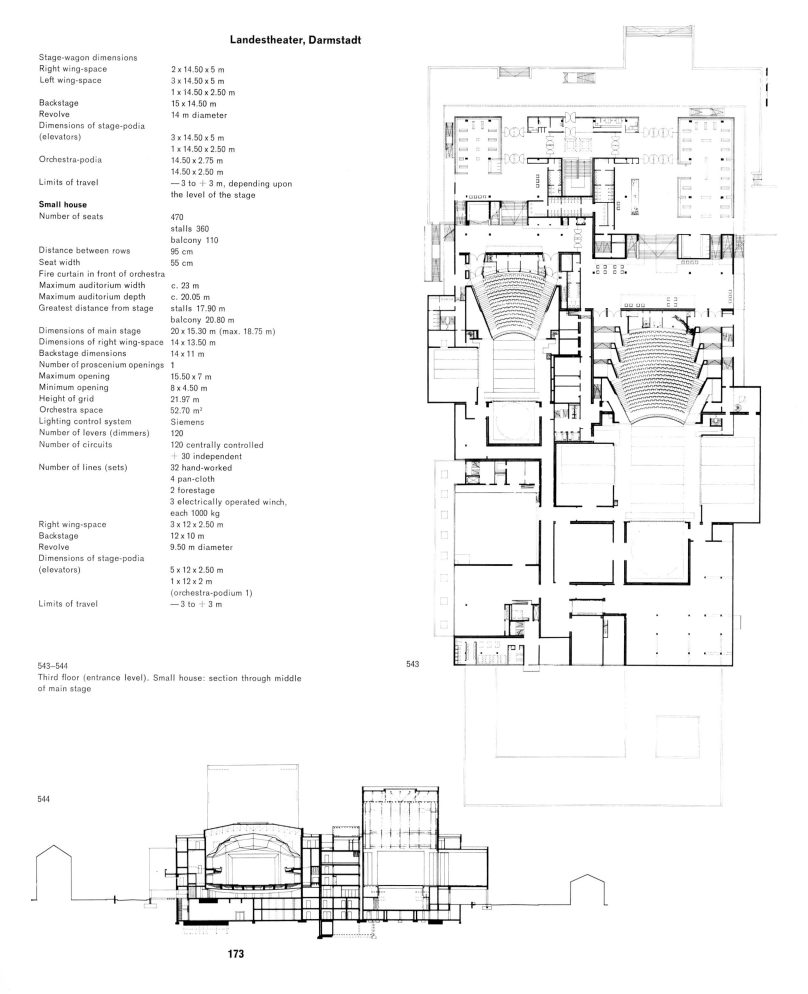

543–544
Third floor (entrance level). Small house: section through middle
of main stage

543

544

173

Landestheater, Darmstadt

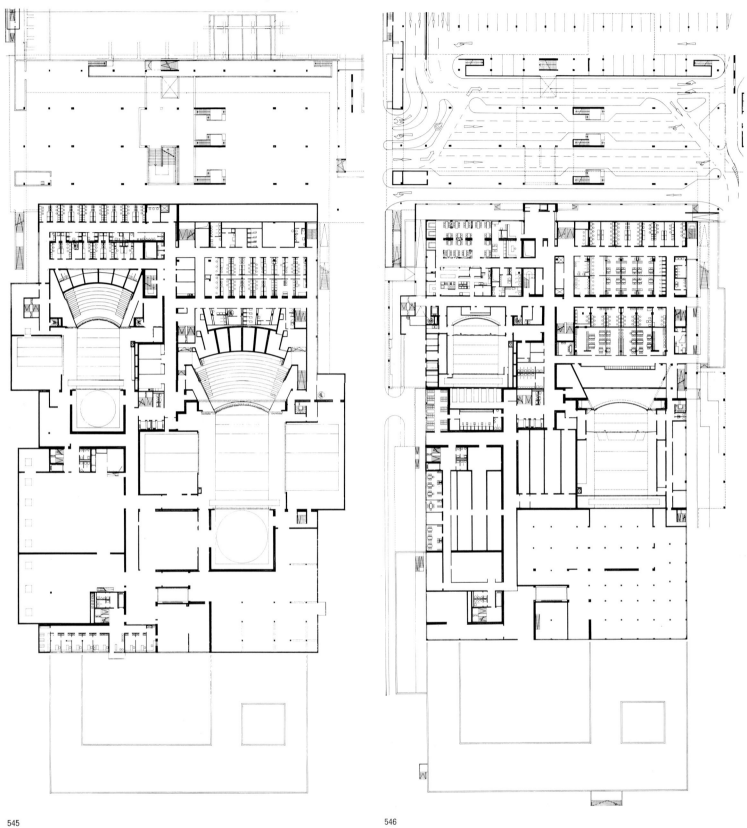

545

546

545—546
Second floor (stage level), first floor (orchestra-pit level, stage
entrance, underground garage)

Ulm Theatre

The squat compact silhouette of Ulm's municipal theatre is the product of its location. On the edge of the old city (and from the outset a subject of dispute), the site was extraordinarily small for a new building, which was to include a large house with eight hundred seats, a studio holding two hundred, and all workshop and storage facilities. It was therefore necessary to build upwards and pile one thing upon another, when otherwise one might have allowed the building to spread.

In plan a succession of interlocking hexagons, the building—compact, as it is, and solid—fits well enough into the surrounding townscape. The massive structure is characterized by large, blind surfaces, very infrequently pierced by ribbon windows. The hexagonal pattern of the ground-plan is not clearly apparent in practice, except perhaps in the auditorium and fly-tower blocks. The foyer is faced by a sloping wall, which resembles a hip-roof.

Handsome twin-flight staircases lead from the cloakrooms to the main foyer and straight single-flights to the balcony-foyer. Multi-angular bands of light play upon the hexagonal theme of the theatre plan. The outward-sloping external wall widens the foyer, but also excludes much of the daylight.

The dished tier of the stalls is adapted to a hexagon and is framed by a balcony, the effect being intimate and unpretentious. The stage-curtain, with a composition by Albert Mavignier, provides the dominant motif.

The stage is equipped with back-stage and wing-space. A revolve is mounted on the back-stage wagon.

The studio-theatre lies under the rake of the auditorium and is also a strictly hexagonal room with a lift-stage and movable seating. It can be infinitely flexible. The swivel-seats are easy to fix. There is no fly-floor, but scenery can be fastened to the ceiling.

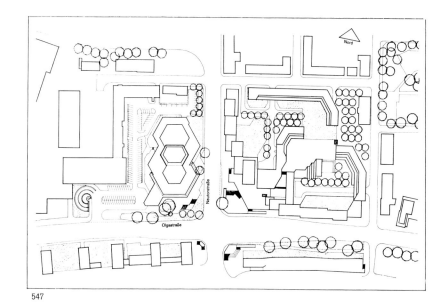
547

548

549

547
Site plan

548—549
South-west view, foyer

175

Ulm Theatre

550

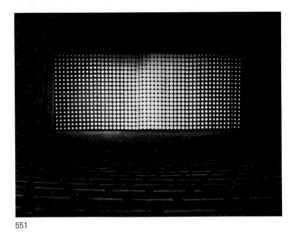

551

550–553
Views of auditorium and experimental
stage

552

553

554

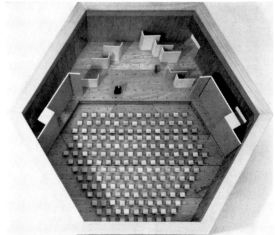

Ulm Theatre

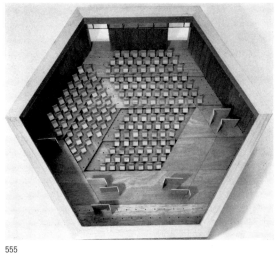

555

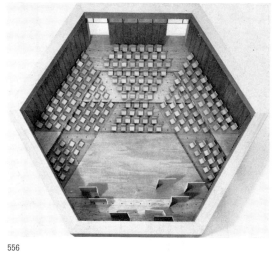

556

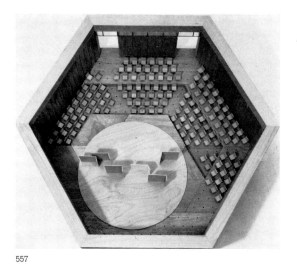

557

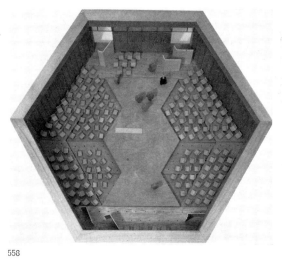

558

559

560

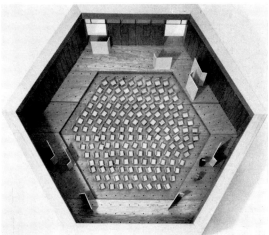

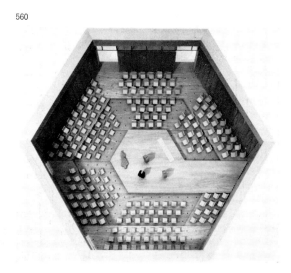

Ulm Theatre

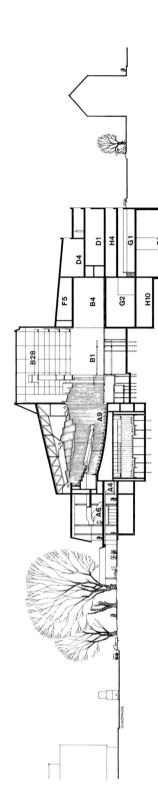

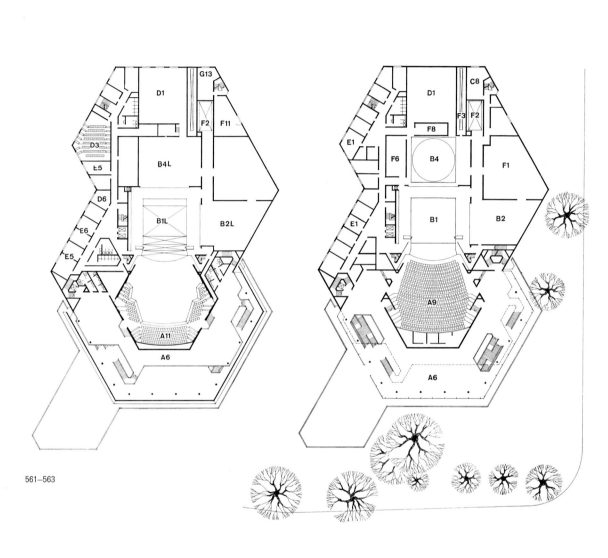

561–563

Client	City of Ulm	Greatest distance from stage	stalls 22.15 m
Artistic categories	opera, operetta, plays		balcony 24.65 m
Competition	1962	Dimensions of main stage	20 x 14 (max. 16.50 m)
Period of building	1967–1969	Dimensions of right wing-space	15 x 12 m
Opening	October 1969	Backstage dimensions	17.25 x 13 m
Architect	Fritz Schäfer	Number of proscenium openings	1, mobile in stage-width and
Painter	curtain: Mavignier		depth
Theatre consultants	Münter and Biste	Maximum opening	12 x 8 m
Stage technical consultants	Münter and Biste	Minimum opening	8.50 x 6 m
Structural engineers	Leonhardt and Andrä	Height of grid	21.40 m
Acoustics	Zeller	Orchestra space	max. 88 m²
Tests (structure)	Henne, Pfefferkorn, Glos	Lighting control system	Siemens
Cost	DM 23,000,000	Number of levers (dimmers)	144
Space enclosed	89,000 m³	Number of circuits	144
Number of seats	817	Number of pre-set banks	4, punched cards
	stalls 626	Number of lines (sets)	50
	balcony 191	Electrically operated	25 (spot-set installation with 4 or
Distance between rows	90 cm		5 spot-lines in a row)
Seat width	55 cm	Manual	25
Fire curtain in front of orchestra		Stage-wagon dimensions	
Maximum auditorium width	25 m	Backstage	12 x 12 m
Maximum auditorium depth	23 m		

Ulm Theatre

561—564
Section, balcony floor, main floor, entrance floor

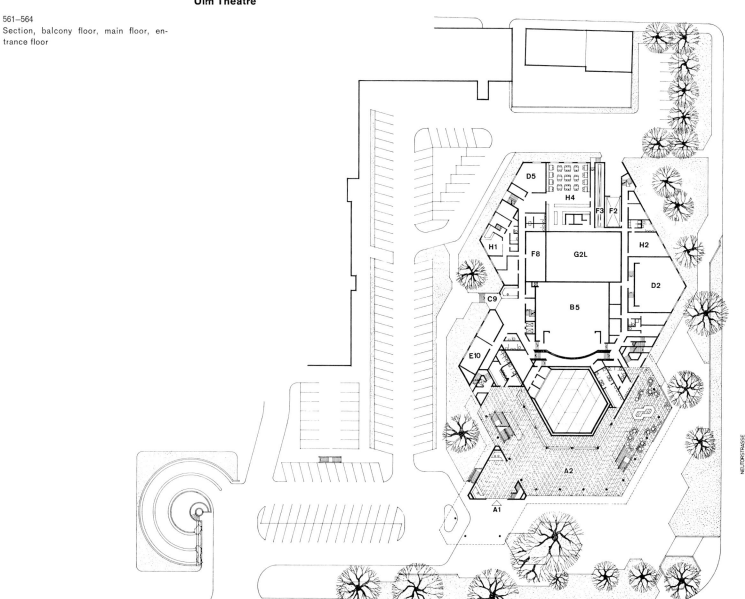

564

		Podium (experimental stage)	
Revolve	11.60 m diameter (backstage wagon)	Number of seats	max. 200, variously arranged according to the type of stage; swivel-seats
Dimensions of stage-podia (elevators)	12 x 1.50 m, 12 x 2.50 m, 12 x 8 m, 12 x 1.50 m	Maximum auditorium width	19 m
Limits of travel	— 2 to + 2 m	Maximum auditorium depth	17 m
Cyclorama	2 armed-battens (curved) with double-height pan-cloth (hung)	Auditorium height	4.50 m
		Lighting control system	BBC 36 pre-settings and punched-card installation
		Number of dimmer-switches	52
		Number of circuits	52
		Hydraulic elevators	16 platforms of various sizes — 0.90 to + 0.90 m
		Ceiling	gridiron-ceiling equipped for hanging scenery
		Walls	slotted all round for fixing scenery
		Lines	provision for hanging curtain

179

Studio Theatre of the Academy of Art, Berlin

The studio-theatre at the Academy of Art in Berlin is a special case, because it is not planned for the habitual presentation of plays. It is intended to provide, within the framework of the Academy's programme, an opportunity to present studio and experimental productions. At the same time it serves as a large hall for lectures and discussions.

The house is unusual in that the stage thrusts across the middle of the auditorium, almost like a bridge, dividing it into two large segments which rise gently on either side. Apart from lighting and a few sets of lines, there is no technical equipment.

The 'studio' is a challenge which is unlikely to be accepted by theatre people. It has been shown again and again that the opening of the stage on several sides, so often practised in American college theatres, finds little response in Europe, at least in this form. The completely built and installed experimental theatre is too much of an established thing to offer the avant-garde adequate playing space and possibilities for developing stagecraft. The experimentalists prefer an empty room, which they can adapt to their particular needs.

565

565–566
Entrance side, auditorium and stage with view of rear auditorium

566

Studio Theatre of the Academy of Art, Berlin

567–568
Section, ground-floor

569
Auditorium

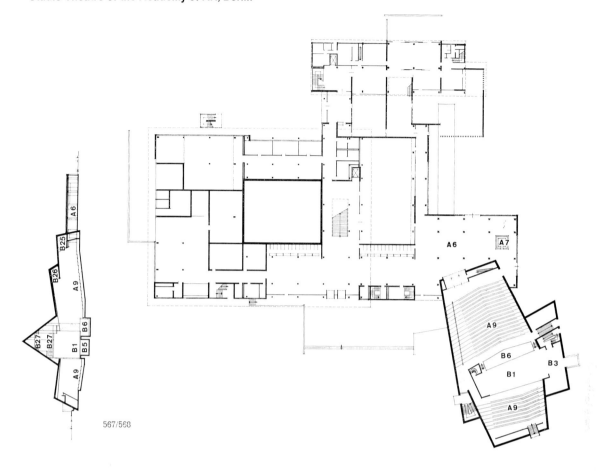

567/568

569

Client	H. Reichhold Foundation, New York
Artistic category	experimental theatre
Period of building	1959–1960
Opening	18. 6. 1960
Architect	Werner Düttmann
Sculptor	Henry Moore
Stage technical consultants	Märkische Maschinenfabrik, Friedrich Huhn
Structural engineer	Hellmuth Bickenbach
Acoustics	Lothar Cremer
Tests (structure)	Hans Dienst
Cost	c. DM 7,400,000
Space enclosed	c. 75,000 m³
Number of seats	650
	small stalls 198
	large stalls 431/518
Distance between rows	95 cm
Seat width	55 cm
Maximum auditorium width (large stalls)	23 m
Maximum auditorium depth (large stalls)	24 m
Greatest distance from stage	21 m
Dimensions of main stage	17.50 x 7.50 m (with orchestra-pit covered 9.90 m)
Dimensions of left wing-space	storage area only
Backstage dimensions	usable as small stalls
Proscenium opening	max. 17 x 7 m
Height of grid	23 m
Orchestra space	34,80 m²
Lighting control system	Bordoni
Number of levers (dimmers)	84
Number of circuits	84
Number of lines (sets)	15 hand-worked

181

Municipal Theatre, Lünen

570

The town theatre of Lünen was probably the first house to be built after the war purely for guest-performances, and not for a regular company of its own. It is without workshops and technical production facilities.

The house is lucidly organized, and has adopted from Gerhard Weber the theme, applied in the Hamburg state opera house, of the balcony divided into separate sledge-like boxes. The latter's white front-railings bring an element of audacity into an otherwise staid design. The auditorium is embedded in a large cube, the entrance front rendered coherent by decoratively emphasizing the foyer stairs.

The conventionally arranged main stage has an ample wing-space. The technical equipment is simple, but practical.

Client	Municipality of Lünen
Artistic categories	guest performances of all kinds, multi-purpose theatre for opera, operetta, plays, concerts etc.
Period of building	1957–1958
Opening	11. 10. 1958
Architect	Gerhard Graubner
Sculptor	Hermann Jünger
Theatre consultant	Gerhard Graubner
Stage technical consultant	Willi Ehle
Structural engineers	Bruno Kohlhaas, Eberhard Lippke, Otto Kremer
Acoustics	Karl F. Darmer
Tests (structure)	Günther Raczat
Cost	DM 3,020,000
Space enclosed	31,000 m³
Number of seats	765
	stalls 643
	balcony 122, divided into boxes
Distance between rows	87.80 cm
Seat width	55 cm
Fire curtain in front of orchestra	
Maximum auditorium width	22.50 m
Maximum auditorium depth	25.30 m
Greatest distance from stage	stalls 22 m
	balcony 26.70 m
Dimensions of main stage	18 x 12.70 m (max. 13.70 m, 17 m)
Dimensions of right wing-space	13 x 13.50 m
Number of proscenium openings	1
Maximum opening	12 x 6 m
Minimum opening	9 x 2 m
Height of grid	17 m (working height 16 m)
Orchestra space	62.50 m²
Lighting control system	Siemens-Bordoni
Number of levers (dimmers)	60
Number of circuits	60
Number of lines (sets)	41 hand-worked
Revolve	12.40 m diameter, can be fitted

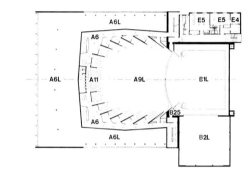

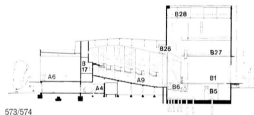

571

572

573/574

570–572
Entrance front, foyer, auditorium

573–574
Upper storey, section

Municipal Theatre, Mönchengladbach

575
Site plan

576–578
View from south, auditorium, foyer

575

The theatre of Mönchengladbach has a charming situation. To get into the town, one has to climb through the outskirts to the top of a hill, where the central area lies. On the edge of the centre, and almost at the entrance to the town, is the theatre. Paul Stohrer was able to exploit the splendid site, adapting the building to the slope with flights of steps and open spaces.

Opened in 1959 and costing 6,5 million marks, the theatre proves, like the Freie Volksbühne, that with comparatively limited means a fully efficient theatre can be built which also fulfils architectural and aesthetic requirements.

Stohrer's aim was to build a small house for a small town, but this has not resulted in a second-rate job. While many theatres simply reflect the architectural fashion of the time, the house at Mönchengladbach still retains its architectonic character.

The light foyer-wing stretches along a contour of the hill, with the auditorium and stage forming a compact complex on the hillside itself and close up to the street. Large glazed surfaces, light wood internal walls, warm brickwork and transparent, open, construction give the building its intrinsic quality.

The theatre is fairly well equipped technically with a wing-stage, a smaller back-stage, a number of stage-wagons and comprehensive lighting.

576

577

578

Municipal Theatre, Mönchengladbach

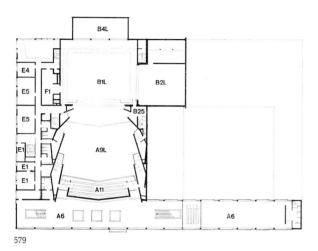

579

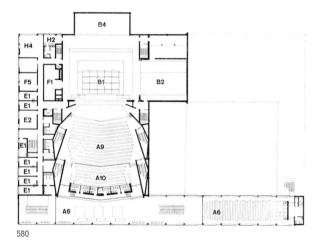

580

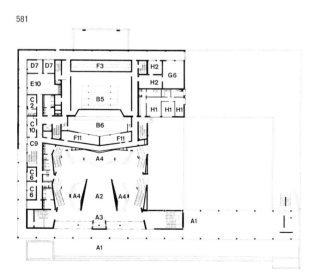

581

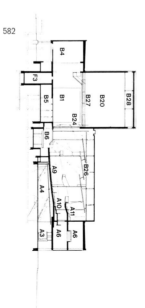

582

Client	Municipality of Mönchengladbach
Artistic categories	opera, operetta, plays
Competition	1955
Period of building	1957–1959
Opening	10. 9. 1959
Architect	Paul Stohrer
Sculptor	Rolf Wagner
Painter	Paul Kamper
Stage technical consultant	Hansing
Acoustics	Reiher
Tests (structure)	Grünastel
Cost	DM 6,500,000
Space enclosed	42,055 m³
Number of seats	794
	stalls 571 + 41 forestage
	+ 16 reserve
	balcony 166
Distance between rows	91 cm
Seat width	46 cm
Fire curtain behind orchestra	
Maximum auditorium width	23.50 m
Maximum auditorium depth	23 m
Greatest distance from stage	stalls 22.60 m
	balcony 25 m
Dimensions of main stage	21.60 x 17.60 m (max. 22.50 m)
Dimensions of right wing-space	13 x 10.90 m
Backstage dimensions	5.70 x 14.80 m
Number of proscenium openings	1
Maximum opening	12 x 8 m
Minimum opening	8 x 8 m
Height of grid	20 m
Orchestra space	98 m²
Lighting control system	Siemens motor-driven
Number of levers (dimmers)	80
Number of circuits	80
Number of lines (sets)	36
Electrically operated	1
Manual	35 + 3 hand-worked winch-sets
	backstage
Stage-wagon dimensions	2 x 12.50 x 4 m
Right wing-space	12.50 x 9.20 m
Backstage	6 x 15 m
Revolve	6 m diameter, mobile
Cyclorama	available

579–582
Balcony floor, stalls floor, ground-floor, section

184

Municipal Theatre, Solingen

Solingen is a scattered town of many separate sections. To link these urban particles, an ambitious community centre has been built with a theatre and large concert hall.

There are few instances, however, which demonstrate so clearly the problem of cultivating the arts in such industrial environments. On a fairly attractive sloping site—above an impressive open flight of steps—stands the large, elongated, structure of the 'House of Culture'.

The long façade, interrupted rather than divided by an entrance hall, is a mere unimaginative succession of glazed bays, hiding behind it an equally monotonous foyer, reached by big ungainly stairs. No architectural consideration has been given to the back of the building, which offers parking space and has a service yard.

The auditorium, with its raked and slightly angled rows of stalls and a balcony which repeats the angular plan, makes a somewhat friendlier impression. The bright, undulating, acoustic ceiling with numerous lines of lights is mildly entertaining.

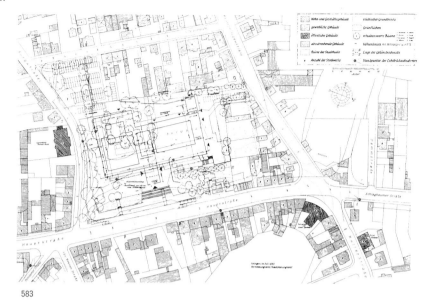

583

583
Site plan

584–586
Entrance side (seen from east), foyer, auditorium

585

584

586

Municipal Theatre, Solingen

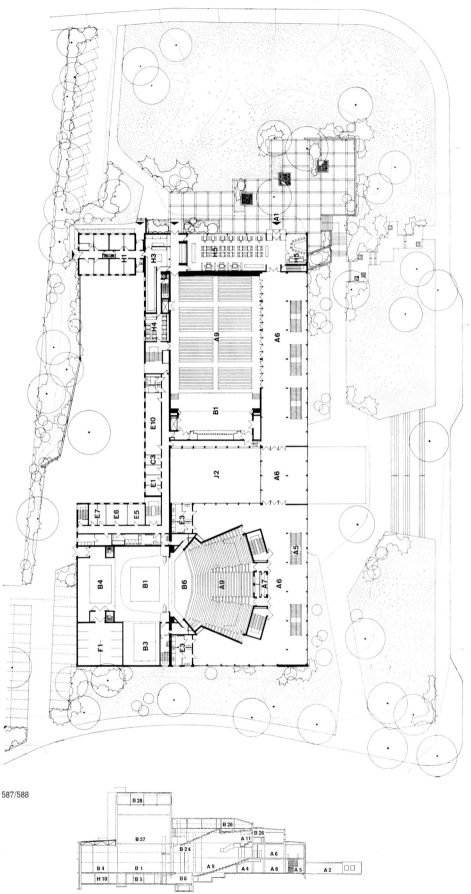

Client	Municipality of Solingen
Artistic categories	guest performances of all kinds
Competition	yes
Period of building	1960–1963
Opening	11. 5. 1963
Architect	Hans Joachim Budeit
Sculptors	Rodewald, Kratz, Dywan
Painter	Schürmann
Theatre consultant	Thomas Münter
Stage technical consultants	Maschinenfabrik Hensel
Structural engineer	Weber
Acoustics	Zeller
Cost	DM 12,900,000
Space enclosed	70,000 m³
Number of seats	811
	stalls 684
	balcony 127
Distance between rows	90 cm
Seat width	55 cm
Fire curtain behind orchestra	
Maximum auditorium width	31.20 m
Maximum auditorium depth	23.95 m
Greatest distance from stage	stalls 24.15 m
	balcony 25.40 m
Dimensions of main stage	20 x 14 m (16.80 m, 21.15 m)
Dimensions of left wing-space	11.80 x 10 m
Backstage dimensions	14 x 9.80 m
Number of proscenium openings	1
Maximum opening	11 x 6.50 m
Minimum opening	8 x 5 m
Height of grid	18.30 m
Orchestra space	156.50 m²
Lighting control system	Siemens-Bordoni
Number of levers (dimmers)	96
Number of circuits	96
Number of lines (sets)	30
Electrically operated	3
Manual-counterweight	27
Stage-wagon dimensions	
Left wing-space and backstage	1.25 x 3.33

587/588

587–588
Principal floor, section

Municipal Theatre, Schweinfurt

589

589
View from south

590
Site plan

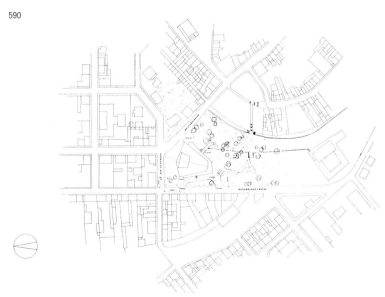

590

The new theatre at Schweinfurt stands in the heart of the old city. As at Ingolstadt, the contrast of old and new is exploited, but in a less pronounced manner.

The spacious Platz der Schwedenschanze made a sizable scheme feasible and, as this is a theatre for touring companies—with a capacity of less than eight hundred seats—the intimate character of the building has also been preserved. The agreeable, gradually ascending, front elevation and roomy foyer belie an auditorium interior, in which decorative effects are paramount. As is so often the case, an attempt has been made to incorporate the acoustic elements in the design, but the cubic sound-diffusing devices at the front of the house, close to the proscenium-opening, divert attention from events on the stage rather than draw attention to them. The glass icicle-like light fittings introduced in the foyer and auditorium are original.

The stage, without wagons or traps, has one wing-stage and a small storage space at the back.

Municipal Theatre, Schweinfurt

591

Client	Municipality of Schweinfurt
Artistic categories	guest performances of all kinds
Period of building	1962–1966
Opening	1. 12. 1966
Architect	Erich Schelling
Sculptor	Trude Karrer
Painter	K. F. Dahmen
Theatre consultant	Hanns Zimmermann
Stage technical consultants	Maschinenfabrik Wiesbaden GmbH (Ltd.)
Structural engineer	Ernst Dorband
Acoustics	Struve, Siemens & Halske AG
Cost	DM 12,000,000
Space enclosed	42,444 m³
Number of seats	785
	stalls and upper stalls 606
	balcony 124
	orchestra pit 55
Distance between rows	90 cm
Seat width	59 cm
Fire curtain behind orchestra	
Maximum auditorium width	25 m
Maximum auditorium depth	24.50 m
Greatest distance from stage	stalls 24.50 m
	balcony 25.40 m
Dimensions of main stage	max. 25 x 16.90 m
Dimensions of right wing-space	16 x 15 m
Number of proscenium openings	1
Maximum opening	12 x 7.50 m
Minimum opening	8 x 4.50 m
Height of grid	17.50 m
Orchestra space	77 m²
Lighting control system	AEG/Strand Electric
Number of levers (dimmers)	104
Number of lines (sets)	37
Electrically operated	6
Manual	31
Counterweight	1
Stage-podia (elevators)	orchestra-podia can be used as forestage

593

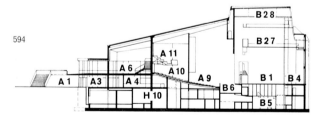

594

592

591–592
Main foyer with stairs to balcony, auditorium

593–594
Principal floor, section

Municipal Playhouse and Festival Theatre, Worms

There are few houses which have been built so strictly to their purpose and within the limitations imposed by local practical possibilities and requirements. The theatre of Worms—a reconstruction—is planned to be used in the normal course of events for widely varying guest-performances by touring companies from the district.

The auditorium is tailored to the size of the town (750 seats to 850 for plays), while the stage is big enough to accommodate more elaborate performances. It is provided with adequate wing-space, but only simple mechanical aids. For example, the lighting is controlled by the traditional switch-board, which can be handled by any troupe; and for the stage, apart from the grid, there is little machinery—which, in any case, is not inevitably associated with the guest-type of theatre.

Externally, the architecture is simple and restrained, with no particularly striking features. It is mostly of the indeterminate sort met with everywhere. The interior, however, has a modest, tranquil gaiety and good proportions. The wide arena-shaped raked stalls, surmounted by a balcony, can be traced back to the original building, which had an interesting stage plan, i.e. the main stage had a broad forestage, entered by two additional portals at the sides. The present stage has adopted the traditional plan with wide proscenium-opening and, in front of the safety-curtain, a forestage.

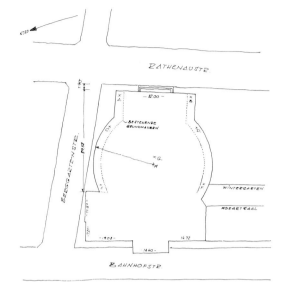

595

Client	City of Worms
Artistic categories	guest performances of all kinds
Period of building	1963–1966
Opening	6. 11. 1966
Architects	City of Worms Architectural Dept., Gernot Heyl in association with Peter Höbel and Heinz Conrad Brinkmann
Sculptor	Gustav Nonnenmacher
Other artists	tapestry: Hermann Kaspar mosaic: Blasius Spreng silver-leaf relief design: Gerhard Pallasch, Rosemarie Pallasch-Fluch glass mosaic frieze: Hilde Gems
Theatre consultants	Thomas Münter, Rudolf Biste
Stage technical consultants	Thomas Münter, Rudolf Biste
Structural engineers	Podgajetz, Rolf Schäfer
Acoustics	Werner Gabler
Tests (structure)	City of Worms, Heinrich Winter

595
Site plan

596
View from south

596

Municipal Playhouse and Festival Theatre, Worms

597

598

597–598
Foyer, view of auditorium and stage

599–600
Principal floor, section

Cost	DM 10,845,000
Space enclosed	47,100 m³
Number of seats	844 with orchestra-stage raised
	stalls 727 (641)
	balcony 117
Distance between rows	91.50–96 m
Seat width	65 cm
Fire curtain behind orchestra	
Maximum auditorium width	c. 27 m
Maximum auditorium depth	c. 23.50 m
Greatest distance from stage	stalls c. 23 m
	balcony c. 23.50 m
Dimensions of main stage	19.20 x 15.30 m (max. 21.30 m)
Dimensions of right wing-space	16.80 x 10.44 m
Backstage dimensions	13.30 x 8 m
Number of proscenium openings	1
Maximum opening	12 x 7.75 m
Minimum opening	8.50 x 5 m
Height of grid	21.48 m
Orchestra space	96 m²
Lighting control system	Siemens & Schuckert AG
Number of levers (dimmers)	120
Number of circuits	120
Number of pre-set possibilities	1 pre-set bank
Number of lines (sets)	
Electrically operated	86 spot, 2 curved-batten,
	1 counterweight
Manual	17 back-cloth
	4 pan-cloth
Counterweight	1
Stage-wagon dimensions	
Right wing-space	2 x 8 x 12 m, divisible into 2 units
	of 4/12 m
	24 x 2 x 1 m
Cyclorama	curved(armed)-batten sets

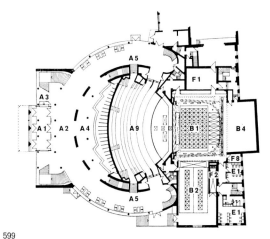

599

600

Pfalzbautheater, Ludwigshafen

There is an old saying that money does not bring happiness, and in connection with theatres one notices constantly that the buildings spoken about are generally those erected with limited financial means (Münster, Ingolstadt, St. Gallen). In Ludwigshafen the new theatre is difficult to justify, for on the other bank of the river—admittedly in another city and province, but within ten minutes' tram-ride—is the Mannheim National Theatre.

But Ludwigshafen, thanks to the profits of the industrial giants, was rich and wanted its own theatre—one for guest-performances. One might reasonably believe that the technical organization could have been harmonized with the neighbouring large house—the Mannheim theatre—to ensure the smooth transfer of performances and in a few guest-presentations, at least the lavish apparatus might have been used. But no; Ludwigshafen built its own house, summoned the Wiesbaden director as ad-

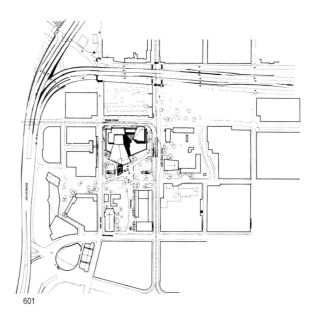

601

601
Site plan

602–603
North view, section

602

603

viser, and in the end concluded a comprehensive guest-performance agreement with Mannheim.

This kind of thing might be overlooked, if in other respects the results were commensurate to the resources expended. But as at Dortmund, so in Ludwigshafen, money was not synonymous with good taste. Certainly the building, which has to serve many purposes and, as well as the theatre, contains several halls and a restaurant, is logically arranged, and the relationship between individual rooms is well balanced; but the rooms themselves are not so happily contrived. While the balcony foyers, spaciously planned, seem low and cramped, the smoking-foyer rises through three storeys.

Nothing has been spared on the décor: the most costly colour schemes, art exploited everywhere, and every item as expensive as possible—proof that he who has all can do all—but theatres are hardly created this way.

The stage is equipped with a generous wing-space and back-stage, complete with under-stage machinery and revolve. The lighting has a very efficient control-system.

191

Pfalzbautheater, Ludwigshafen

604

605/606

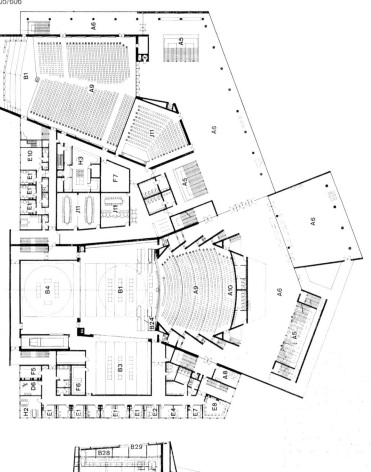

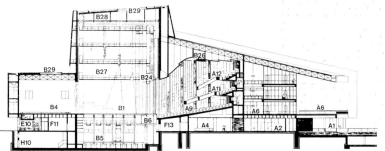

Client	City of Ludwigshafen
Artistic categories	opera, operetta, plays
Competition	1960
Period of building	1963—1968
Opening	21. 9. 1968
Architects	Alfred Koch, Edwin Steinhauer, Günter Nörling, Gerhard Troitzsch
Artists	Ernst W. Kunz, Blasius Spreng, A. Gangkofner
Theatre consultant	Helmut Drese
Stage technical consultant	Hanspeter Sajak, M.A.N.
Structural engineer	Fritz Spiegel
Acoustics	Karlhans Weisse
Tests (structure)	Adolf Ruhl
Cost	DM 33,000,000
Space enclosed	148,766.50 m³
Number of seats	1175
	stalls 786
	1st balcony 194
	2nd balcony 195
Distance between rows	90 cm
Seat width	distance between axes 53—63 cm (balconies)
Fire curtain in front of orchestra	
Maximum auditorium width	22.96 m
Maximum auditorium depth	23.90 m
Greatest distance from stage	stalls 24.75 m
	1st balcony 28.20 m
	2nd balcony 31.50 m
Dimensions of main stage	26 (at back 24) x 21.18 m
Dimensions of left wing-space	15 x 17.76 m
Backstage dimensions	19.55 x 15.54 m
Number of proscenium openings	1
Maximum opening	14 x 8 m
Minimum opening	8 x 6 m
Height of grid	25 m
Orchestra space	82 m²
Lighting control system	magnetic-amplifier
Number of levers (dimmers)	200
Number of circuits	200
Number of lines (sets)	56
Electrically operated	5
Manual	51
Pan-cloth	2
Counterweight	12
Stage-wagon dimensions	
Backstage	14 x 14 m
Revolve	13 m diameter, in backstage-wagon
Dimensions of stage-podia (elevators)	orchestra-podium 14 x 3.50 m and 14 x 3 m
	3 others 3 x 14 m
	2 others 2.50 x 14 m
Limits of travel	—3 to + 3 m
Cyclorama	available

604
View of auditorium from stage

605—606
Principal floor, section

Municipal Theatre, Rüsselsheim

The Rüsselsheim town theatre, too, is a typical guest-performance house in a town which has grown up round an automobile factory. In a purely industrial community of this kind, a theatre is a social catalyst. Stage-house and auditorium are linked together in a large oval, from which the front segment has been cut off. Here the wide glazed façade of the foyer opens on to a green open space. The roof slopes down continuously to the foyer, checked only by the short counter-movement of the auditorium fume-vent structure. A small management and stage-office wing is annexed to the back.

The auditorium preserves a sense of intimacy, with 821 seats, of which about 200 are disposed in a wide-embracing balcony.

The safety-curtain is placed behind the orchestra-pit, resulting in a comparatively extensive forestage, which will cause some problems when plays are presented. The stage has no wing-spaces, but an ample backstage. A wagon with a built-in revolve is planned for a later phase of building.

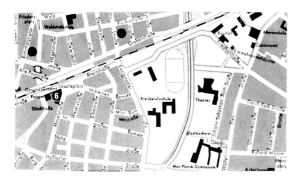

607

608

609

607
Site plan

608–609
Entrance front, view of auditorium and stage

Municipal Theatre, Rüsselsheim

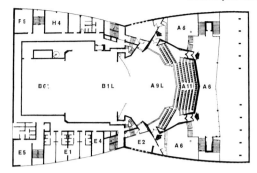

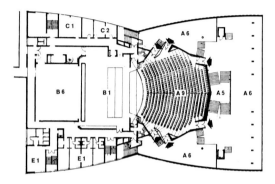

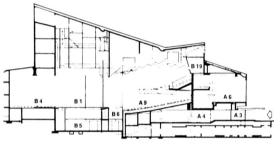

610–612
Balcony floor, main floor, section

Client	Municipality of Rüsselsheim
Artistic categories	opera, operetta, concerts, plays
Period of building	1965–1969
Opening	6. 9. 1969
Architects	Borough of Rüsselsheim Architectural Dept., Chief Architect Otto; design by Dietrich Hirsch
Painter	Dieter Ritzert
Theatre consultant	Adolf Zotzmann
Stage technical consultant	Adolf Zotzmann
Structural engineer	Peter Knodt
Acoustics	Hermann Schäcke
Tests (structure)	W. Fuchssteiner
Cost	c. DM 13,000,000
Space enclosed	49,000 m³
Number of seats	865
	stalls 670
	balcony 195
Distance between rows	86 cm
Seat width	52 cm
Fire curtain behind orchestra	
Maximum auditorium width	23 m
Maximum auditorium depth	23 m
Greatest distance from stage	stalls 23.20 m
	balcony 24.20 m
Dimensions of main stage	14 x 11.60 m (max. 19 m)
Backstage dimensions	15 x 12 m
Number of proscenium openings	1
Maximum opening	13.20 x 7.50 m
Minimum opening	9.50 x 4.50 m
Height of grid	18.90 m
Orchestra space	65 m²
Lighting control system	ADB
Number of levers (dimmers)	100, with pre-set equipment
Number of circuits	120
Number of line-sets	32
Electrically operated	2
Manual	28
Counterweight	1
	4 winch-operated
Stage-wagon dimensions	
Backstage	1 x 2 m
Dimensions of stage-podia (elevators)	14 x 2 m
Limits of travel	—1 to + 3 m
Cyclorama	available

Designs not yet Executed

Essen Opera House

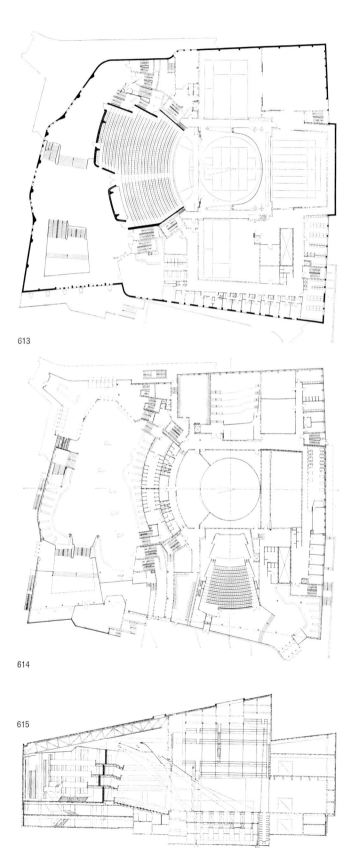

613

614

615

This section consists of theatres for which designs suitable for building exist, but which on various grounds have been abandoned or postponed, and those for which designs have just been completed and are now in process of realization.

The oldest project of this group is Alvar Aalto's for a new opera house at Essen. As far back as 1959, a competition was organized and financed by a private consortium of wealthy patrons. Aalto was awarded the first prize, but only ten years later, in 1969, the town council decided to build the new opera house.

The design aroused great interest from the beginning, because of the convincing way in which the auditorium and the fly-tower are linked together. The roof rises from the auditorium in a vast slope—the pitch is steeper in the final version than in the competition entry. Thus the entire complex is moulded into a uniform block, varied only by a lower structure on the side of the left wing-stage. The original vigorously curved plan was largely straightened out in the subsequent design in order to improve the interior, but much of the lively grace of the first scheme has been retained. The auditorium is divided into two sections: the larger, deeply receding and slightly staggered on plan; the other, smaller and more intimate. The stage is constructed as a big wagon-stage, with three large subsidiary stages, and an extremely flexible proscenium opening.

Alvar Aalto: Opera House Essen
Competition 1959, final version approved for building 1969

613–615
Main stage floor, entrance floor, section

616
Photo of model: north-west side

616

Zürich Opera House

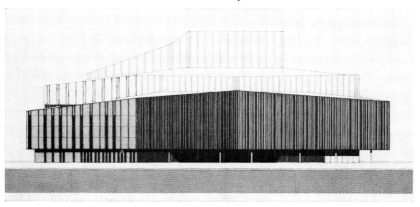

617

In 1961, on the basis of a competition held by the city of Zürich, the Swiss architect, W. Dunkel, was commissioned to develop further his design for the Zürcher Stadttheater, home of the Zürich opera. The classical building by Fellner and Helmer (1891), beautifully sited on the lakeshore, of course already existed, but it no longer answered present-day needs as a modern opera house.

The new scheme makes conspicuous use of the lakeside site. The house is planned as a spacious balcony-theatre; the stage has been laid out as a large wagon-stage with three subsidiary stages; the workshops are outside and separate. Unfortunately, there is no hope of the design being realized for the time being, as new traffic regulations concern the opera house area, and until these have been finally clarified, work on the opera project is inevitably postponed.

618

Zürich Opera House

W. Dunkel in collaboration with Jos. Stutz and W. Schindler:
Opera House Zürich
Competition 1961, further design studies, position at spring 1970

617
West side

618—619
Photos of model: auditorium and foyer

620—621
First balcony level, section

619

620

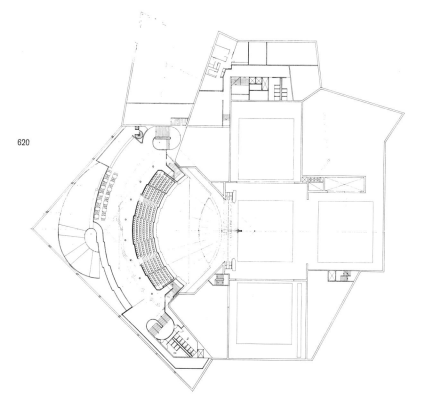

621

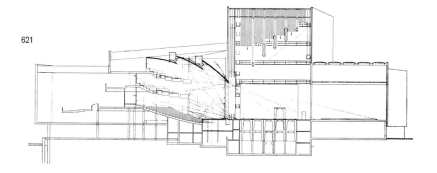

Zürich Opera House / Playhouse

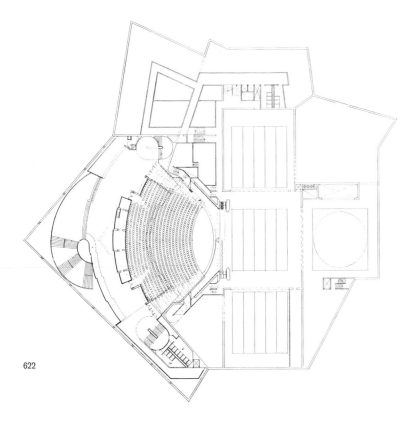

622

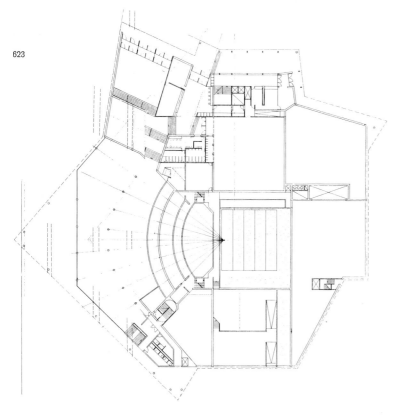

623

The same consideration applies to the proposals for the Zürich playhouse, which have been carried much further. After the first prize had been won by Jørn Utzon in the 1963 competition, his design was examined in close collaboration with the theatre authorities in relation to the building's specific needs, and these studies had proceeded to the extent that the scheme was ready for submission for final approval.

Utzon's design offers an ingenious solution to the awkward traffic situation with a spacious raised forecourt, enabling vehicles to circulate freely beneath. An equally spacious, gradually evolving sequence of foyers precedes the auditorium, which is planned as a balcony-theatre.

The stage-section can be opened wide by means of mobile proscenium-wings, the stage proper being designed as a wagon-stage with back and wing stages, the left one reduced to a roomy storage space. The roof of the fly-tower is steeply inclined, so that its front edge is raised only slightly above the multi-undulations on top of the foyers.

Jørn Utzon: Zürich Playhouse
Competition 1963, further design studies, position in spring 1970

624–625
First floor, photo of model

622–623
Principal floor, foyer gallery

Zürich Playhouse

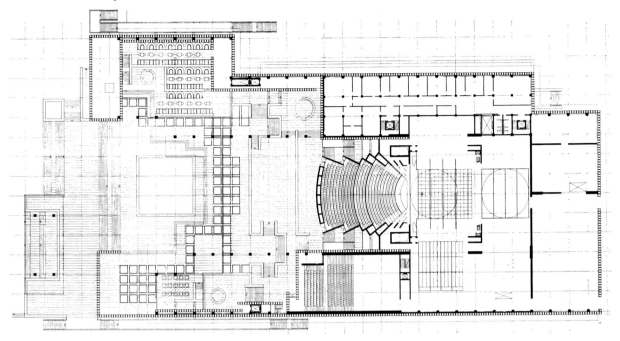

624

625

201

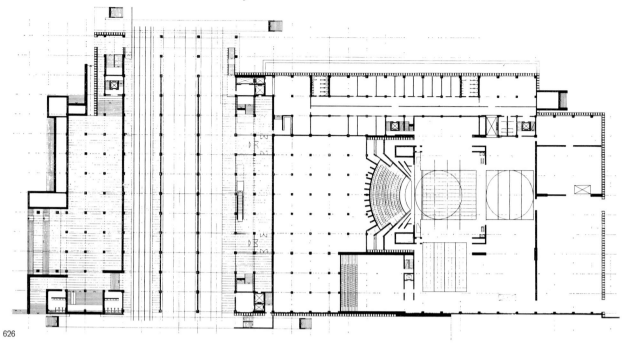

626

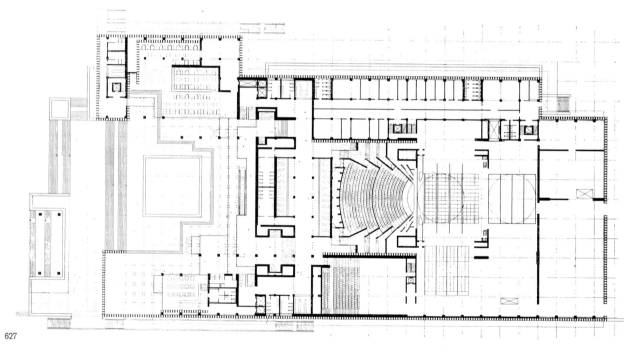

627

626–628
Basement, ground-floor, section

628

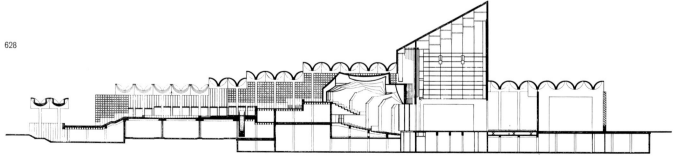

Badisches Staatstheater, Karlsruhe

629

The project for the Baden state theatre in Karlsruhe has had a chequered career. In 1959—60 a competition was held for a new theatre to be built on a site close to the castle (Schloss), for which Paul Baumgarten evolved a scheme comprising five 'round' polygons. In the end, however, it was decided to use this site for the Federal court building, and not for the theatre, which was now to be erected somewhat further away from the historic town centre. Baumgarten did not feel in a position to transfer his design to the new position, and as he had been appointed architect for the court building, a second competition for the theatre was announced in 1963. Helmut Bätzner was awarded the commission and invited to develop his proposals. After protracted and detailed study, however, the scheme was shelved owing to financial difficulties. But in 1969 the town council decided to revive it and the project was subjected to further revision.

Paul Baumgarten: Badisches Staatstheater, Karlsruhe

629
Competition design 1960

Helmut Bätzner: Badisches Staatstheater, Karlsruhe
Competition 1963, final version approved for building 1969

630
Photo of model: west side

630

Badisches Staatstheater, Karlsruhe

The theatre is to have two houses, the larger with one thousand seats and the smaller with three hundred and fifty. The auditoria converge at an angle of sixty degrees and form in the stage area a single interrelated players' complex.

Here in Karlsruhe the Frankfurt stage plan, with its huge turntable-stage carrying an in-built smaller revolve (in this instance, centrally placed), has been adopted for the first time. The foyer is fanned wide out by the angular plan, with stairs opening on to various levels so that an impression of great spaciousness results.

The work of revision chiefly affects the small house, which is conceived as a one-room theatre. The conventional confrontation of audience and players is admittedly still apparent, but the house is infinitely flexible. The stage can be thrust out arena-like into the audience, or a hexagonal central stage can be used with the audience grouped on the surrounding podia. The whole ceiling is equipped for technical and mechanical exploitation.

631–632
Photos of model: auditorium

633
Section through large house

631

632

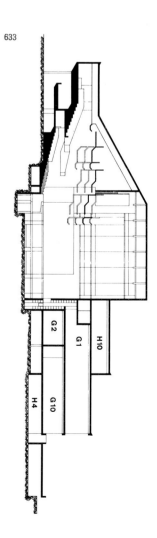

633

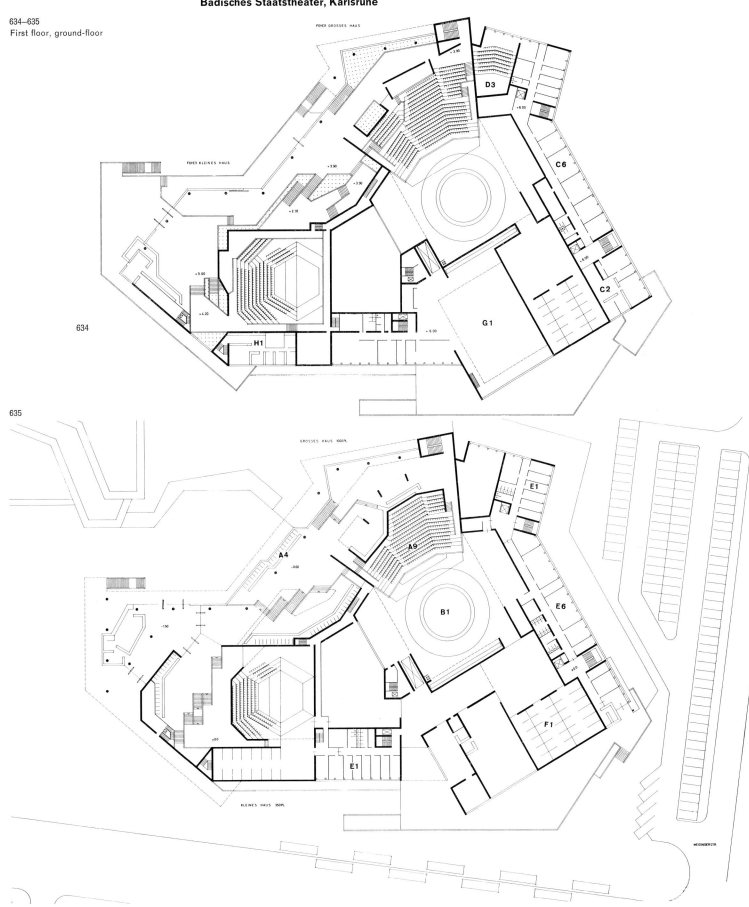

634

635

Municipal Theatre, Münster

636

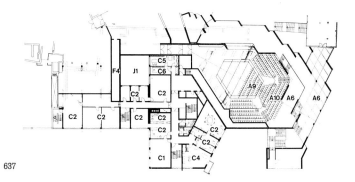

637

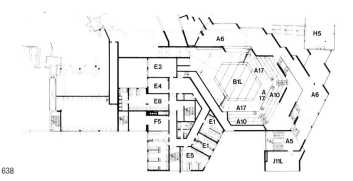

638

639

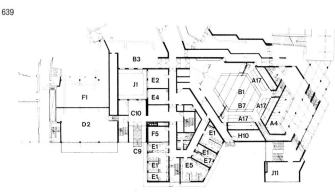

640

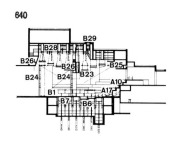

Lack of funds has continued to obstruct the completion of the municipal theatre at Münster. The building already erected (by architects Harald Deilmann, Ortwin Rave, Werner Ruhnau and Max von Hausen) comprised only a minimal programme (see page 109 et seq.), namely the auditorium and stagehouse, in which the building of the left wing-space was not provided for until a later stage. It is true that workshops and scene-stores were built in a second phase, but the complex of production and management offices and rehearsal rooms, as well as a very versatile studio remain projects, so that the theatre has to be satisfied with makeshift facilities in crucial spheres.

The studio has already been considered in the previous section (see page 79). It could be used in many different ways to suit the specialized cultural needs of a small university town, and we have previously alluded to the advantage of its particular adaptability to simple transformations. For the progressive theatre, too, it would open up many new possibilities, which unhappily are now impossible to test.

Municipal Theatre, Münster

Max C. von Hausen, Ortwin Rave, Werner Ruhnau: Municipal Theatre, Münster, 2nd and 3rd phases, 1966

637–640
Second floor, first floor, ground-floor, section

636, 641
Photos of models

642–643 a
Seating plans (1:500)

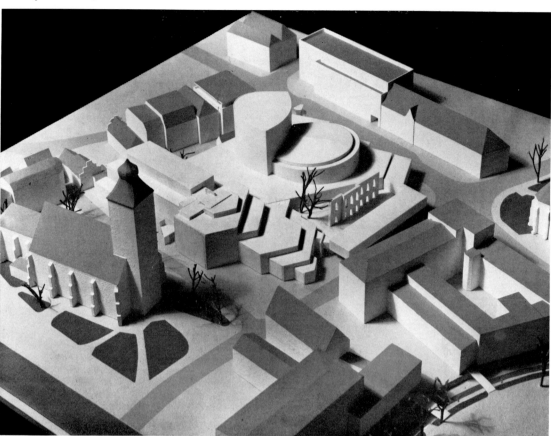

641

642–643 a

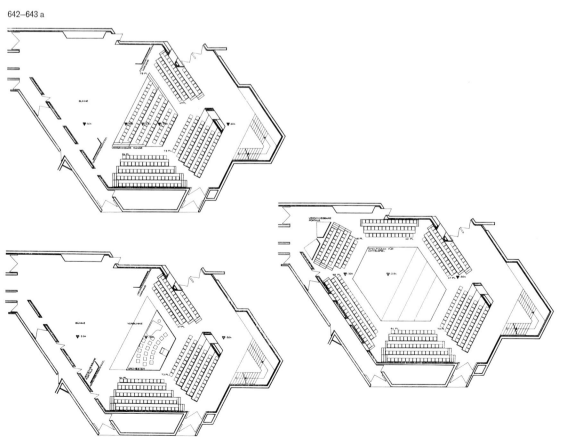

City Theatre, Basle

A representative new building for the city theatre in Basle (opera, playhouse, ballet) is under construction. The early history of this competition was also long and chequered. In the second stage, held at the end of 1964, architects Felix Schwarz and Rolf Gutmann were awarded the first prize and entrusted with elaborating the final design (which is now taking shape).

The architectural form is inevitably influenced by the immediate proximity of the Elisabethenkirche. The architects have avoided a too emphatic counterpoint, interpreting the fly-tower not as the antipole of the church tower, but linking auditorium and stagehouse with an upward-curving roof. The building is planned as an open angle, and has no overwhelming effect on the church.

The dimensions—in contrast to many German houses planned at the beginning of the sixties—are not excessive and have taken into consideration the problem, recently apparent, of filling and financing overlarge theatres. The large house has 950 seats, the small 300. The auditorium and stage lie in one axis of the complex, with workshops and scene-stores concentrated in the right angle. The stage is designed as a wagon-stage, with left-hand wing-space and backstage.

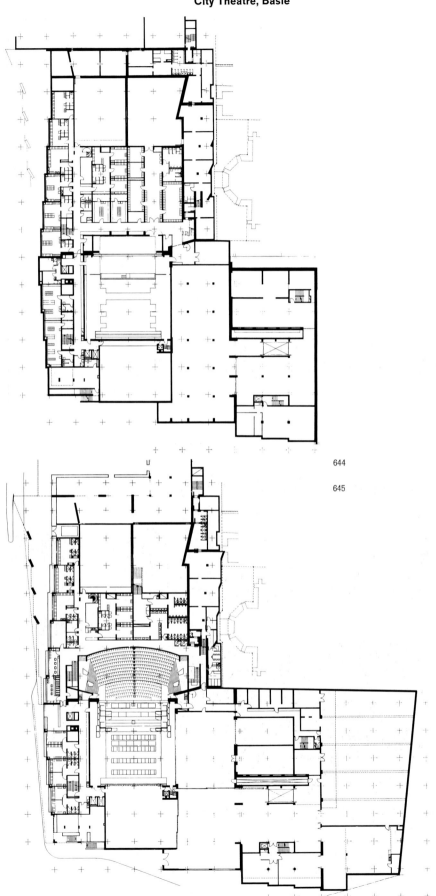

644

645

646

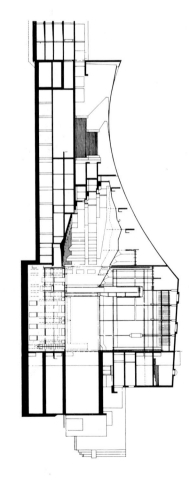

Frank Gloor, Rolf Gutmann, Felix Schwarz:
City Theatre, Basle
Competition 1964, design approved for
building 1968

644—646
Basement, ground-floor, section

647—648
Photos of models: south-east side, auditorium

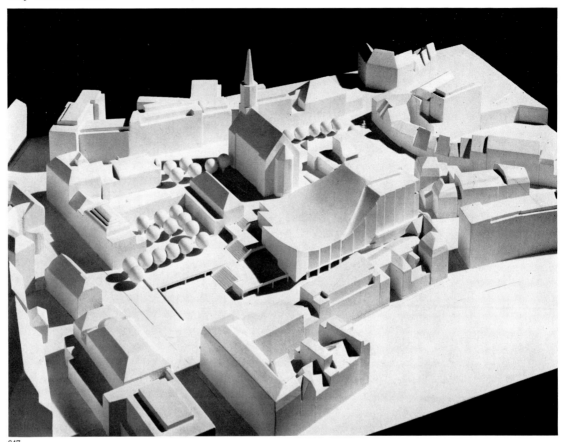

647

648

Town Theatre, Winterthur/Switzerland

Frank Krayenbühl: Town Theatre, Winterthur
Competitions 1966 and 1968, design approved for building 1968

649—651
First floor, ground-floor, section

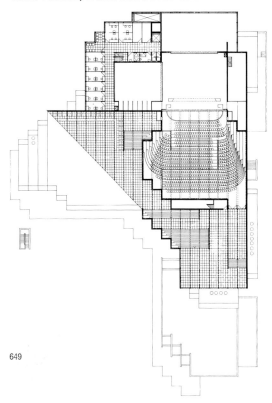

649

At Winterthur, after a three-stage competition prepared and assessed with extraordinary care, the scheme of Frank Krayenbühl was accepted in 1968. The thoroughness with which the competition was carried out meant that the final designs presented projects which were already almost ready for tender. Krayenbühl's is another angle layout, but without the pivot being, as at Basle, the stage area. Here the auditorium is the centre, from which radiate two spacious foyers with box offices and cloakrooms and a theatre-café. Behind extends the massive block of the stage-house and artists' dressing-rooms. Scene-store and workshop facilities are very modest, for the Winterthur theatre is exclusively played by visiting companies.

The external form of the building, immediately conspicuous for its angular shape, is unusual. In architectural mass, the theatre comprises three slightly irregular blocks rising on a north-south axis to the

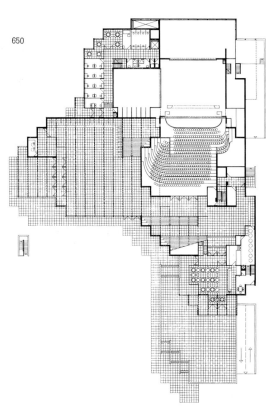

650

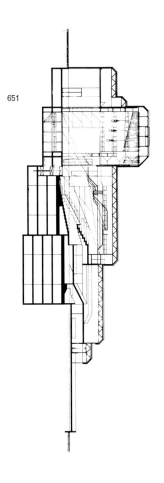

651

Town Theatre, Winterthur/Switzerland

fly-tower, each block terminating in a series of stair-
like steps on the east side. The auditorium is asym-
metrically planned and surmounted by a balcony extending deep into the room on one side. The stage
is equipped with a backstage and wing-space to the
left. The main stage is trapped.

652
Photo of model from south

652

653

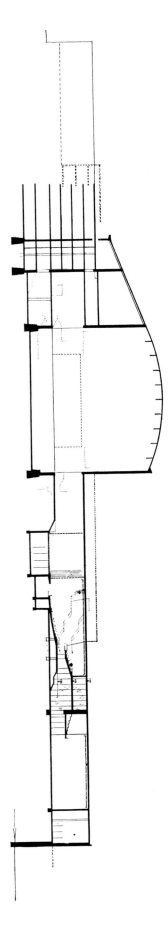

Hans Scharoun: Competition design for Kassel State Theatre, 1951

653
Photo of model

654–655
Sections

656–657
Stage floor, balcony floor

In the fifties, the theatre projects of Hans Scharoun attracted much lively discussion. The scrapping of his work on the Staatstheater at Kassel (later built under other direction—see page 128 et seq.) amounted to a scandal, and we publish here his Kassel designs of 1951, because they reflect the essence of his architectural philosophy of the period. Scharoun had planned an entire theatrescape, which stood in direct relation to the site above the Karlsaue on the edge of the Friedrichsplatz. From three sides the architectural volumes climb gradually towards the fly-tower, which in its turn has multitudinous connections with the building as a whole. The stage has an extremely wide proscenium opening, calculated to minimize the separation of players and audience; but this type of 'Cinerama' stage has not worked well in practice, because the action evolves too much in breadth and consequently the sense of dramatic suspense is lost.

654

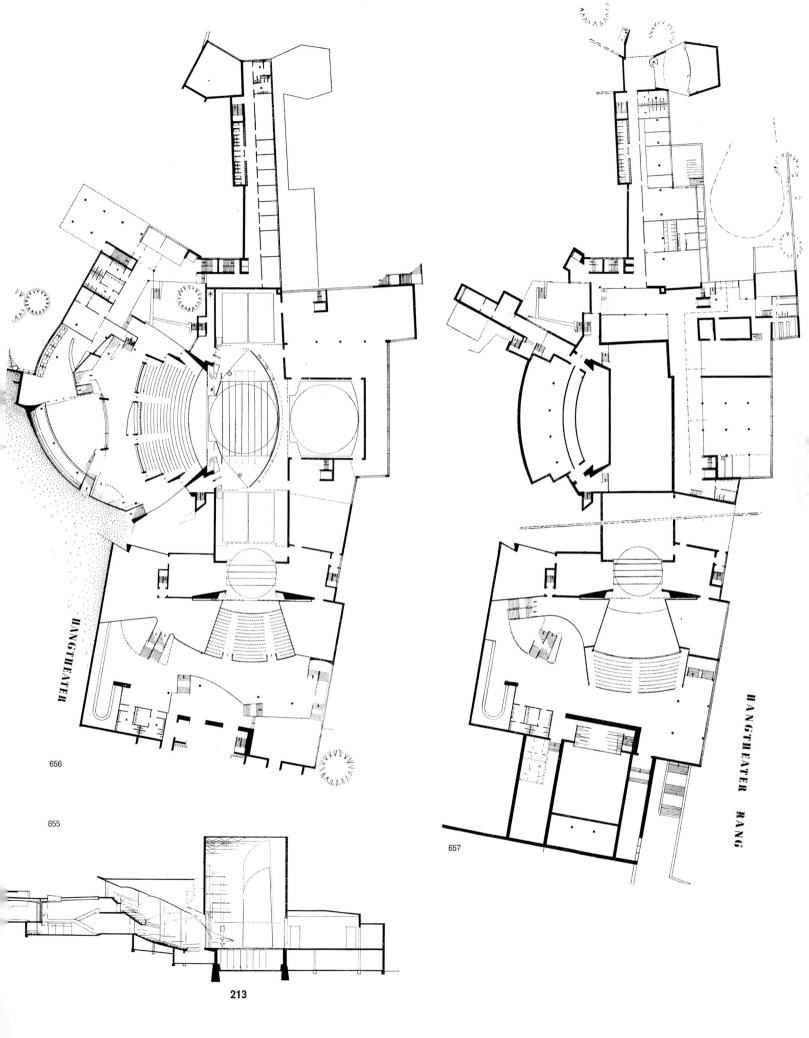

656

655

657

Municipal Theatre, Wolfsburg

Hans Scharoun: Municipal Theatre,
Wolfsburg
Competition 1968, design approved for
building 1969

658–660
Balcony floor, ground-floor, section

661–662
Photos of models: north side, auditorium

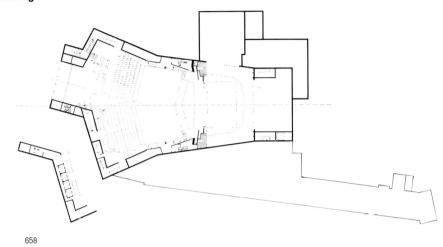

658

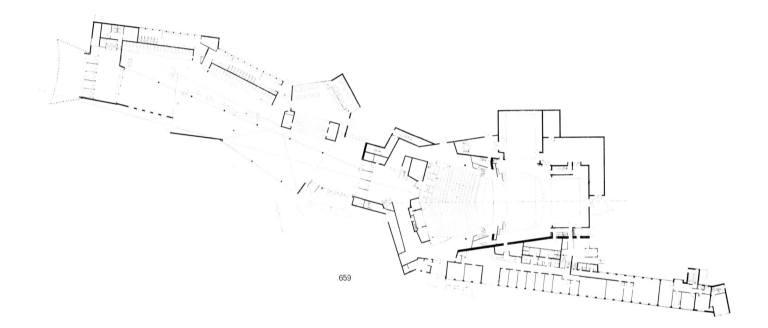

659

660

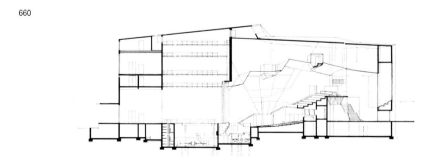

661

662

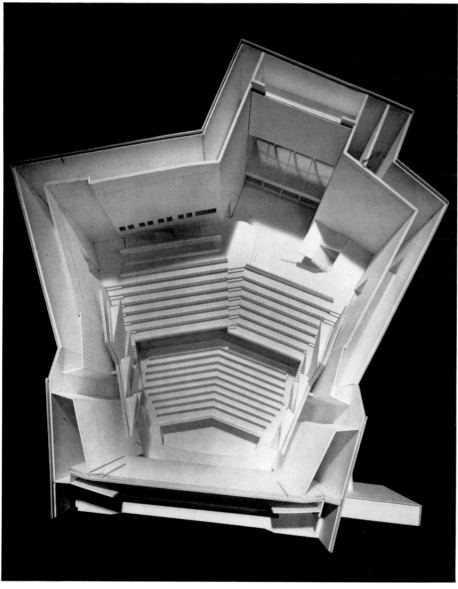

More than fifteen years elapsed between the Kassel project and the designs for Wolfsburg. Scharoun was awarded first prize in a competition held in 1968 and the following year was commissioned to build. The vicinity of Aalto's interesting community centre was certainly a happy choice. The site is on the edge of a wood, and Scharoun deliberately exploits the trees as background scenery to his scheme. Two elongated buildings stretch like great tentacles into the country-side, the low 'tract' of the foyer and the two-storey dressing-room and management wing. Between them stand the high blocks of the auditorium and the stage-house. The contrast in heights is intentionally stressed as in no other theatre design. Elsewhere the aim has been to conceal the height of the fly-tower, but Scharoun uses it as the distinguishing feature of his theatre.

The house is relatively intimate in character and tailored to the size of the town and district. Wolfsburg, too, is a guest-performance theatre without large workshop and scenic construction resources of its own. With the close proximity of the Braunschweig theatre, there would be little advantage in a resident company.

In comparison with Scharoun's earlier theatre designs, the stage is remarkably conventional. Its guest-performance use precluded automatically the development of individuality in staging. Thus the stage is not of the wide 'cinemascope' type, but breadth and depth enjoy a normal mutual relationship (39 x 26 feet). The safety curtain is behind the orchestra-pit and forms a fairly extensive 'buffer' zone.

Hanover Playhouse

At Hanover, after much—hotly disputed—toing and froing, a protracted period of planning and a second competition, a decision over the new playhouse was finally taken in 1969. Claude Paillard, architect of the St. Gallen theatre, was given the job. His lively

663

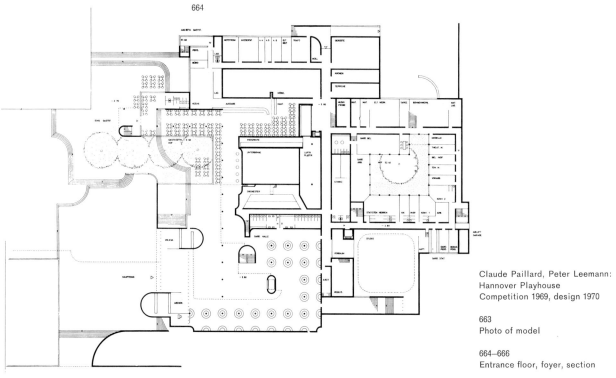

664

Claude Paillard, Peter Leemann:
Hannover Playhouse
Competition 1969, design 1970

663
Photo of model

664—666
Entrance floor, foyer, section

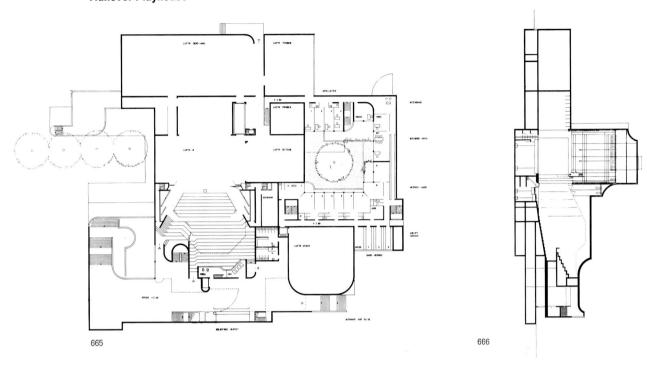

665

666

solution was preferred to a design, in many respects more conventional but one more consistently worked out, by Dieter Oesterlen.

The boom in German theatre-building is undoubtedly over. The theatres which are now being erected are inevitably much smaller than in the fifties and early sixties. The enormous houses, faced with a very wide choice of entertainments for leisure (television is not the theatre's only rival; week-end excursions, for instance, are another), can no longer be filled. In addition, the larger theatrical enterprises absorb such heavy subsidies on upkeep that the municipal and provincial authorities are today neither willing nor able to maintain them. Already quality is often sacrificed to quantity. Events like those at Darmstadt are not untypical. The large double scheme with its two houses was planned in the early 1960s, and will be finished at the beginning of the seventies. But, during the discussions over the appointment of a director, the possibility was seriously

considered of getting the Wiesbadener Staatstheater to take charge of opera. Yet the amalgamation of the Bochum and Gelsenkirchen theatres has not resulted in an increase in the number of playgoers, nor in reduced costs. A rationalized approach to theatre capacity will clearly be imperative in the future.

Switzerland still lags behind in theatre-building. Smaller communities, like St. Gallen and Winterthur, have taken a lead, and at Basle a new house is under construction; but in Zürich—notably in the case of the playhouse—very complete plans have been shelved, because of the prior claim of a new traffic system. Both theatres, moreover, are out of date to the extent that it is hard to put into practice conceptions which correspond to the standards reached by the two houses in the war. However slight a comprehensive technical armoury may be as a guarantee for the quality of the performance, it is bound to offer the essential minimum of tools for the purpose.

Bibliography

Books

Aloi, Roberto: Architetture per lo spettacolo, Milan 1958

Graubner, Gerhard: Theaterbau – Aufgabe und Planung, Munich 1968

Hollatz, J. W.: Das neue Essener Opernhaus – Wollen und Werden, Essen 1964

Job, Heinrich / Ostertag, Roland: Theater für morgen, Projekt Vol. 8, Stuttgart 1969

Kallmorgen, Werner: Theater heute, Darmstadt 1954

Kranich, Friedrich: Bühnentechnik der Gegenwart, 2 Vols., Munich/ Berlin 1929

Maisons de la Culture – Amiens/Grenoble/Rennes, Paris

Modern Architecture in Germany – Theaterbau in Deutschland nach 1945, Ed.: Institut für Auslandsbeziehungen, Stuttgart

Münz, Ludwig / Künstler, Gustav: Der Architekt Adolf Loos, Munich 1964. English edition, London 1966

Ruhnau, Werner / Kriwet, Ferdinand: Multiperspektivisches Theater–Mixed Media, Freunde neuer Kunst Dortmund, Museum am Ostwall, Dortmund 1968

Southern, Richard: Seven Ages of Theatre, London 1962

Stäubli, Willy: Brasilia, Stuttgart 1965

Theater, Darmstädter Gespräch 1955, Darmstadt 1955

Veinstein, André: Le théâtre expérimental, Paris 1968

Special (and Commemorative) Publications

Wettbewerb für den Neubau des Stadttheaters Basel, 1964

Deutsche Oper Berlin – Zur festlichen Eröffnung des Hauses, 1961

Schauspielhaus Bochum – Festschrift zur Eröffnung, 1953

Bonn Center, 1969

Theaterneubau Bonn, 1965

A Budapesti Nemzeti Szinház Tervpályázata, 1965

Theaterbau Dortmund, 1966

1832–1970 – Eine Dokumentation über das Düsseldorfer Schauspielhaus, 1969

Ideenwettbewerb für den Neubau eines Opernhauses in Essen, 1959

Stadttheater Ingolstadt, 1966

Istanbul Kültür Sarayi, 1969

Das neue Staatstheater Kassel – Festschrift zur Eröffnung der neuen Häuser am 12. und 13. September 1959

Die Technik im Großen Haus der Bühnen der Stadt Köln, 1957

Festschrift zur Eröffnung des Stadttheaters Krefeld, 1952

Stadttheater Krefeld, 1963

Neuer Pfalzbau Ludwigshafen am Rhein, 1968

Malmö Stadsteater – Malmö's Municipal Theatre, 1944

Das neue Theater in Münster, 1956

Recklinghausen – Zur Eröffnung des Festspielhauses 11. Juni 1965

Stadttheater Rüsselsheim, 1969

Das neue Salzburger Festspielhaus, 1960

Festschrift der Württembergischen Staatstheater Stuttgart, 1962

Theater der Stadt Trier, 1964

Ulmer Theater – Neubau 1969

Das Ulmer Theater im neuen Haus, Sonderbeilage der Südwestpresse, 1969

Städtisches Spiel- und Festhaus Worms – Einweihung des wiederaufgebauten Hauses am 6. November 1966

Informationen Schauspielhaus der Stadt Wuppertal, 1966

Stadttheater Würzburg – Festschrift, 1966

Periodicals

In addition, the following periodicals have been scrutinized for this book, so far as they have been available in libraries. When no individual numbers are given, the annual volumes from 1950 were examined:

L'architecture d'aujourd'hui, Boulogne-sur-Seine

Architectural Forum, New York

Architectural Record, New York

The Architectural Review, London

Der Architekt, Essen

Architektur und Wohnform, Stuttgart

architektur wettbewerbe, Stuttgart

Architektura CSSR, Prague

Ark – Arkkitehti, Helsinki

Architekten, Copenhagen

Arkitektur, Stockholm

Baukunst und Werkform, Nürnberg

Baumeister, No. 3/1969, Munich

Bauwelt, Berlin

Bochum baut, Schauspielhaus Bochum, 1953

Bouw, Rotterdam

Bouwcentrum, No. A 11.4/1958, Rotterdam

Bühnentechnische Rundschau, Berlin

Building, London

Darstellung plus Technik, Würzburg

Deutsche Bauzeitschrift, Gütersloh

Deutsche Bauzeitung, Stuttgart

Internationale Lichtrundschau, Amsterdam

Merkblätter über sachgemäße Stahlverwendung, No. 289: Stahlkonstruktionen im Theaterbau, Düsseldorf

Norske architektenkonkurranser, No. 138/1967, Oslo

RIBA Journal, May 1963, London

sar:s tävlingsblad, Stockholm

Schweizerische Bauzeitung, Zürich

The Structural Engineer, March 1969, London

Werk, Winterthur

Index of Names

The numbers in standard type give the pages on which the relevant name is mentioned. Those in bold type refer to the pages on which the theatres designed by a particular architect are illustrated.

The names of technical experts, artists, etc., quoted in the Documentation section (p. 92 et seq.) under technical data, are not included in this list.

Index of Names

221

Photographic Credits

Sources of illustrations, so far as can be ascertained:
Number

4	Ullstein-Bilderdienst, Berlin	502	Sigrid Neubert, Munich
81	Simo Rista, Helsinki	503	Helmut Bauer, Ingolstadt
85	Hedrich-Blessing, Chicago	504	Stichting 'Prometheus', Amsterdam
94	Pius Rast, St. Gallen	505	Donau-Kurier, Ingolstadt
108	Behr, London	508–510	Romain Urhausen
109	Robert Kirkman	514	A. Sickert, Innsbruck
116, 119	Wm. J. Toomey	515	Erich F. Birbaumer, Innsbruck
122	Allan Hurst	519	Pius Rast, St. Gallen
124–127	Mann Brothers, London	521–522	F. Mauersberg, Zürich
128–130	Colin Westwood, London	523	Pius Rast, Zürich
151	Martti I. Jaatinen, Helsinki	528–533	Manfred Hanisch, Essen
152–153	Jouko Könönen, Helsinki	548	Stadtarchiv, Ulm
182	Pawel Mystkowski, Warsaw	549	Wilhelm Pabst, Holzhausen
183	Jan Siudecki, Warsaw	550–551	Stadtarchiv, Ulm
185	Jerzy Piasecki, Warsaw	552–553	Wilhelm Pabst, Holzhausen
186	ZAIKS	554–560	Siegel, Ulm
190	Jerzy Piasecki, Warsaw	565–566, 569	Kessler, Berlin
200–201	Jan Regal, Gottwaldow	570	Bodo Niederprüm, Remscheid
206	Bob Serating, New York	571–572	Rudolf Dodenhoff, Worpswede
207	Katrina Thomas, New York	576	Dülberg, Soest
215–216	Ezra Stoller, Mamaroneck	577–578	Bodo Niederprüm, Remscheid
219	Louis Checkman	589, 592	Robert Ruthardt, Karlsruhe
220–221	Ezra Stoller, Mamaroneck	596–597	Helmut Hertel, Worms
252	Lois M. Bowen, Cambridge/Mass.	598	Helga Günther, Wiesloch
253	Clemens Kalischer, Stockbridge	602–604	Robert Häusser, Mannheim
269–270	Young + Richardson, Sydney (Beton-Verlag, Düsseldorf)	608–609	Lang, Rüsselsheim
272–273	Panda Ass., Toronto	625	Häussler, Zürich
276, 279	H. R. Jowett, Willowdale	629	Robert Ruthardt, Karlsruhe
280–281	Roger Jowett, Willowdale	631	Manfred Schaeffer, Karlsruhe
303–304, 306–307	Eberhard Troeger, Hamburg	636	Dieter Rensing, Münster
312–313	Ursula Seitz, Frankfurt	647–648	Peter Grünert, Zürich
314	Seitz-Gray, Frankfurt	652	Michael Speich, Winterthur
315	Ursula Seitz, Frankfurt	653	Walter Köster, Berlin
316	Ulfert Beckert, Offenbach	661	Heidersberger, Wolfsburg
324	Schmölz & Ullrich, Cologne	663	Hans Wagner, Hanover
325–326	Rudolf Dodenhoff, Worpswede		
323	Stadt Bochum, Presseamt, No. 2670/66		
333–334	Stadt Bochum, Presseamt		
339, 341	Eberhard Troeger, Hamburg		
342	Hamburgische Staatsoper, Bildarchiv		
343	Eberhard Troeger, Hamburg		
348–349	Fred Waldvogel, Zollikon		
350	Max Hellstern, Zürich		
351	Fred Waldvogel, Zollikon		
354	Plan und Karte GmbH, Münster, No. P. K. 712		
355–356, 361–363	W. Heller, Telgte		
364	De Sandalo, Frankfurt		
366	Dr. Salchow, Cologne		
367–368	Hugo Schmölz, Cologne		
369–371	Schmölz & Ullrich KG, Cologne		
377–378	Robert Häusser, Mannheim		
379, 381	Artur Pfau, Mannheim		
382–384	Robert Häusser, Mannheim		
394	Martin Schindolar, Linz		
395	Lucca Chmel, Vienna		
396	Martin Schindolar, Linz		
402	Gregor Stühler, Bochum		
405	Moegenburg, Leverkusen		
415	Günther Becker, Kassel		
417–418	H. Urbschat – H.-J. Fischer, Berlin		
423–427	Residenzverlag – Dapra, Salzburg		
433–435	H. Urbschat – H.-J. Fischer, Berlin		
436	Heinz Oeberg, Berlin		
437	H. Urbschat – H.-J. Fischer, Berlin		
443, 445–447	Walter Faigle, Stuttgart		
453–454	H. Urbschat – H.-J. Fischer, Berlin		
456	Heinz Köster, Berlin		
461	Rudolf Dodenhoff, Worpswede		
462	Schmölz & Ullrich KG, Cologne		
463	Rudolf Dodenhoff, Worpswede		
469–472	Hatt, Stuttgart		
478–480	Breucker, Waltrop		
485–488	Udo Ernst Block, Hagen		
493–495	Walter Schutte, Wuppertal		
496	Schmölz & Ullrich KG, Cologne		
501	H.-W. Hämer, Ingolstadt		